SAVING ENDANGERED SPECIES

SAVING ENDANGERED SPECIES

Lessons in Wildlife Conservation from Indianapolis Prize Winners

EDITED BY Robert W. Shumaker

FOREWORD BY **HARRISON FORD**

JOHNS HOPKINS UNIVERSITY PRESS
BALTIMORE

Johns Hopkins University Press
2715 North Charles Street
Baltimore, Maryland 21218-4363
www.press.jhu.edu

Library of Congress Cataloging-in-Publication Data
Names: Shumaker, Robert W., editor.
Title: Saving endangered species : lessons in wildlife conservation from Indianapolis
Prize winners / edited by Robert W. Shumaker ; foreword by Harrison Ford.
Description: Baltimore : Johns Hopkins University Press, 2020. |
Includes bibliographical references and index.
Identifiers: LCCN 2020005967 | ISBN 9781421439563 (hardcover) |
ISBN 9781421439570 (ebook)
Subjects: LCSH: Wildlife conservation. | Endangered species—Conservation. |
Biodiversity conservation.
Classification: LCC QL82 .S275 2020 | DDC 333.95/416—dc23
LC record available at https://lccn.loc.gov/2020005967

A catalog record for this book is available from the British Library.

*Special discounts are available for bulk purchases of this book. For more information,
please contact Special Sales at specialsales@press.jhu.edu.*

Johns Hopkins University Press uses environmentally friendly book materials,
including recycled text paper that is composed of at least 30 percent post-consumer waste,
whenever possible.

*To the people who dedicate themselves to saving
wild things in wild places*

CONTENTS

Reach Beyond

Harrison Ford

2018 Recipient of the Jane Alexander Global Wildlife Ambassador Award

Orangutan
Pongo sp.

I want to begin by saying thank you to all who have worked to help preserve the natural world.

I grew up in Chicago. In the city, I fell in love with nature at the Lincoln Park Zoo, the Museum of Natural History, on summer farm vacations, in Boy Scout camp, and in biology class. I saw in nature the presence of something beyond humanity . . . mysterious, powerful . . . the presence of, well, God, I suppose.

Later in life, I suffered an unnatural embarrassment of riches—something called *Star Wars*—and found myself in a position to support those things that I cared about. I was living in Jackson, Wyoming, at the time, and among the people that I met there were a number who were supporters of a new organization called Conservation International. Peter Seligmann, the founder of Conservation International, encouraged me not to just support the organization with my newfound wealth, but to join their board. I've been a board member there for more than 20 years.

Protecting nature is first and foremost a moral imperative, yet saving nature is *really* about saving ourselves. At Conservation International, we have a motto: Nature doesn't need people, people need nature. Our communities, our families, our lives depend on clean air, fresh water, enough food, and a stable climate.

Survival itself is what's at stake.

Our obstacles are not just the complexity and enormity of the task of saving nature. We need to push back against elected officials that denigrate and deny science as part of a strategy to disaggregate us and turn us against each other for their political benefit—and to protect the status quo, a status quo that cannot be maintained because of the damage we are doing to the planet that sustains us.

Protecting nature is the only way we can continue to survive on this planet. We must present this truth to the world, unfiltered, unvarnished, unobscured.

Harrison Ford with a young orangutan at a rescue and rehabilitation center in Nyaru Menteng, Borneo, during filming for The Years Project. Courtesy: The Years Project

And so I ask each of you: *reach beyond those who agree with us. Find those who need to hear this story and learn how to reach them.*

If we succeed in this, we can realize an Earth not only with cheetahs, sharks, and kestrels. It will be an Earth with *us*, too.

We don't have any time to waste.

ACKNOWLEDGMENTS

This volume is a celebration of people who have made an authentic difference in preserving the natural world. All of them have gone about their work with passion, dedication, and clarity of purpose. It is a joy and privilege to share their stories.

It has also been a joy and privilege to work with the people who have helped to create this book. They care deeply about animal conservation, which has been evident through their generosity and spirit of collaboration.

Karen Burns offered enthusiasm, thoughtful comments, important insights, and her characteristic dedication to quality. She improved and elevated every aspect of the project that she touched.

Melanie Laurendine managed an astounding number of critical details with confidence and finesse. Her talent was consistently evident, and her contribution was invaluable.

Jo Hohlbein provided a critical eye and artistic expertise. Her efforts connect the reader directly to the diversity of life on Earth. Neal Cross added a compelling, new dimension to the text with his exquisite illustrations on the chapter openers.

Communication, coordination, and delivery of essential aspects of the manuscript required an international effort. This would not have been possible without the remarkable assistance of Renee Willis, Christine Crais, Betsy Didrickson, Karen Becker, Frank Pope, and Saba Douglas-Hamilton.

At Johns Hopkins University Press, Tiffany Gasbarrini offered an endless supply of patience, wisdom, and pure professionalism. She also has the most wonderful vocabulary of anyone I know. You have been an exceptional editor. Esther Pilar Rodriguez and Juliana McCarthy kept us on schedule, and the kind flexibility of Angela Piliouras at Westchester Publishing Services was much appreciated.

The Indianapolis Prize simply would not exist without Myrta Pulliam. You are a force for good.

The Eli Lilly & Company Foundation, the Lilly Endowment, and the Cummins Foundation Inc. have provided essential support for the Prize. Your contribution has been profound.

Anne, William, Carly and Jackie Shumaker have offered me optimism and unflagging encouragement. I am forever grateful.

SAVING ENDANGERED SPECIES

CONSERVATION SCIENCE, BIODIVERSITY, AND THE INDIANAPOLIS PRIZE

DR. ROBERT W. SHUMAKER
President and CEO of the Indianapolis Zoo

American Bison
Bison bison

In May of 2016, the American bison (*Bison bison*) was officially named the National Mammal of the United States, joining the Bald Eagle (*Haliaeetus leucocephalus*) as a symbol of the country. These two iconic species also share the dubious distinction of having almost gone extinct as a direct result of human influence.

American bison (frequently and incorrectly referred to as "buffalo") once numbered in the millions across the continental United States. Historically, their numbers were estimated in the unfathomable range of 30 to 60 million individuals. For thousands of years, Plains Indians, such as the Arapaho and Shoshone, relied on bison as an essential resource and also considered them to be important cultural and religious symbols.

The introduction of guns, settlers, railroads, and commercial hunting to the American West forever changed the ecological history of bison. During the first half of the 1800s, devastation of the massive herds was already under way. By the early 1870s, about 5,000 bison were being killed every day, primarily for commerce but also for sport. As part of westward expansion by settlers in the 1880s and the associated campaigns against indigenous peoples, a government-approved effort led by the US Army was begun to exterminate bison. It nearly succeeded, and American bison were brought to the brink of extinction.

By 1884, about 300 bison remained in the United States.

In 1886, William T. Hornaday traveled to Montana on a mission to collect live bison to display on the grounds of the Smithsonian Castle, primarily as a reference for taxidermists. Hornaday was shocked to see how bison populations had been depleted, and as a result, he became a passionate advocate for the conservation of the species. The bison he brought to the Castle were a hugely popular educational display, ultimately leading to the founding of the Smithsonian National Zoo, with Hornaday as the first director.

In 1896, Hornaday became director of the Bronx Zoo (now known as the Wildlife Conservation Society, or WCS). In 1907, he initiated the first-ever zoo-based conservation effort by transporting and reintroducing 15 zoo-born bison to the Wichita State Forest in Oklahoma.

The trajectory of zoo-based conservation efforts in the United States can be confidently traced back directly to Hornaday's bison reintroduction. That unprecedented and historic effort was the intellectual model that established the role for modern zoos as conservation organizations. It also occurred about a century before the term *conservation biology* was coined.

In his now classic 1985 article, Michael E. Soulé described conservation biology as a new scientific discipline that "addresses the dynamics and problems of perturbed species, communities, and ecosystems." It serves as a complement to existing fields such as biology and ecology and shares with them a focus on accumulating and distilling knowledge. But with strong ties to the environmental movement, conservation biology was (and is) distinct. It operates with a clear mission of preserving and protecting biodiversity around the globe. From that perspective, it has an "ethical norm" not typically found in traditional branches of academia. As Soulé explains, this makes it a "crisis discipline," meaning that conservation biologists must frequently "act before knowing all the facts; crisis disciplines are thus a mixture of science and art, and their pursuit requires intuition as well as information."

Soulé proposed two sets of assumptions that describe how conservation biologists understand the way natural systems function as well as how humans can impact those systems. His predictions have been remarkably durable and remain foundational for the field. The first set describes four functional attributes of conservation biology. First, *"Many of the species that constitute natural communities are the products of coevolutionary processes."* Essentially, a single species does not evolve in isolation from other species in its environment. Natural communities are composed of many different types of organisms. While this may seem like an obvious assumption, it leads to the significant realization that species in a community are interdependent and that some species may be highly specialized in the ways they survive. The complexity of interactions among species may not be obvious, and the loss of a single species may have many unintended consequences for a natural system. Losing a single species can potentially have a devastating impact on the entire community, in both the short term and long term. Viewed from a different perspective, the introduction of nonnative species can lead to serious consequences that disrupt a natural system.

Soulé's second assumption states: *"Many, if not all, ecological processes have thresholds below and above which they become discontinuous, chaotic, or suspended."* The size of an ecological system matters. If it becomes too small or too large, the system may fail completely. When it comes to applying this concept to habitat preservation, size definitely matters in terms of maintaining sufficient resources and diversity of species. Without the proper amount of habitat, a diversity of species simply can't survive in a healthy balance with one another.

The third assumption deals with reproduction and the importance of sufficient genetic diversity within a population: *"Genetic and demographic processes have thresholds below which nonadaptive, random forces begin to prevail over adaptive, deterministic forces within populations."* As with habitat size, a certain number of individuals are essential for the long-term survival of a species. The minimum size of the population varies depending on the natural history of the species being considered.

The fourth functional assumption is related directly to conservation efforts: *"Nature reserves are inherently disequilibrial for large, rare organisms."* For these species, protected areas may not allow for the normal flow of new genes in and out of the population to ensure robust populations for the long term.

In addition to these functional assumptions, Soulé also offered a second set of four ethical, or "normative," assumptions that are embraced by conservation biologists. These encompass human values and philosophies, and although they absolutely have applications when it comes to conservation, none are readily testable by the scientific method. First, *"Diversity of organisms is good."* The well-known conservation biologist E. O. Wilson coined the term *biophilia*, which means that humans "have the urge to affiliate with other forms of life." We crave the company of other species, both plant and animal. Associated with this is the idea that extinctions are bad. Natural processes leading to the extinction of species have always existed, but the point here is that human influence has led to an unsustainable and regrettable acceleration of species extinctions. These diminish the natural world and our experience in it.

Second, *"Ecological diversity is good."* While clearly related to the first of the ethical assumptions, this one acknowledges the importance of truly wild landscapes and habitats. Gardens of all sorts can be quite wonderful and satisfying, but they do not replace the biological complexity found in truly wild places. Both have tremendous value, and one cannot replace the other. The third assumption is profound in its simplicity: *"Evolution is good."* Soulé's own words say it best: "Assuming that life itself is good, how can one maintain an ethical neutrality about evolution? Life itself owes its existence and present diversity to the evolutionary process. Evolution is the machine, and life is its product. One possible corollary of this axiom is an ethical imperative to provide for the continuation of evolutionary processes in as many undisturbed natural habitats as possible."

And last, *"Biotic diversity has intrinsic value,"* Soulé emphasizes, "irrespective of its instrumental or utilitarian value. This normative postulate is the most fundamental. In emphasizing the inherent value of nonhuman life, it distinguishes the dualistic, exploitive world view from a more unitary perspective: Species have value in themselves, a value neither conferred nor revocable, but springing from a species' long evolutionary heritage and potential or even from the mere fact of its existence."

The challenges facing conservation biologists have changed dramatically since Soulé published his seminal work. The demand for resources of all types appears insatiable, the climate is warming, species are disappearing at an alarming pace, and the human impact on the natural world is so profound that the term *Anthropocene* is being promoted as the name for our current geological age. Richard Louv, author of *Last Child in the Woods*, gets to the heart of the matter when he suggests that children rarely spend time outdoors and have become marginalized from wild things and wild places. As Louv states, "For a new generation, nature is more abstraction than reality."

Largely in response to this new reality, conservationists Peter Kareiva and Michelle Marvier believe that the concept of "conservation biology" should be reconsidered and expanded. While still embracing Soulé's fundamental concepts, Kareiva and Marvier believe that the role humans play in conservation should be more strongly incorporated into the field. In their view, humans have traditionally been categorized as either a "threat to biodiversity" or the "saviors" who can preserve and protect the wild. Instead of labeling people as one or the other, they believe that "we need a more integrative approach in which the centrality of humans is recognized in the conservation agenda. Although modern conservation science will continue to rely heavily on the biological disciplines, it must also embrace economics, psychology, political science, ethics, business management, marketing, anthropology, and other disciplines spanning the social sciences and humanities."

Kareiva and Marvier bring other important dimensions to the discussion of conservation biology. For example, they update Soulé's concept of coevolution and natural communities. Since 1985, many wild areas have changed in response to such stresses as global warming or the introduction of invasive species. These ecosystems have not coevolved over time and have suffered damage in response to the external threats they face. It is unlikely that these scenarios would have been predicted 35 years ago, when Soulé first defined the field of conservation biology. The rehabilitation of these areas presents a relatively new and important opportunity.

Other notable topics in the field today are not specifically addressed by Soulé's functional assumptions. For example, the successful reintroduction of captive-bred individuals from "assurance" populations housed in zoos and other conservation facilities has successfully bolstered communities living in the wild. This technique is used much more often now than in the past and will certainly continue to be an important aspect of conservation biology into the future. The notion of "ecosystem services" (the benefits humans gain from healthy and well-functioning natural systems), such as clean water, have become a legitimate reason to advance conservation. Finally, discussion of the intersection between human rights and conservation initiatives should exert tremendous influence on how the field moves forward. As a result of the significant changes that have occurred since the publication of Soulé's classic paper, Kareiva and Marvier propose a new set of four functional assumptions, or postulates, that describe the current state of conservation biology.

First, *"Pristine nature, untouched by human influences, does not exist."* This assumption recognizes the fact that the results of human activities are absolutely pervasive around the globe, and it is nearly impossible to identify wild areas that are exempt. As a result, humans must be considered in all conservation initiatives. Second, *"The fate of nature and that of people are deeply intertwined."* The factors that impact species across diverse ecosystems, whether positively or negatively, are likely to have the same effects on humans. As Kareiva and Marvier state, "All people need functioning, unpolluted ecosystems for everything from food and materials to medicines and protection from natural disasters. The ecosystems that provide these services to humanity are the same ecosystems on which many other species also depend." This is not meant to contradict or replace the assumption that other species have inherent value. Rather, recognizing the importance of healthy ecosystems for humans provides additional incentives to protect and preserve wild things and wild places. Third, *"Nature can be surprisingly resilient."* There are numerous examples of species and ecosystems that have recovered after enduring tremendous pressures and the resulting damage. Recognizing the recuperative powers of nature is not a license to abuse the environment. Rather, it offers genuine optimism for conservation biologists. When external forces such as pollution, deforestation, overfishing, or poaching are eliminated, nature has the demonstrated ability to rebound. This is an important factor when planning conservation initiatives.

Fourth, *"Human communities can avoid the tragedy of the commons."* Overconsumption or depletion of natural resources is not inevitable. Kareiva and Marvier make the case that local communities have repeatedly shown a strong willingness to embrace long-term sustainability and avoid a short-term benefit only if they understand the import of their actions. In many cases, decision making by communities is more reliable than government policies for promoting a conservation ethic. Combined with this is the understanding that many issues, ranging from carbon emissions to rhinoceros poaching, may occur locally but have a global impact. It is no longer sufficient to act only at the local level; a broader perspective must be considered.

Complementing their functional postulates, Kareiva and Marvier offer a set of statements, the adoption of which they believe is essential for conservation efforts to be successful. First, and highly consistent with their central premise, *"Conservation must occur within human-altered landscapes."* From their perspective, it is no longer realistic or desirable to focus preservation efforts only on relatively undisturbed landscapes that are separate from humans. It is essential that all areas, even those that have been heavily affected by human behaviors, should be considered for restoration. They assert, "Conservation needs complementary strategies that simultaneously maximize the protection of nature and that of human well-being in the areas where people hunt, harvest, and live." Second, *"Conservation will be a durable success only if people support conservation goals."* This tenet recognizes that, too often, conservationists focus on the negative, leading potential supporters to believe there is nothing they can do to reverse the situation. In fact, positive and optimistic messaging is essential for garnering public support. Frequently, conservation efforts are most successful when tied to economic benefit for local people. Ultimately, behavioral change by people is the essential factor for ensuring long-term success.

Third, *"Conservationists must work with corporations."* Major corporations exert a massive influence on consumer choices, energy policies, resource extraction practices, and ultimately on the state of the natural world. Conservationists have an obligation to help businesses develop and implement ethical and sustainable practices that support biodiversity. Fourth, *"Only by seeking to jointly maximize conservation and economic objectives is conservation likely to succeed."* Conservation biologists must work to identify options that, ideally, benefit people and natural systems equally. And last, *"Conservation must not infringe on human rights and must embrace the principles of fairness and gender equity."* Kareiva and Marvier make their point eloquently: "People deserve a voice in their own fates as well as in the fates of the lands and waters they rely on. Not only is this arguably the right thing to do from an ethical perspective, it will probably improve conservation outcomes."

How then do these various assumptions and postulates become integrated into one field of study? Anna A. Sher and Richard B. Primack, both conservation biologists, offer a useful and concise description. They define conservation biology as "an integrated, multidisciplinary scientific field that has developed in response to the challenge of preserving species and ecosystems." They identify three primary goals:

1. To document the full range of biological diversity on Earth.
2. To investigate human impact on species, genetic variation, and ecosystems.
3. To develop practical approaches to prevent the extinction of species, maintain genetic diversity within species, and protect and restore biological communities and their associated ecosystem functions.

Reminiscent of Soulé's ethical assumptions, Primack has offered his own ethical principles:

1. The diversity of species and ecosystems should be preserved.
2. The untimely extinction of populations and species should be prevented.
3. Ecological complexity should be maintained.
4. Evolution should continue.
5. Biodiversity has intrinsic value.

Primack's simple statement about the value of "biodiversity" is definitive, and the implication is clear: that which has intrinsic value deserves respect and protection. The impact of this is profound when we consider that "biodiversity" refers to the complete variety of life, including plants, animals, fungi, and microorganisms. It can refer to the number of life-forms in a particular habitat, an ecosystem, geographic region, or on Earth. It also includes the level of genetic diversity that exists within species, as well as the range of different types of ecosystems and biological communities that exist.

Biodiversity occurs across the globe, but the highest diversity of species is consistently found close to the equator. An important and well-known concept developed by Norman Myers describes the richest areas of biodiversity that are also threatened by human influence as "hotspots." Two specific criteria qualify a region as a biodiversity hotspot: it must have a high percentage of plant species that are not found anywhere else on Earth, and it must have no more than 30% of its original vegetation remaining. Stated simply, a "hotspot" is an area with immense biological value that is in danger of disappearing without meaningful conservation action. According to Conservation International, there are 36 biodiversity hotspots around the world today, yet they cover only 2.4% of the surface of the earth. This tiny fraction of the world supports around half of all plant species and about 43% of the birds, mammals, reptiles, and amphibians. Conservation International describes hotspots as "among the richest and most important ecosystems in the world—and they are home to many vulnerable populations who are directly dependent on nature to survive. By one estimate, despite comprising 2.4% of Earth's land surface, forests, wetlands, and other ecosystems in hotspots account for 35% of the 'ecosystem services' that vulnerable human populations depend on."

Preserving global biodiversity in all its forms is the goal that unites conservation biologists. As an increasing percentage of the human population moves to cities and becomes increasingly disconnected from the natural world, the challenges to achieving this goal increase. Ecologist and conservationist James R. Miller sees a direct connection between the general public's lack of awareness of and concern for the loss of biodiversity and "the estrangement" that most people now have from nature. He notes how pervasive this is among children, particularly those living in urban settings. Research by J. Allen Williams Jr. into the content of award-winning children's books supports this point. From 1938 to 2008, depictions of natural environments and animals have significantly declined, replaced by stories about "built environments." He concludes that in these influential books, "natural environments have all but disappeared." Of course, this mirrors what is occurring around the world.

Eric W. Sanderson, a conservation ecologist with the Wildlife Conservation Society at the Bronx Zoo, and his colleagues study the impact of humans on nature. They conclude, "The influence of human beings on the planet has become so pervasive that it is hard to find adults in any country who have not seen the environment around them reduced in natural values during their lifetimes—woodlots converted to agriculture, agricultural lands converted to suburban development, suburban development converted to urban areas." Of course, human impact is not limited to the land. Benjamin S. Halpern and his team studied 20 different marine ecosystems around the world and reached a stunning conclusion.

They could find no area that was unaffected by humans, and 41% of the areas they studied were heavily affected by humans.

The United Nations' Sustainable Development Goals report for 2019 states that the "average abundance of native species in most major land-based habitats has fallen by at least 20%" over the past century. The IUCN Red List, a comprehensive source for information on the world's animals, plants, and fungi, notes that 25% of all mammals, more than 40% of amphibian species, almost 33% of reef-forming corals, and 34% of conifers are threatened with extinction.

It is true that extinctions have always been a normal and natural part of the evolutionary process. However, the rate at which animal extinctions have occurred over the past century is at least 100 times higher than what can be considered "natural." Human influence is responsible for this massive and unsustainable acceleration. Sanderson eloquently makes the point, "The global extent of the human footprint suggests that humans are stewards of nature, whether we like it or not. The long-term impact of human influence, positive or negative, benign or catastrophic, depends on our willingness to shoulder responsibility for our stewardship."

The Indianapolis Prize, the world's leading award for animal conservation, was founded to celebrate the work of exceptional stewards of nature who shoulder their responsibility with passion, integrity, and pure devotion for preserving biodiversity. Recipients of the Prize are individuals who have achieved major victories in advancing the sustainability of an animal species or group of species. The Prize is awarded biennially by the Indianapolis Zoo; applications are reviewed by a nominating committee, which identifies six finalists, and a jury, which selects the winner. In addition to honoring great conservationists, the Prize is philosophically devoted to engaging, enlightening, and empowering the general public on the topic of advancing conservation. In this way, the Prize embraces the idea that any true and enduring conservation success must include people as a primary factor in the equation. In the 2018 prize cycle, which included a gala and national lecture tour by the winner, at least 2.2 billion media impressions were earned internationally. This level of exposure fulfills another specific goal of the Prize, which is to elevate conservationists as heroes and role models, especially for younger generations.

Along with the Indianapolis Prize, the Jane Alexander Global Wildlife Ambassador Award was established to recognize the contributions of public figures who advocate for the conservation of biodiversity. The Award was named in honor of actor and conservationist Jane Alexander, who was also its first recipient.

To date, there have been seven winners of the Indianapolis Prize and three recipients of the Jane Alexander Global Wildlife Ambassador Award.

DR. GEORGE ARCHIBALD, 2006. When Dr. Archibald, an ornithologist and cofounder of the International Crane Foundation, first met a female whooping crane named Tex, who had imprinted on humans, his goal was simple: form a bond strong enough that she would lay an egg. His unique approach, which included dancing alongside her, created a remarkable relationship. She successfully produced a chick, which helped make a future for the species a reality. Dr. Archibald was the first recipient of the Indianapolis Prize and is well known for his devotion to understanding crane behavior and applying that knowledge to successfully support breeding and reintroduction efforts.

DR. GEORGE B. SCHALLER, 2008. Known as one of the founding fathers of modern wildlife conservation and widely regarded as the world's preeminent field biologist, Dr. Schaller is relentless in his pursuit to save endangered species across the globe. Since 1952, his successes have been numerous and span the animal kingdom. He has worked tirelessly to help lions in the

Serengeti, gorillas in Central Africa, tigers in India, jaguars in Brazil, and giant pandas in China, to name only a few of his efforts. Dr. Schaller has inspired countless field biologists and continues to actively conduct fieldwork.

DR. IAIN DOUGLAS-HAMILTON, 2010. Dr. Douglas-Hamilton is recognized as one of the world's foremost authorities on African elephants for his decades-long studies of their natural history and behavior. His investigations led to the first world-wide awareness of the ivory poaching crisis and were instrumental in bringing about an end to the international trade in elephant ivory. Dr. Douglas-Hamilton pioneered GPS tracking survey techniques and, since founding Save the Elephants in 1993, has nurtured a new generation of researchers and conservationists within northern Kenya and around the world.

DR. STEVEN C. AMSTRUP, 2012. While working in the Arctic, Dr. Amstrup, chief scientist for Polar Bears International, discovered something disturbing—the sea ice polar bears rely on for traveling, hunting, and raising their young was disappearing. Amstrup has conducted research on all aspects of polar bear ecology in the Beaufort Sea and is regarded as the most influential scientist working on the conservation of these iconic bears. Dr. Amstrup and his team are determined to create a better future for them.

JANE ALEXANDER, 2012. The inaugural Jane Alexander Global Wildlife Ambassador Award was presented to its namesake in recognition of her decades-long commitment as a champion for wildlife. Ms. Alexander considers being a conservationist her most important and challenging role. The Tony and Emmy award-winning actor's advocacy for wild things and wild places has included involvement with the Wildlife Conservation Society, the Audubon Society, and Panthera. An accomplished author, Ms. Alexander's most recent book, *Wild Things, Wild Places*, tells about her travels with field biologists over the past 35 years. Jane Alexander is an Honorary Chair of the Indianapolis Prize.

DR. PATRICIA CHAPPLE WRIGHT, 2014. Dr. Wright, primatologist, anthropologist, and conservation biologist, is particularly devoted to lemurs. She rediscovered a species of lemur thought to be extinct for more than 50 years and also discovered a new species—the golden bamboo lemur. She has had tremendous success fostering collaboration among scientists, local communities, and the government to save lemurs and sustain their unique ecosystem on the island of Madagascar. She was central to the establishment of Ranomafana National Park, which provides critical habitat for lemurs and many other rare species of plants and animals.

DR. CARL JONES, 2016. There may be no other conservationist credited with saving as many species as Dr. Jones. He has truly changed the fate of animals on the brink of extinction. Much of Dr. Jones's work has focused on the animals found on the island of Mauritius. As a chief scientist for the Durrell Wildlife Conservation Trust and scientific director of the Mauritian Wildlife Foundation, he has developed and led programs that have resulted in some of the most striking animal population recoveries in the world, including that of the Mauritius Kestrel—once the world's rarest bird—the Echo Parakeet, and the Pink Pigeon. He helped develop the first national park in Mauritius and championed the idea of "ecological replacement," a conservation tactic in which a similar species is introduced to an area outside of their historic range to fulfill an important ecological role once held by an extinct species.

SIGOURNEY WEAVER, 2016. The award-winning actor Sigourney Weaver has been an advocate for the mountain gorillas of Rwanda since her starring role in the 1988 film *Gorillas in the Mist*. She is a recipient of the Jane Alexander Global Wildlife

Ambassador Award and serves as honorary chair of the Dian Fossey Gorilla Fund International. Ms. Weaver narrated BBC's highly popular series *Planet Earth*, joined other conservationists at the United Nations General Assembly in 2006, and has earned multiple honors, including the Explorers Club Communication Award and the National Audubon Society's Rachel Carson Award.

DR. RUSSELL A. MITTERMEIER, 2018. With a career that has spanned more than five decades, Dr. Mittermeier has focused on advancing conservation in all corners of the globe. He has described 21 animal species new to science, and an additional 8 are named in his honor. With deep subject matter expertise in primatology, herpetology, and conservation science, he has authored and edited (at last count) more than 40 books and more than 700 scientific and popular papers. He has done fieldwork in more than 30 countries, with special emphasis on Suriname, Madagascar, and Brazil. He was the president of Conservation International from 1989 to 2014, and executive vice-chair from 2014 to 2017. Dr. Mittermeier is currently the chief conservation officer for Global Wildlife Conservation. He is a *Time* magazine "Hero for the Planet," and travels the globe devoting himself to the preservation of biodiversity hotspots and high biodiversity wilderness areas.

HARRISON FORD, 2018. Harrison Ford's devotion to planet Earth is truly heroic. A recipient of the Jane Alexander Global Wildlife Ambassador Award and dedicated supporter and board member of Conservation International for many years, Mr. Ford believes nothing is more important than preserving the environment. He has been the voice for many wildlife films and documentaries and is a "hands-on" conservationist. This was most clearly demonstrated by his work in Indonesia to understand the unsustainable palm oil crisis affecting species like orangutans. He has been instrumental in the protection of more than 40 million acres on three continents as part of the Global Conservation Fund.

As part of the 2018 Gala, Harrison Ford narrated a short film on the significance of the Indianapolis Prize. He posed key questions in this thought-provoking commentary:

> Who are your heroes? Who are the people who move and inspire you? There are heroes who accomplish great things in the face of great odds. Whose feats of audacity and achievement make them seem larger than life. But then there are heroes of another sort. Whose feats may not seem larger than life but are interwoven deeply into the fabric of life on Earth. Heroes who work tirelessly, selflessly, to save what might otherwise be lost. In the world of conservation, our heroes are the people who strive to save Earth's wild places and the animals that inhabit them. But animals and habitats are only part of the story. Because conservation is also about helping people live in harmony with the wild next door. It's recognizing traditions and practices that have been part of a culture for centuries. For others, it's about survival, for what we do today affects our planet for generations to come. This is not in question. The facts are in. The science is done. We know what we need to do to save our wild places. And we need to recognize the people who are leading the way. The Indianapolis Prize exists to honor and inspire conservation: to support the efforts to these extraordinary pioneers and help them keep fighting the good fight. It's about conserving and protecting the most vulnerable creatures and the wildest places on Earth. The challenges have never been greater, but neither has our will to make a difference. These are the people of conservation. You can call them researchers or scientists or conservationists. But let's call them what they really are: These are heroes. Real heroes.

In this volume, each of these 10 heroes offers their own perspective on the state of wildlife conservation and the future of the natural world. These are the voices of the greatest conservationists of our time.

Dr. Rob Shumaker with community game scouts in the Simanjiro Plains in northern Tanzania.

Further Reading

Alexander, J. 2016. Wild Things, Wild Places: Adventurous Tales of Wildlife and Conservation on Planet Earth. Alfred A. Knopf.

Chazdon, R. L., and T. C. Whitmore, eds. 2002. Foundations of Tropical Forest Biology: Classic Papers with Commentaries. University of Chicago Press.

Louv, R. 2008. Last Child in the Woods. Algonquin Books of Chapel Hill.

Wilson, E. O. 2002. The Future of Life. Vintage Books.

References

Halpern, B. S., et al. 2008. A Global Map of Human Impact on Marine Ecosystems. Science 19:948–952.

Kareiva, P., and M. Marvier. 2012. What Is Conservation Science? Bioscience 62 (11): 962–969.

Miller, J. R. 2005. Biodiversity Conservation and the Extinction of Experience. Trends in Ecology and Evolution 20 (8): 430–434.

Myers, N. 1988. Threatened Biotas: "Hot Spots" in Tropical Forests. The Environmentalist 8 (3): 187–208.

Primack, R. B. 2014. Essentials of Conservation Biology. Sinauer Associates.

Sanderson, E. W., et al. 2002. The Human Footprint and the Last of the Wild. BioScience 52 (10): 891–904.

Sher, A. A., and R. B. Primack. 2020. An Introduction to Conservation Biology. Sinauer Associates.

Soulé, M. E. 1985. What Is Conservation Biology? BioScience 35 (11): 727–734.

CHAPTER 1

DANCING WITH CRANES

Their Story Is My Story

DR. GEORGE ARCHIBALD
2006 Recipient of the Indianapolis Prize

Whooping Crane
Grus americana

As the rain poured down, and with the darkness shattered only by lightning, I carried Tex gently in my arms down the grassy hill from our shared nest. When I spoke her name, she responded with low soft purring sounds that seemed to confirm a sense of security. Holding one of the last remaining Whooping Cranes on Earth during that violent storm, I felt a powerful bond with her and to cranes everywhere. My unusual pair-bond with Tex became well known in those early days and garnered awareness for her species—but for me, the story of Tex will always be a metaphor for the complicated dance performed by the many people who worked to save one of the world's most threatened families of birds.

My first memory is of golden sunlight on green grass and a mother duck and her brood of yellow ducklings. Too young to walk, I crawled after them. My friends claim I imprinted on birds then, and have been following them ever since. My second memory is of feeding coconut to domestic ducks in Sherbrooke, Nova Scotia, Canada, and my third memory is one of anger after discovering several wild ducks that my father had shot hanging on the back porch. One thing is certain: my earliest memories are of birds, and since childhood, I have had a passionate interest in nature, and birds in particular.

My loving parents, Donald and Lettie Archibald, recognized and appreciated this special interest of their little son. Both were teachers who shared an interest in learning and nature. Dad loved farming, fishing, and hunting, while Mom was a skilled gardener. Our rural home beside the St. Mary's River was surrounded by wilderness from which deer, moose, bears, and eagles sometimes appeared. Our field provided pasture for a cow, a horse, and space for a large vegetable garden.

I am the second born of six children—two girls and four boys. My siblings and I shared close relationships with one another and with nature, expressed in different degrees through gardening, farming, fishing, and hunting. I was the only one captivated by birds. My brother Don once commented that I was fortunate to have a strong passion for something that provided such a clear direction.

I am of primarily Scottish descent. My ancestors, the Archibalds and MacLeods, left Scotland for a better life in Canada. My parents embraced the traditional Scottish value of thrift. Wash water was never discarded but used to water the gardens. Three small sheds that others would have destroyed were transported to our property and neatly placed beside the forest. They became homes for my menagerie of birds, including peafowl, pheasants, chickens, geese, ducks, and pigeons. Despite their limited financial resources, my parents graciously purchased food for the many hungry avian mouths. I inherited the frugal gene from my parents, which later came in handy during the lean, early years of establishing a nonprofit organization.

My first birds during childhood were four Rhode Island Red laying hens, followed by five white leghorns reared from eggs and hatched by a broody hen. The chicks developed into three hens and two handsome and ferocious roosters. To promote domestic peace in the chicken house, Dad butchered one of the roosters. I was upset and pled the case that chickens might someday become endangered! I was sad that chickens seemed unable to fly long distances, and I wanted to help them. So, I carried them to the roof of the barn, and after they recovered from the stress of transport, I pushed them off. Alas, they did not progress well in flight, and undoubtedly, their egg production was curtailed by this flight therapy. It brought me hours of great joy to watch the behavior of my domestic birds. Hens returning to roost in the evening fascinated me, as each selected its special spot on the perch. Why the same spot, I wondered? And why did people always sit in the same seat in church?

In autumn and spring, a flock of wild Canada Geese flew over our valley with raucous calls that stirred my spirit. In the forest, I was thrilled to discover the nests or broods of Ruffed Grouse. Fishermen would sometimes leave me for hours on coastal islands to search for nests of Eider Ducks, Common Terns, Herring and Black-backed Gulls, and Double-crested Cormorants. Occasionally, I brought home a few eggs from these wild birds and hatched them under chickens. The young were hand-reared and then released back into the wild. I have fond memories of newly fledged terns and gulls flying down to grab food from my uplifted hands. It brought me a deep sense of satisfaction that the captive-reared birds became wild and free.

During these formative years, I did not have much exposure to small birds. The feeding of wild birds in winter was not practiced by anyone I knew. I did not have binoculars or a field guide, and little birds were difficult to see. Large birds were easy to identify, and as a project in biology class, I compiled a ring binder on the waterfowl of North America.

While growing up, perhaps my greatest thrill was a visit every few years to the Provincial Wildlife Park near Shubenacadie, Nova Scotia. Mammals and birds could be seen alive and up close. It helped me realize the importance of captive animals in cultivating the interest of young people in the appreciation and conservation of nature.

Except for a pair of peafowl, my childhood bird collection was dispersed to others after I graduated from high school. I intended to become a medical doctor and pursued premedical studies through a bachelor of science in biology and chemistry at Dalhousie University in Halifax. During my undergraduate years, I dedicated summer vacations to earning income from jobs related to nature. The first summer, I raised and released Mallard Ducks and banded Black Ducks for the provincial government in Nova Scotia.

During the following two summers, I was employed to study and care for cranes and other birds at Al Oeming's Alberta Game Farm. There in the northwest, I was uplifted to experience Sandhill Cranes in the wild and interacted with eight species of captive cranes that I fed and watered daily. My interest in conservation grew. I knew cranes were special, but why? Was it their rarity? Was it that some species are as tall as humans? Or, was it because they are monogamous and pairs dance together and call in synchronized duets? I was fascinated that the calls of migrating Sandhills were heard before the birds could be spotted through binoculars in those cold blue spring skies in Alberta. I was hooked!

Although I adored the wildlife park in Nova Scotia and the game farm in Alberta, deep down, I wanted more than captive animals could offer. Unaware of the possibility of ornithology as a profession, I decided on medicine as a career and birds as a hobby. After all these big decisions had been made, in November of 1967 in the company of a close friend and colleague, I attended the world's fair in Montreal. After one day of doing the tourist thing, I decided to hitchhike south to Ithaca, New York, to visit the famed Laboratory of Ornithology at Cornell University. There I met a man who changed my life, Professor William Dilger.

On that cold November day in 1967, I walked the corridors of the Cornell Laboratory of Ornithology, admired the original bird paintings by Louis Agassiz Fuertes, and then heard the distinct sound of parrots. At the end of a long, dark corridor, bright light and birdcalls poured from an open door. Timidly I walked into a room filled with cages of small colorful parrots. This room led to the office of Professor Dilger, an ethologist at Cornell University, best known for his behavior studies on parrots and for providing scientific insight into the age-old controversy between nature versus nurture.

Surprised to see an unannounced stranger, Professor Dilger invited me to join him for a chat. Dressed in lederhosen and smoking a long, curved Burmese pipe, Dilger immediately put me at ease by requesting I address him by his first name (a custom not practiced at Dalhousie). During the next hour, I had the undivided attention of a kindred spirit as I shared my knowledge of cranes with a truly eccentric individual in a colorful office filled with books, papers, aquaria, and birdcages. Without asking the typical questions about background and achievements, Bill invited me to come to Cornell to study cranes. Without a thought, I nodded. I told him I hoped to start as his graduate student in September of 1968.

That last summer in Canada, I became a seasonal park naturalist at magnificent Fundy National Park. It was a total delight to share with visitors the world's highest tides and the brilliant abundance of songbirds in the Acadian forests. I learned two important skills: how to identify tiny songbirds and how to speak effectively in public. I found it difficult to believe I was being paid to have so much fun. It was a dream job! But I was in for a great shock.

I had failed to read the fine print in the letter from the National Research Council announcing my fellowship. It stated that this support from the Canadian government could be used only at a Canadian institution. Cornell was in the United States. Stunned and dismayed, I called Bill for advice. He replied, "To hell with it. Come anyway, George. We'll find something." His magnetic personality and great warmth bolstered me. At the end of that summer, I was sad to leave my country, my family, and my friends, with only $800 (Canadian) to my name. But I knew I had made the right decision, so off I went to the United States.

In September of 1968, I arrived at the expensive Ivy League school nearly penniless. In my naivety about travel, I had placed my wallet in my suitcase. To this day, that suitcase has never been located. Professor Dilger helped me land a research assistantship at Cornell's Laboratory for Ornithology, support that provided both tuition and a respectable salary.

The lab is in the countryside several miles from Cornell's main campus complex in Ithaca, New York. My goal was to establish a captive population of cranes at the lab to conduct a comparative study of their behavioral displays. Within a week of my arrival, I started to prepare for the arrival of cranes. A small pond in a weed-filled field across the road from the lab was soon fenced, and an abandoned shed dragged to the site to provide shelter for two female Sandhill Cranes from the Alberta Game Farm. In another field stood an abandoned complex that, until recently, had been the site of Cornell's mink research. I secured the mink complex at the suggestion of another mentor, Professor Tom Cade. It would all soon become the home for 56 cranes. It was also home for me and my Labrador retriever, Fuji. The dilapidated buildings were scheduled to be leveled at the end of 1971, so I had them for only three years.

I dedicated my summer of 1969 to the removal of rows of mink cages, many of which I sold, using the funds to excavate ponds and build high fences for cranes. The old office building provided a room for food storage, two rooms in winter for the cold-sensitive crowned cranes from Africa, and one small room for Fuji and me. To make my space feel larger, I installed a large picture window (found at the local dump) to provide a commanding view of the enclosure for Wattled Cranes. My next objective was to secure cranes and funds to care for them, at what soon became known as the Cornell Cranium.

At this time, Dr. Sewall Pettingill was the director of the Laboratory for Ornithology. Some years before his arrival at Cornell, he was involved in a search for the then-unknown nesting grounds of the Whooping Cranes in northern Canada. He knew cranes, and he was considered royalty in the academic community. One day, he asked to see me in his office. He questioned the wisdom of my interest in developing a large captive collection of cranes at Cornell. "Cranes are well known and highly respected. If things do not go well, it will not be the best reflection on the lab." I assured him of my dedication and competence to manage the project. He remained reflective, with a definite twinkle of support in his conservative eyes. Another member of my graduate committee was Professor Oliver Hewitt (Ollie). Ollie was a tiny man with a warm heart, who had access to a fleet of university vehicles! Enthusiastic about my dreams, he agreed to provide vans and fuel to fetch cranes for the Cranium.

The next step in my efforts to gain support for my project was to visit the Bronx Zoo office of the highly respected Dr. William Conway, director of the prestigious New York Zoological Society. While I explained the project, Dr. Conway remained silent but attentive. Then he cleared his throat, stared at me, and said, "Who do you think you are? Cranes are revered, costly, and rare birds that require top-level professional management. You have a heavy academic program to face. How can you possibly care for so many cranes with zero financial resources?" I replied that I had 22 years' experience living with birds, I had raised Sandhills and cared for eight species of cranes at the Alberta Game Farm, and that I was willing to live with the cranes, study them, raise funds to support them, and complete my doctorate concurrently. Unmoved, he asked me if I would like to join him on a walk around the zoo. On that walk, we talked and soon discovered that we indeed were kindred spirits—his doubts about me seemed to melt away. Before departing the zoo that day, I had the promise of $5,000 cash for the Cornell Crane Research Project, and one female White-naped, two Eurasians, two Blue, two Grey Crowned, four Sarus, and six Demoiselle Cranes. I was in crane heaven!

I soon assembled a collection of 56 cranes of 9 species (on loan from the government, zoos, and private individuals), including the Black Crowned (*Balearica pavonina*), Grey Crowned (*Balearica regulorum*), Demoiselle (*Anthropoides virgo*), Blue (*Anthropoides paradiseus*), Wattled (*Bugeranus carunculatus*), Sandhill (*Grus canadensis*), Sarus (*Grus antigone*), White-naped (*Grus vipio*), and Eurasian (*Grus grus*). I was now able to focus on my research. I observed three other species, Hooded (*Grus monacha*), Red-crowned (*Grus japonensis*), and Whooping Cranes (*Grus americana*), at other centers in the Northeast. I analyzed the behavior of the Brolga from films and sound recordings taken by Australian colleagues. Unfortunately, information was lacking for 2 of the world's 15 crane species, the Siberian (*Leucogeranus leucogeranus*) and Black-necked Cranes (*Grus nigricollis*). There was only a single Siberian Crane in captivity in the United States, and there were no known Black-necked Cranes in captivity outside of China, which was locked in the throes of the Cultural Revolution.

Cranes are social and communicative birds whose behavior can be divided into two categories: vocal and visual. With an excellent tape recorder on loan from Cornell's Library of Natural Sounds, I recorded the calls from each species. Using a small Super 8mm movie camera, I filmed the repertoire of threat postures and dances. The volume of recorded information influenced me to concentrate my analysis on the comparative evolutionary relationships of cranes based on a single display—the dramatic unison call—a duet performed by a mated pair of cranes.

Male and female cranes look alike. Males are sometimes larger. Unable to determine gender by outward appearance, zoos often unknowingly paired cranes of the same gender together. At the Cranium, I made an interesting discovery that the sex of crane species, except for crowned cranes, can be determined by the unison call display. During this display, which signals both mate fidelity and aggression toward others, the male crane typically elevates his wings and gives one long call compared with the two higher-pitched calls of the female. It is an easy way to tell the boys from the girls, and thus an important tool in captive management.

By comparing the dozens of characteristics of the unison call among the 13 species of cranes in my study, I projected a model of their evolutionary relationships. Twenty-five years later, Dr. Carey Krajewski compared the DNA of all 15 species of cranes from blood samples collected at the International Crane Foundation (ICF). The model projected by that DNA study was nearly identical to the model revealed by my behavioral research many years earlier.

It was great fun caring for the cranes, learning about their communication systems, and piecing together what the data suggested about their evolutionary relationships. Often, I discussed my findings with my colleagues at Cornell and with Bill Conway at the Bronx Zoo. One day, Bill commented to me that I would be wasting my life if I pursued a career in academia. I was needed on the battleground of conservation. I was intrigued, but how was that to be expressed after completing my doctorate?

Aldo Leopold's *A Sand County Almanac*, written in Wisconsin during the 1930s and 1940s, was a profound introduction to conservation for me. Leopold expressed in words how I felt about cranes: "... When we hear his call we hear no mere bird. We hear the trumpet in the orchestra of evolution. He is the symbol of our untamable past, of that incredible sweep of millennia that underlies and conditions the daily affairs of birds and men. . . . The sadness discernible in some marshes arises, perhaps, from their once having harbored cranes. Now they stand humbled, adrift in history."

Leopold's sentiments about cranes deeply moved me—feelings confirmed by replies to letters I wrote to ornithologists overseas. I was seeking information about the status of the world's cranes. Many responded that little was known about cranes and that the last observations had been many years before. Perhaps the cranes of Asia and Africa were exposed to the same pressures that had reduced the Whooping Cranes in North America to fewer than 20 birds by 1940.

Knowing that my Cornell Cranium would be leveled in December of 1971, I applied for a grant from the New York Zoological Society to study cranes in Japan and Australia, where five crane species awaited my observations comparing displays in captivity with the same in the wild.

The autumn of 1971 witnessed the return of my Cranium cranes to their owners, the completion of the first draft of my thesis, and success with the oral exam. As scheduled, the Cranium was demolished. I was off to Japan with a brief stop in Baraboo, Wisconsin, to see a fellow graduate student, Ron Sauey, and Aldo Leopold's property and shack beside the river where he was inspired to write *Marshland Elegy*. I didn't know at the time that a life-changing idea would take root during my visit. In Baraboo, just a few miles from the abandoned farm where Aldo Leopold and his family helped "heal" the land, Ron Sauey was born in 1948, the same year Leopold died fighting a spring wildfire. Ron's parents, Norman and Claire Sauey, built a beautiful home and facilities to accommodate a herd of Arabian horses on 65 acres on the north side of Baraboo. The harsh winters proved too severe for the valuable equines, and the Saueys and their herd eventually moved to a much larger property in Florida, leaving the farm buildings near Baraboo empty.

Since childhood, Ron had a deep interest in nature, and like me, parents who understood and nurtured him. Also like me, he went birdwatching frequently and kept birds in captivity. He had several pheasant species that he maintained in a building with 12 fenced runs. But not only was Ron passionate about nature, he was determined to build a career working with the natural world, much to the consternation of his otherwise supportive father. How would he make a living looking at birds and wildflowers?

After completing a bachelor of science in biology, Ron came to the Cornell Laboratory for Ornithology for graduate studies. The fall of 1971 marked Ron's first and my last semester at Cornell. It was an extremely busy time for me, completing the first draft of my thesis, passing oral exams, returning cranes to their owners, and preparing for work in Japan. Although our offices were near each other, I had not met Ron until I overheard him telling someone he was from Wisconsin. I had a special interest in Wisconsin through Aldo Leopold. After introducing myself, I asked Ron if he knew about Leopold's work there. I was amazed that Ron's home was just 10 miles from Leopold's shack beside the Wisconsin River, and that the Leopold Reserve was among his favorite birding spots.

A few weeks before I left Cornell, Ron and I volunteered to spend one Sunday afternoon helping with a census of the waterfowl of Lake Cayuga. We had a conversation that would change our lives forever. A magnificent pair of Wattled Cranes was the last to leave the Cornell Cranium. Ron had seen them through the perimeter fence and was impressed. He commented that it seemed a pity that my assemblage of cranes was dispersed just after the colony had been established, and some pairs of cranes had started to breed. We agreed that a world center was needed for the conservation of cranes. Jokingly, I commented that cranes migrated across continents, and a special branch of the United Nations was needed to coordinate conservation programs among politically polarized nations whose boundaries cranes could not recognize.

Ron told me about his family's empty horse farm in Baraboo. Ideas percolated. A few weeks later, just before Christmas, on my way to Japan to study Red-crowned Cranes, I spent several days in Baraboo and visited the Leopold shack. The Wisconsin winter and the open spaces with farms and forests reminded me of Nova Scotia. The big red horse barn on the property was fairly new and elegantly designed—fitting habitat for regal birds! Ron's parents agreed to rent us the farm for $1.00 per year to create our Crane Branch of the United Nations. They were delighted that the abandoned farm would be used to create a career for their gifted son. The rent was just right, but it was the responsibility of the cofounders to raise support for operations.

During the following year, through the generosity of his parents—while I worked first in Japan and then in Australia—Ron supervised the construction of 15 large aviaries on the farm. We exchanged extensive correspondence concerning the mission and goals of our crane center. We settled on a simple mission statement: *The mission of the International Crane Foundation is the study and preservation of cranes worldwide.*

Five goals, in order of priority, included research, public education, habitat protection, captive breeding, and reintroduction. ICF's registration as a nonprofit organization was secured in 1973. We had plenty of enthusiasm and ideas, but we knew nothing about properly managing a nonprofit organization.

There was an old white farmhouse on the Sauey property. During those early years, that is where we all lived, including many volunteers. The local grocery store generously gave us a charge account. I purchased inexpensive but wholesome food and filled the refrigerator at the farmhouse we called the White House. Sometimes our store debt exceeded $800. The meager donations that came from tours and speaking engagements paid the grocery bill and the farmer's cooperative where we bought poultry food for the cranes.

When I had worked as a bird keeper and crane researcher at the Alberta Game Farm during the summers of 1966 and 1967, the director had mentioned on several occasions that the enormous black and white Red-crowned Cranes dwarfed all other cranes in their magnificence. Throughout the ages, these cranes have been depicted in art and folklore as symbols of good luck, long life, happiness, and marital fidelity.

In the late 1960s, there were only two pairs of Red-crowned Cranes in captivity in the United States. I observed one pair in Massachusetts. They lived in a large, rocky pasture shared with goats and donkeys. I broadcast recorded unison calls of wild Red-crowned Cranes near their enclosure. The two captive cranes suddenly became alert, and each bird walked to adjacent mounds of earth beside a ditch along the far side of the pasture. With the bright red patch of bare skin expanding down over the back of their heads, and their bodies held rigid in threat posture, the cranes emitted a trumpetlike territorial duet, the unison call. Instantly, this "pair" was identified as two males!

After they finished calling, and with wings tightly closed, the cranes elevated their wings vertically above their backs while bending forward toward each other and rotating their heads sideways to contract their crimson crowns against a backdrop of black and white. During my observations of twelve other species of cranes, I had never seen such a spectacular display. I named it the Arch Threat Display. It appeared that the two male cranes were threatening each other. In just a few seconds, they had revealed something unique and fabulous. I felt like I had discovered a hidden treasure.

I traveled to Japan to study Red-crowned Cranes in the wild after completing my studies at Cornell. On the way, I stopped in

Honolulu to see the other pair of Red-crowned Cranes in the United States. To my amazement and delight, as revealed by my new unison call sexing method, I immediately identified them as two females. I explained to the zoo director that there was another mismatched pair in Massachusetts and that the only two pairs in North American zoos had no hope of ever producing offspring. I also explained that, by the time I had returned from my overseas fieldwork in two years, there would be a newly formed center specifically for cranes in Baraboo, Wisconsin. Would he send the two females to Baraboo to pair with the two males from Massachusetts? As usual, I had my fingers crossed that I could secure the males on loan and that everything would work out.

And it did.

When I returned from Japan and Australia to Baraboo in December of 1973, the four Red-crowned Cranes had arrived—two females from Hawai'i and two males from Massachusetts. One of the males and one of the females were feather perfect. Placing them side by side in a divided pen, I hoped that love would blossom. They immediately started unison calling together, and I was thrilled. Some weeks later, they were finally placed together in the same pen under supervision. They walked side by side, danced, performed the unison call, and seemed compatible. Eventually, they were allowed together without supervision. One morning when I came to feed them, to my horror, I discovered the male had killed the female. Two months later, the male died from liver cancer that had spread to his brain, likely causing his abnormal behavior.

The other pair of Red-crowned Cranes had serious physical handicaps. One wing of the male was detached from its socket and dangled around his leg. The female was so old and arthritic she could barely walk and could not crouch. They were unable to perform natural copulation because of their physical limitations, but that spring, the elderly female laid two eggs. Unable to crouch fully to lay her eggs, she awkwardly squatted above the nest, and each fragile egg had a distance to travel before landing in the nest. Observing this unusual situation, I added a deep bed of straw to her nest, and henceforth each new egg gently bounced home.

The following spring, I artificially inseminated the female, producing ICF's first captive-produced crane chicks—Tancho and Tsuru (Japanese words for red-crowned and crane). At one month, Tancho died, but Tsuru flourished, and until he moved to our new site in 1981, delighted me with a daily flight in the sky overhead. One day he joined a flock of migrating Tundra Swans, and I thought we would lose him, but after a short time at the end of their "V," he broke rank and returned for breakfast. His parents produced many offspring in subsequent years that we distributed to zoos. More Red-crowned Cranes were brought in from zoos in Europe and Japan, and soon there was a healthy captive population of these magnificent cranes in the United States.

I have always been described as an eternal optimist, but the next chapter in my crane saga nearly broke my spirit to continue.

The captive population at ICF had grown to the point that during the winter of 1977–1978, a 10-acre, securely fenced field was home to a flock of about 60 cranes of 7 species. That spring I returned to Baraboo in mid-March from fieldwork in Afghanistan. It was a mild, balmy day. When I first walked into the field with the assortment of cranes, a juvenile Blue Crane walked up to me and collapsed. I noticed several other cranes looked ill. I was witnessing the beginning of a disease outbreak. During the weeks that followed, 25 sick cranes had to be tube-fed every few hours throughout the day and night. Only three survived. The chick house where many of the ill birds had been reared became the hospital where most of them perished. For the first time in my life, I was exhausted and somewhat psychologically paralyzed. Twenty-two cranes died from a formerly unknown disease that attacks the liver and spleen.

With assistance from the University of Wisconsin and the National Wildlife Health Laboratory (NWHL) in nearby Madison, the disease was eventually identified as a type of herpes virus that was subsequently named Inclusion Body Disease in Cranes (IBDC). A test for the virus was developed. The outbreak at ICF resulted in an important medical discovery. Testing for IBDC has now become standard procedure in the management of both wild and captive cranes.

By the end of the outbreak, I was discouraged and tired. Our flock was reduced by more than 60%, our site was contaminated, our funds were scarce, and most of the staff members were volunteers. How was ICF to survive?

The secretary of the Smithsonian Institution in 1978, Dr. S. Dillon Ripley, was a renowned ornithologist and aviculturist. We had met when he served on the board of directors of the Cornell Laboratory for Ornithology while I was a graduate student. He enjoyed observing my captive cranes in the Cornell Cranium. In the summer of 1978, after the dust settled from the disaster, I called Dr. Ripley for advice about the future direction for ICF.

With his typical flair for optimism and bright ideas, Dr. Ripley encouraged me to contact all the people who had made substantial financial contributions to ICF and invite them to join our board of directors. Within two weeks, 18 major supporters met with Ron and me. Sixteen of them joined the board. In 1979, just one year after an epidemic had threatened to destroy ICF, our new board of directors met and unanimously voted to buy a new property. From the ashes of tragedy arose a new, clean ICF supported by an enthusiastic and gifted board of directors and a reasonably paid staff.

My adventure with Whooping Cranes had first begun in May of 1954 in a one-room schoolhouse in Stillwater, Nova Scotia, where I was eight years old and the only student in the third grade. The formerly unknown nesting grounds of the Whooping Cranes in northern Canada had recently been discovered, and a dramatization about a pair of Whooping Cranes was broadcast on the weekly radio program, *Science of the Air*. The pair of cranes de-

scribed the dangers on their 3,000-mile migration from wintering grounds in Texas and, finally, their relief on reaching an
enormous impenetrable wetland complex—a place unknown to
humans. Suddenly the sound of a low-flying aircraft was followed
by the cries of the female crane, "Help, help! They found us. Now
we will be shot, stuffed, and placed in a museum." The male crane
comforted her, "No dear, this a safe place inside Wood Buffalo National Park. The wood bison survive here, and so will we!"

The broadcast had a profound effect on me. From that point
forward, I was deeply concerned about the welfare of Whooping
Cranes. The radio broadcast also demonstrated the power of effective education in shaping the opinions of youngsters. That was
the beginning of my fascination with the welfare of our continent's
tallest bird, one of the rarest species on the planet. The migratory
flock had been reduced to just 16 individuals by 1942. In 1954, there
were 24, and by 1966, when the governments of Canada and the
United States first collected eggs from wild nests to establish a captive flock, there were about 44 birds.

In 1966, when I was an undergraduate student at Dalhousie
University in eastern Canada and employed by the Alberta Game
Farm near Edmonton, some 300 miles south of the nesting area
of the Whooping Cranes, I had my first experiences with cranes
in the wild as the calls of migrating Sandhill Cranes floated down
from the skies. I was amazed that such a loud sound was produced
by specks so high in the sky. I was also fascinated by reports in the
news about the historic lift of Whooping Crane eggs from the wild
nests. The eggs were transported in a portable incubator across the
continent to the Patuxent Wildlife Research Center in Maryland,
where they were hatched, and the chicks were reared to start a captive flock. I would never have believed at the time that, three
years later, as a graduate student at Cornell University, I would be
recording the behavior of Whooping Cranes at Patuxent. That is
where I first met Tex.

Beginning in 1966, the Whooping Cranes at Patuxent were raised from eggs collected from nests of wild cranes. Whooping Cranes typically lay two eggs per clutch, but usually rear only one chick. Removing one egg from each nest and hatching the eggs in incubators did not harm productivity in the wild, and established a captive flock as a safeguard against extinction. There were about 15 cranes at Patuxent that year. Most of them were in a large fenced field, where it was hoped that pairs would form. Another enclosure contained two cranes—a male named Canus, taken from the wild following a wing injury, and Tex, a female. Other cranes were somewhat afraid of humans, but Tex was just the opposite. Whenever someone approached her enclosure, if she liked the way they looked, she approached and often danced. I returned to Patuxent several times during my three years at Cornell to study the Whooping Cranes. Tex appeared to have zero interest in Canus, but a great interest in humans.

Tex's father, Crip, was a juvenile Whooping Crane migrating south across Nebraska when one of his wings was broken. He was captured and eventually ended up at the San Antonio Zoo, where some years later, he paired with an injured female crane named Rosie. They became an excellent breeding pair, and produced many eggs and chicks, but unfortunately, none of the young cranes survived, until the arrival of Tex in 1966. Wanting to protect her, the zoo director took Tex from her parents and raised her in his home for three weeks before sending her to the government facility at Patuxent.

Unfortunately, such exposure exclusively to humans during her early life irreversibly imprinted Tex on humans. During the next decade, all efforts to pair Tex with a male Whooping Crane failed. Tex never laid an egg at Patuxent. When Crip and Rosie produced Tex in 1966, there were only 44 of their kind alive in the wild flock. Although the pair lived for many years after Tex hatched, they never produced more offspring. Tex was the sole recipient of their valuable genes.

I reasoned that if Tex had a human companion during the spring breeding season, she might be stimulated to ovulate and lay an egg. With the help of my Cornell colleague Dr. Cam Kepler, we convinced the powers that be to send Tex to the International Crane Foundation, with the understanding that I personally would attempt to bring her into egg production. The summer of 1976 was the beginning of a seven-year saga that culminated with the production of a single chick named Gee Whiz, the historic hatch that proved to be the foundation for the species' recovery.

In Baraboo, Tex's home was a wooden, unheated shelter, adjoining a larger outdoor enclosure. During the summer of 1976, the indoor shelter was subdivided by chicken wire to provide an office and sleeping space for me, with Tex on the adjoining side with food, water, and a door to her outside pen. From the start, Tex liked me. We often did the courtship dance, and while I worked at my desk, she stood nearby preening. When she wanted me to follow her, she elevated her beak, faced in the direction she wanted to move, and emitted a soft purr. I followed her, and the walk often turned into a dance.

Crane dancing kept me in shape—it was Texercise! The motions included bowing, jumping, running, and tossing small sticks in the air. The vigorous sequence usually lasted several minutes. By late summer, I had moved back to my home but visited Tex as time allowed. The separation did not seem to stress her. She always wanted to dance. From mid-March through late May of 1977, I spent all my daylight hours with Tex and continued with office work between dances. She finally came into breeding condition and laid a single egg. But the egg was slightly deformed, with wrinkles on the pointed end. Of course, it was infertile, as there was no male Whooping Crane at ICF at that time from which to collect semen and perform artificial insemination. But I had guessed correctly, and we proved that she could lay an egg.

The Audubon Park Zoo in New Orleans agreed to send two males on breeding loan to ICF. We named them Tony and Angus. Tony was a poor specimen with a broken beak, crooked toes, unkempt plumage, a strange raspy voice, and an aggressive personality. He was never a viable donor for Tex. Angus was feather perfect, an excellent semen producer, and mild-mannered. In 1978, through artificial insemination, Tex produced a single fertile egg! Unfortunately, the chick died while hatching. Not long after that, Angus perished from injuries sustained as he flew into the side of his enclosure when a hot air balloon that floated overhead frightened him. His death was an enormous loss for us.

In 1979, I again worked with Tex, but she laid only one softshelled egg that broke. In 1980, because I was away, a colleague tried to work with Tex, but she disliked him and never laid an egg. In 1981, our curator of birds danced with Tex as time allowed. She came into breeding condition but still never laid an egg. Finally, in 1982, before moving to our new site six miles away, I decided to make an all-out effort to get a chick from Tex.

I built a small shed, moved it to the crest of a hill in a hayfield adjacent to Tex's enclosure, and equipped the shed with a desk, chair, manual typewriter, battery-operated radio, and a sleeping bag. That was my home from late March through May. Writing and office work kept me occupied much of the day, broken only by walks and dances with Tex, and mail delivery at noon. When people entered our field, Tex became defensive. In contrast, when wild Sandhill Cranes flew over or landed nearby, Tex ignored them.

During this time, fresh Whooping Crane semen was sent from Patuxent in Maryland twice weekly and administered to Tex. In late May, Tex laid an egg! We immediately placed it under a pair of reliable captive Sandhills, and I remained with Tex night and day, hoping for a second egg. Our routine was quite amusing. Tex's nest containing a dummy egg was beside my shed. Members of a crane pair alternate incubation responsibilities. After incubating for several hours, Tex would leave the nest to forage for earthworms in our field. I would then place my folded sleeping bag over the nest, over which I placed my little table and chair. After some time, when she returned, I moved my materials back into the shed, and she resumed incubation.

It was the night of May 25, 1982. Total darkness, deluges of rain, flashing lightning, crashing thunder, and, within a few feet of my tiny shed on the grassy hilltop, the soft purr of a very wet human-imprinted Whooping Crane named Tex. From my comfortable sleeping bag behind a small wooden door, I spoke words I hoped would bring her comfort as she faithfully incubated the dummy egg. She answered with more purrs. But when warnings of tornados were announced over the radio, I decided we had reached a breaking point. Abandoning hope that Tex might lay a second egg, I emerged from my shelter and picked up the huge bird that I had courted from dawn till dark over the last seven weeks. Her nest was saturated, and so was she. She did not resist me cradling her with legs folded in incubation posture, as I made my way down the hill to her permanent residence. As I was unable to hold both a flashlight and a crane, we continued in the darkness and the ferocity of the elements. When I spoke, she answered. She never struggled, and I sensed that she felt safe. Soon she was secure in her dry home. I cherish that memory of such a unique connection between man and bird.

Unfortunately, there was no second egg. After two weeks, Tex's egg was taken from the Sandhills and brought to a dark room that contained a box with a bright light inside and a small round opening. By holding the egg against the hole, the bright light lit up the contents of the egg. There was a chick developing. Hooray! However, as with Tex's other eggs, there were problems. The pointed end was wrinkled, and the egg was losing weight so rapidly that the survival of the chick was threatened. After consulting with Dr. Bernard Wentworth at the Department of Poultry Science at the University of Wisconsin, we were encouraged to hydrate the egg by submerging it for 10 minutes in ice water. The temperature drop would cause contraction of the liquid contents in the egg. Atmospheric pressure on the water would then force water into the vacuum. It worked. The egg gained weight and hatched.

But the new chick was underweight and incapable of swallowing water and food. It appeared that dehydration was causing constriction of the esophagus. Despite subcutaneous injections of fluids, the chick continued to lose weight. Finally, we were forced to gently thread a tiny tube down the chick's esophagus to inject food. The chick's health rapidly improved, and soon he was eating and drinking. We named him Gee Whiz, after Dr. George Gee from the Patuxent Wildlife Research Center who had collected and sent the semen. Gee Whiz eventually paired with a female Whooping Crane named Ooblek, and they have produced many offspring to contribute both to the captive flock and to release efforts to establish new wild flocks.

In 1990, I joined the 10-person International Whooping Crane Recovery Team (Canada-USA), and I continue in that role to help guide research and conservation programs for the only self-sustaining wild population and to help with captive management and release programs.

A few years ago, one of my greatest pleasures was to visit a pair of reintroduced wild Whooping Cranes nesting on a cranberry farm about 60 miles north of Baraboo, Wisconsin. The female of this pair was an offspring of Gee Whiz—so I fondly thought of her as my "daughter." For several years, the pair produced only infertile eggs, but eventually, a researcher checking on their nest was thrilled to be greeted by a chick in the nest—my granddaughter! It brings me great satisfaction that our efforts with Tex proved successful, and I consider it symbolic for most of our programs that require many years of patience, perseverance, and faith before the tide turns in favor of conservation.

In 1976, there was only one Siberian Crane, a critically endangered species, in the United States. Her name was Phyllis, and she arrived in Baraboo on a breeding loan that summer, after more than 30 years at the Philadelphia Zoo. For many years, she had been on display in a rather small enclosure shared with waterfowl. At ICF, she was given a large, grassy, private enclosure, and a house. The space, solitude, and stimulation from other pairs of cranes displaying nearby stimulated Phyllis to begin performing a series of calls we later described as pre-copulatory calls. We sensed her motivation to become reproductively active.

An old male Siberian Crane, thought to have hatched in 1905, had survived both world wars living in a zoo in Switzerland. On a frigid and windy night in November 1976, Wolf arrived on a breeding loan in Baraboo, Wisconsin. He was 71 years old at the time! As we lifted the plywood crate that contained Wolf and took him from the van, Phyllis began calling. Wolf answered from the crate. It was an incredibly touching moment to hear two birds communicating that had not heard the voice of their own species for many decades.

They were placed in adjacent enclosures and immediately appeared to be attracted to each other. Within a few weeks, Wolf was placed with Phyllis. Their enclosure was lined with old Christmas trees to provide the ambiance of the Russian taiga where some Siberian Cranes nest. Floodlights were installed to simulate the almost continual daylight to which Siberian Cranes are exposed on their breeding grounds during late spring and summer. When they started painting the bases of their necks with dirt in what appeared to be a sexual display, we provided a bucket of black marsh mud to mimic a more natural substance. I cherish the memory of watching Phyllis and Wolf late at night with their enclosure bathed in bright light and engaging in bursts of activity including dancing, nest building, and long bouts of pre-copulatory calling that some-times ended with actual copulation. To our delight, Phyllis laid her first egg! We collected the eggs as they were laid to encourage continued production. To our amazement, they produced 12 eggs, but unfortunately, all the eggs were infertile.

There was a lone Siberian Crane in captivity at the Hirakawa Zoo in Japan. Blown off course during migration, the juvenile fe-male had been rescued by children and rehabilitated at the zoo. She was named Hirakawa, and she matured into a magnificent bird. Believed to be a male at the time, Hirakawa was sent to ICF as a semen donor for Phyllis. When placed in a nearby enclosure, Hirakawa began displaying with Wolf, not Phyllis. I immediately subdivided the enclosure containing the pair, with Wolf occupy-ing the pen between the two females.

That spring, Hirakawa began laying eggs, but despite our efforts with artificial insemination, the eggs were infertile. To increase the chances of fertility, another male was imported from Germany, and in 1981, we achieved the first captive breeding of Siberian Cranes. We named the chick Dushenka, which means "little loved one" in Russian. We were honored to receive a congratulatory letter from Indira Gandhi. It was a hatch heard around the world! Wolf later produced viable semen samples and is listed in the Siberian Crane studbook as the sire of two chicks in 1982. Five years later, at the age of 82, Wolf died. His longevity record is chronicled in the thirty-fifth edition of the *Guinness Book of Records*.

China is home to the world's greatest diversity of cranes—8 of the 15 species. Of these, 6 are threatened. China's foremost orni-thologist was the late Professor Cheng Tso-hsin. Graduating with a PhD from the University of Michigan in 1922, he was the youn-gest candidate ever to receive such a doctorate from that institu-tion. Until his death in 1998, Professor Cheng worked tirelessly at the Institute of Zoology in Beijing as the nation's foremost author-ity on birds.

His major life work was the massive book, *A Synopsis of the Avifauna of China,* published in 1987. Decades in the making, this monumental volume was confiscated and presumed destroyed during the early years of the Cultural Revolution that swept China between 1966 and 1976. However, unlike many of his colleagues who perished, Professor Cheng and his family survived. For several years, he cleaned latrines. As the political sky cleared toward the end of the 1970s, survivors returned to their institutions, and miraculously, the rough draft of *A Synopsis of the Avifauna of China* was located in a warehouse.

During my time as a graduate student from 1968 to 1971, I wrote Professor Cheng asking about the status of cranes in China. I received a one-line typed reply, "China has eight species of cranes, and little is known about their status." After ICF was established in 1973, I wrote to Professor Cheng again and received a similar reply. But his answer came during a period when scholars were persecuted in China. I was relieved that he was alive. In August of 1979, while visiting my family in Nova Scotia, I wrote a letter to Professor Cheng explaining that I would be in East Asia in autumn and welcomed an opportunity to visit him if he could provide an invitation. I gave him the address of my hotel in Tokyo and the date that I would be there in early October. My letter carried colorful Canadian stamps.

After working in Russia and South Korea that autumn, I finally arrived at the hotel in Tokyo. There was a letter waiting for me at my hotel. It was from Professor Cheng, inviting me to come to Beijing in early November. I soon had a visa and booked a flight to Beijing. It was late in the evening when I arrived at a very dark and dingy airport. An enormous illuminated portrait of Chairman Mao looked down at the visitor's entrance. Professor Cheng and three colleagues—Ding, Zhou, and Liu—all wearing navy blue Mao suits, greeted me warmly. During the next two years, Ding and Zhou would discover the wintering grounds of Siberian Cranes at Poyang Lake, and Liu would locate seven extremely rare Crested Ibis breeding near Xian.

The three younger scientists were all smiles but did not speak English. Professor Cheng did all the talking and apologized that his English was "a bit rusty." He was such a warm-hearted and jovial man. I instantly bonded with him. My apprehensions about the visit soon vanished.

The Friendship Hotel near the Institute of Zoology was to be my home for the next week. That first night I was so excited that I couldn't sleep. A few Black-necked Cranes, the only species of crane I had never seen, resided at the Beijing Zoo. From a map in the lobby, the zoo appeared to be only several kilometers from the hotel—right for some distance and then left for some distance. The right was easy, but which left? It was pitch dark, and street signs, if visible, were all in Chinese.

Still awake, at about 3:00 a.m., I donned my jogging gear and headed out. At a major intersection, from the left, I heard the distant bugles of cranes—as if they were calling to me. As I jogged along, the infrequent calls became louder until, finally, I reached a high stone wall that appeared to surround the zoo. By following it, I found the closed and locked entrance gate. Continuing along, I was delighted to discover a large gap in the wall and workers sleeping on the ground around small fires. Apparently, they were rebuilding that portion of the wall during the day.

Tiptoeing among the sleeping workers, I was soon inside the zoo as the first rays of dawn made it possible to follow paths. Soon I reached a large pond with an island. There were many birds on the water and the island. With increased light, I could make out the unmistakable form of a Black-necked Crane. What a moment— at long last, to see a Black-necked Crane! Suddenly people were everywhere. The gates of the zoo had been opened, and many people were walking through the zoo for exercise or as a shortcut to another street. I followed the flow in the direction of what I presumed would be the entrance gate I had passed in the darkness.

I was shocked upon leaving the zoo. Streets that had been almost empty were now jammed with traffic. Blue-suited pedestrians so covered the sidewalks that it was impossible to run. Somehow, in the confusion, I made it back to the hotel, jumped in the shower, then threw on my suit just before the doorbell rang. It was Ding, Zhou, Liu, and an interpreter. "Dr. Archibald, did you have a good rest?" If they only knew.

Miraculous things also happened the following year in connection with the long-shot hatch of Gee Whiz, the Whooping Crane chick resulting from my unusual courtship of Tex. Three weeks after the hatch, I was invited to tell the big story on the popular *Tonight Show Starring Johnny Carson*. I flew to Los Angeles the day before the taping. Before leaving Baraboo, I had one last dance with Tex in the enclosure and the big grassy field where we had first danced six years before. The following morning in my hotel, I was concerned that my story with Tex might make me the laughingstock of the masses. Then, the phone rang. It was the ICF administrator. "George, I am so sorry to tell you this, but last night Tex was attacked and killed by a pack of raccoons." Shocked and deeply affected by the strange timing of Tex's death, I made my appearance before 22 million people on television. Johnny Carson, Ed McMahon, and Doc Severinsen could not have been more considerate. At the end of the 15-minute interview, I explained the tragedy. The studio audience groaned, and throughout the country, there was a new awareness for the plight of cranes.

As the millennium turned, I reflected on the new century and what it held for cranes, for me, and for those who had been with me throughout the International Crane Foundation's journey. How would the leadership move forward—with me or without me? I knew that founders could become liabilities. After 27 years of leadership, it was time for me to assume a new role. Our excellent deputy director, James Harris, became the president and CEO. I moved my office to my home but continued to work full time in a role that involved fundraising, leading group trips to wonderful crane landscapes, spearheading new programs, and helping the staff without micromanaging or undermining the new administration. My overriding goals were to help the team through encouragement, financial security, and advice.

I have been blessed with knowing many kindred souls throughout my life, and my vision for my future is time in the field where I can share, learn, and develop ideas with old friends and new. With them, and through them, I see a safer world for cranes and people. To continue my work and dreams, we must invest in the conservation leaders of tomorrow. I will continue to work toward that end, in the persevering Scottish way instilled by my parents, until I can joyfully give way to the new pioneers of crane conservation.

I am sometimes asked if I am thrilled with the success of ICF. Thrilled is not the right word. I have moments of a warm glow that

Dr. George Archibald and a Sarus Crane chick in Australia. Courtesy: International Crane Foundation

the dream of two college kids has matured beyond their wildest expectations, but as long as I am alive, my overriding thought will be of keeping the engines running and of the programs that will continue long after I have joined the cranes of heaven. The dream is still in progress, and I have faith. I always have.

Further Reading

Archibald, G. 2016. My Life with Cranes. Edited by B. Didrickson. International Crane Foundation.

Cheng, Tso-hsin, 1987. A Synopsis of the Avifauna of China. Parey Scientific.

Didrickson, Betsy. 2010. Little Book of Crane Lore. International Crane Foundation.

Mirande, Claire, and James T. Harris. 2019. Crane Conservation Strategy. International Crane Foundation.

CHAPTER 2

THE NATURAL HISTORY OF A FIELD BIOLOGIST

DR. GEORGE B. SCHALLER

2008 Recipient of the Indianapolis Prize

Chiru
Pantholops hodgsonii

During the summer of 1952, I made a survey of bird species in northern Alaska in the area that would become the Arctic National Wildlife Refuge, protecting the last great wilderness in the United States.

In the spring of 2019, I joined a Chinese team on the Tibetan Plateau to evaluate the impact of climate change on the landscape and the livelihood of the local Tibetan communities in a newly created protected area.

During the intervening 67 years, I conducted wildlife surveys and studies and promoted conservation in 32 countries. However, the focus of my efforts has changed over the years. I spend less time just watching animals living their natural lives, the thing I enjoy most. Instead I ask myself the question, "What facts do I need to help protect and manage a species and its habitat?" Every perceptive person now realizes that the ever-increasing human population is having a devastating impact on the ecology of our small planet. In the past 50 years we have used up more of the planet's resources than in all previous human history combined. Air, water, and soil pollution affects all living beings with toxic residues. Man-made climate change shifts and fragments habitats, threatening the survival of many species, including the human one. No one even knows the level of biodiversity lost because we have little idea how many millions of species there are, most having not yet been identified.

But we do know that everything in nature is interconnected. How many species can we lose before a system collapses? Everything we make, buy, and use comes from nature: destroy nature and we destroy ourselves. Yet human inertia, blindness to reality, and political expediency cause us to ignore potential solutions. And then there is climate change, which too many people prefer to deny, or treat with purposeful ignorance. The fossil fuel addiction that has led to global warming, together with human population growth and the ever-increasing consumption of resources, is driving us toward ecological disaster. Rising sea levels will inundate coasts, grassland will turn to desert, habitats will fragment, and many local species will become extinct. As a field biologist, I wonder whether what I do now will soon become irrelevant. And I wonder also how best to adapt to the rapidly changing environment.

To ponder the state of the world depresses me, and I have always treasured an escape into nature. "I was a born naturalist," wrote Charles Darwin in his autobiography. I lack such self-assurance about my own vocation's evolution, yet it is in my mind and heart. A series of lucky circumstances pointed me toward a life in the wilderness. After a childhood in Germany, I ended up in my uncle's home near St. Louis, Missouri, where I went to high school. Noting my pet menagerie of opossums, ring-necked snakes, and others, my cousin, Ed Barnes, who had attended the

University of Alaska, urged me to head north, and I enrolled at the University of Alaska in 1951. The wildlife department opened a new world to me. Graduate students studied everything from mountain goats to grayling fish, and I joined some in the field. I noted that one could actually make a living by watching animals. Encouraged by a professor to attend graduate school at the University of Wisconsin in Madison under the guidance of ornithologist John Emlen, I applied and was accepted in 1955. This shaped my fate, as over the next half a century, I studied various iconic species in places of natural splendor.

The summer of 1956 saw me back in Alaska as assistant to an expedition led by Olaus and Mardy Murie to northeastern Alaska. Olaus was president of the Wilderness Society and a well-known conservationist. We tallied birds, plants, insects, and spiders and took notes on grizzly bears, wolves, and caribou herds. Observing and tramping through the mountains of the Brooks Range, our goal was to gather the kind of information that would lead to the protection of the region. Olaus stressed that we were not just there to collect scientific facts but also to look deeply into nature, to consider "the precious intangible values," the moral and spiritual values, of the place. I have never forgotten this advice. Through the effort of Olaus, Mardy, and others, the Arctic National Wildlife Refuge was established in 1960 and enlarged in 1980 to 30,000 square miles (77,700 km²).

This 1956 trip was sponsored by the New York Zoological Society (now known as the Wildlife Conservation Society), which manages the New York zoos and has an international conservation program. It was my first contact with the organization that became my enduring professional home. The society, especially under its general director, William Conway, increasingly linked zoos to field conservation, even to assembling a staff for that purpose. I joined that staff in 1966 after brief studies of tool-using by California sea otters and nesting of white pelicans in Yellowstone National Park.

Now I had wonderful freedom of selecting my projects—as long as I raised the grants to support the fieldwork.

One day, while a graduate student at the University of Wisconsin, I entered the office of "Doc" Emlen, as we called him. He asked me, "Would you like to study gorillas?" Impulsively I answered "yes." Doc and I, together with our wives Ginny and Kay, now planned for a study of mountain gorillas in Central Africa, again sponsored by the New York Zoological Society. First we would do a general survey of gorilla distribution, and then Kay and I would study these apes in detail in their main habitat of the eight Virunga volcanoes that straddle the border of the Belgian Congo, Rwanda, and Uganda. Gorillas "are exceedingly ferocious," wrote one author, and they are "frightfully formidable apes," stated another. There was concern among some academics that I, a mere graduate student, would be unable to conduct the study. Nonetheless, we left for Africa in February 1959 and surveyed the gorilla's range.

With the help of local African supporters, Kay and I then moved to an isolated board hut on a meadow called Kabara. It was surrounded by forest, at 10,000 feet elevation, and we were on the Congo side of the Virunga volcanoes. Daily I followed the trails of gorilla groups through wet and dense vegetation to seek contact with them. Most groups numbered 10 to 25 animals, each led by a 400-pound silverback male. At first meeting, the males tended to roar and beat their chest with open palms, and their groups were visibly nervous. But after a few contacts, the gorillas realized that I presented no threat. I often settled myself on the lower branch of a tree so we could see each other better. I finally developed a rapport with several of the 10 groups that foraged near our cabin.

The faces of gorillas surrounded by lustrous black hair are distinctive, and I soon knew many by name. Never were they ferocious, and indeed they were as curious about me as I was about them. One female with an infant even climbed into the same tree with me, and we sat beside each other. So well were some groups habituated that at dusk I could stay with them as they built their night nests on the ground by bending in the available vegetation. Then I too slept on the ground near them, though without building a nest, close enough to hear stomachs rumble. In this way, Kay and I for the first time learned details about the private life of gorillas. After a year, in June 1960, our idyll was shattered when the Congo erupted in violence after Belgium gave it independence. We had to close the project down. Yet in spite of the political turmoil that has continued in the region to the present, the gorillas have survived, thanks to dedicated officials and park guards and also thanks to the benefits local communities derive from tourists who visit these beautiful relatives of ours in considerable number as a result of a program developed by primatologist Amy Vedder and conservationist Bill Weber.

Kay and I had met as undergraduates at the University of Alaska, and my attraction to her blonde beauty had redoubled as we discovered our shared interests. When we married in 1957, we aimed for a life of adventurous travel, but after our time in the Congo, we decided to have children before embarking on another overseas project. Our sons Eric and Mark were born in 1961 and 1962. And in 1963 we moved to India. I was asked by the Johns Hopkins Center for Medical Research and Training to study wildlife as possible hosts for diseases that also affect humans. With our sons we moved into a bungalow in the remote Kanha National Park of central India. There for 14 months I studied several deer species, a wild cattle called gaur, and blackbuck antelope. One member of this ecological community of particular interest to me was the tiger. Little was at that time known about India's wildlife, species having been mainly studied along the sights of a rifle. The tiger was described by one British hunter as the "embodiment of devilish cruelty, of hate and savagery incarnate." Such derogatory verbiage stimulated hunters in their competition to slaughter as many tigers as possible. One British hunter killed 158 tigers, including 31 cubs, between 1850 and 1854. One maharajah, still hunting in 1965, had butchered 323 tigers to date.

I naturally wanted to learn about a tiger's life undisturbed in its forest realm. I looked for tigers by car and on foot, easily recognizing individuals by their distinctive stripes. I soon knew the resident tigers around our bungalow. These included a large male and three females, two of which had cubs. They preyed mostly on deer and wild pigs, but sometimes they killed a cow or buffalo that had strayed from the village. Then I would sit on a branch in a nearby tree to observe the nocturnal doings of tigers on a kill. This revealed a new aspect about them. Tigers were thought to be solitary and asocial. One night, for example, I watched a tigress with her four cubs by moonlight. Above me in the tree several vultures ruffled their feathers, patiently waiting for a meal. Once the tigress roared, *aaouuu*, and from far away she received an answer. Several hours later the male tiger appeared and peacefully mingled with the family, the cubs rubbing their cheeks against his. Then he continued to patrol his territory. Tigers, I learned, are mostly solitary but not asocial, in that individuals know each other and meet on occasion. India has been making a major effort to protect its tigers, and all hunting of them has been prohibited. Studies of tigers there have continued without interruption by Ullas Karanth and others, and I greatly enjoy my occasional visits to India to learn about their results.

Soon after our return to the United States, the director of Tanzania's national parks suggested that we join the newly established Serengeti Research Institute to study the impact of lions and other predators on the great herds of wildebeest, zebras, and gazelle in the park. Kay, the boys, and I moved there in mid-1966 and remained for three and a half years, the most enchanting time of our lives. Kay homeschooled our boys, and with other biologists and their families there studying wildlife, we created a congenial small community.

The lion is the only cat that lives in groups, called prides, though pride members may be widely scattered. I had to recognize individuals before I could learn that a pride usually had about 10 to 25 members, and that prides occupied overlapping ranges, each some 12 to 60 square miles in size. And then there are also wandering male lions, nomads that are not part of a pride. One such male, which we had marked with an ear tag, roamed over 1,800 square miles (4,662 km^2) of forest and plain. What do lions do at night? We followed a nomadic pair, a male and female, continuously for nine consecutive days. During that period they traveled 67.5 miles but did not hunt, instead scavenging meat from hyena kills. Lions sleep and rest about 20 hours a day, making it at times difficult for an observer to stay awake to watch lions sleep. Fortunately other researchers helped with the lion project, including Stephen Makacha. I was interested in working with Tanzanian assistants, and I was fortunate to have Stephen. We amassed much detailed data on the societies of predators and their prey.

My gorilla, tiger, and lion studies had been done in national parks, all of which had a measure of security. From each we took away much information and many treasured memories. However, now I wanted to contribute more directly to conservation by working on new species and in new areas that had been neglected. The pattern of my life had been established: like a nomadic lion I took my small pride of one female and two sons with me on travels.

When World Wildlife Fund–Pakistan indicated that it would like to host me on a project there, I was keen to accept. I like mountains. And Pakistan boasts some of the world's greatest ranges, the Himalaya, Karakoram, and Hindu Kush. Much of our time between 1970 and 1975 was devoted to Pakistan. The family moved to the city of Lahore from 1972 to 1974, where our boys, now almost teenagers, attended the Lahore American School. Accompanied by former army officer Amanullah Khan and avid trekker

Pervez Khan, our surveys took us to far-off valleys including politically unsettled border areas with Afghanistan, something that required a bit of courage on my part. Our main goal was to delimit the distribution and status of wild sheep and goats. And also of snow leopards. So we clambered up and down slopes to find ibex, spiral-horned markhor, and urial and, on the border with China, the magnificent Marco Polo sheep.

Snow leopards are difficult to observe because their smoky-gray coat blends so well into the rocky terrain, and they can spot a person from far away in these barren mountains. Once, offering hours of transcendence, a female snow leopard in the Hindu Kush mountains allowed me near her. She had killed a domestic goat. As I slowly labored up the slope toward her, she retreated a short way and watched me from behind a boulder, only her head visible. Then she reclined in full view for three hours. At dusk she returned to her kill. I stayed with her that night in my sleeping bag as she fed and wandered around. My surveys contributed to the creation of two protected areas in these mountains, and finding the massive horns of Marco Polo sheep stimulated me to survey species in neighboring countries. There was much I could still do in Pakistan. However, as I wrote in one of my books, "I feel rootless, unconnected, always traveling in my mind onward as if with a hunger that is never quite satisfied."

Having studied several species of large cat, my mind turned to the jaguar, about which little was known. Starting in 1975, I visited various South American countries to check on the status of wildlife. Brazil has drawn me back again and again, and so far I have made 20 surveys in that country. Most have been under the auspices of two government departments, the Instituto Brasileiro de Desenvolvimento Florestal and the Instituto Chico Mendes de Conservacao de Biodiversidade. My main Brazilian colleague has been Peter Crawshaw. We have concentrated on two large and quite different habitats. One is the Pantanal, in southwest Brazil and extending into Bolivia and Paraguay, at about 69,000 square miles (179,000 km²) the world's largest wetland. The other is the Amazon rain forest, which in Brazil extends over about 1.26 million square miles, one-eighth of the country's area.

Much of the Pantanal is divided into private cattle ranches, known as *fazendas*. Seasonal flooding inundates much of the area, except where dikes have in recent years been built. One fazenda, named Acurizal, 137 km² (53 sq mi) in size, is located on dry ground along the Paraguay River at the base of a hill range that marks the Bolivian border. With permission of the owner we began wildlife research there in 1977. We studied jaguars, capybaras—which, with a weight of up to 40 kg (88 lbs), are the world's largest rodents—and also the rust-colored marsh deer and the Paraguayan caiman or alligator. During this time, Kay had to stay mostly home in the United States with our two boys, who needed to go to school. However, during their holidays we all enjoyed the Pantanal together. Eric and Mark made plaster of paris casts of the large, round jaguar paw prints in mud along the river, and they fished for piranhas to provide us with dinner.

We attached radio collars to two female jaguars and one male puma. The two big cat species live in the same area, with the jaguars having ranges of 13 to 15 square miles and the puma of 12 square miles. Our surveys on the fazenda revealed 43 potential prey species (excluding bats and small rodents) for the cats, with a total biomass of 380 kg/km². But the biomass of livestock on the fazenda was ten times that of wildlife. Naturally the cats went after some of such easy meals. Intolerant of the few cattle losses, the ranch hands killed several jaguars on the ranch, terminating our project there. Peter, with another American coworker, Howard Quigley, moved to a fazenda in the southern Pantanal, where their study of four jaguars, one puma, and four ocelots, each wearing a radio, produced much valuable information. The jaguar situation has in recent years improved. Many fazenda managers and owners now protect the jaguar, because tourists flock there to see them. In the past, local cowboys wore pistols to blast any jaguar they encountered, but now a visitor is escorted to a fazenda homestay, a pleasant lodge whose main aim is to provide good fishing and a photo session with a jaguar. On recent visits, I have seen jaguars lie casually on a riverbank, confident in their power as they ignore our boat a mere 40 feet away.

I thoroughly enjoyed our study of the blunt-nosed capybara in the northern Pantanal. The capybaras occur there mostly in groups of 5 to 25, grazing together near ponds into which the animals dive on perceiving danger. Groups are quite stable in membership, a small one consisting of just one male and one female and a litter of young, whereas large groups have several adults of both sexes. Capybaras scent-mark their range by rubbing the sebaceous gland on their snout onto bushes and by squirting urine mixed with musk. Disease, predation, poaching, and other mortality affect the populations, but because females give birth to as many as seven young in a litter, there seemed at the time to be no serious problem.

The Paraguayan caiman is abundant in the Pantanal, the reptiles sunning themselves singly and in groups on sandy riverbanks. They are of moderate length and up to 40 kg in weight, males being somewhat larger than females. When former president Teddy Roosevelt and his son Kermit visited the Pantanal in 1913, they for unknown reasons disliked caimans. Mindlessly they "killed scores of the noxious creatures" and simply abandoned the bodies. By contrast, Peter and I were thrilled by our study of the species, especially by its nesting behavior. The female gathers leaf litter into a mound near water and lays a clutch of 20 to 40 eggs inside it. She then guards that nest, lying on or by it. If she leaves briefly, a crab-eating fox or coati may prey on the eggs. Peter and I spent nights in a blind near a nest to observe the hatching. The female opens the nest to allow the young to come out when she hears them squawk. If an egg is cracked but has not hatched, she gently picks it up in her massive, toothed jaws and tenderly squeezes it open. This assures that all young hatch simultaneously, and together they can then move to water, the hatchlings yipping and the mother grunting to maintain contact.

In late 1979, the World Wildlife Fund (WWF) had, through the efforts of the American journalist Nancy Nash, signed an agreement with China for a joint study of the giant panda. I was asked to collaborate with a Chinese team, and so I left the jaguar study in the efficient hands of Peter Crawshaw and Howard Quigley. On May 15, 1980, the head of WWF, Sir Peter Scott, his wife Philippa, Nancy Nash, and I, together with a Chinese delegation, entered panda habitat in Sichuan's Wolong Nature Reserve. As informed, we were the first-ever foreigners invited into the panda's realm. We climbed up a steep slope toward a mountain research camp at an elevation of 8,200 feet. It had been established in 1978 by Professor Hu Jinchu, China's premier panda researcher, and named Wuyipeng, meaning Fifty-One Steps. On the way up we found two panda droppings composed of bamboo stem fragments. We picked them up, and measured and examined them with reverence.

In December of that year, we began an intensive panda study around Wuyipeng. The Chinese team consisted of 10 members, including Hu Jinchu as camp leader and Pan Wenshi, who is affiliated with Peking University. And soon Kay joined us. Pandas were difficult to observe in their dense bamboo habitat. We needed to radio-collar some to obtain basic information beyond examining droppings. However, I was apprehensive about tranquilizing such a rare national treasure of China. I asked Howard, with his extensive experience of sedating animals, to briefly leave the Pantanal project and assist us. We set a foot snare baited with a bit of meat. In it we caught a young male panda, which Howard tranquilized and collared without problem, much to our relief. Our team named the panda Long-Long, meaning "dragon," and also echoing the name of the reserve, Wolong. Later, an adult female was caught, which after discussion was named Zhen-Zhen, "precious" or "treasure."

As a quote from one of my books describes, "From these and others—there were about fifteen pandas in the study area—we discovered that pandas were intermittently active day and night for some fifteen hour, and that their overlapping ranges were small, averaging about two square miles each. Pandas ate up to thirty pounds of bamboo a day, and as many as eighty pounds when juicy shoots were in season." These simple facts took intensive effort to collect in this dense, dank, and cold environment. There were problems too. Poachers killed two of our five radio-collared pandas in snares. One of the bamboo species flowered and died, as it does at intervals of 45 years before recovering from seeds, causing concern that pandas might suffer from lack of food. And then there was Zhen-Zhen. Her home range included our camp. Smelling food in our communal hut, she moved in and made herself at home. Rather temperamental, she sat at one end of the hut while we cowered at the other. For a change of scene, she entered Kay's and my tent when we were in the field and slept on our bed, leaving several dropping as mementoes. We finally moved her to another part of the park, where she returned to a normal panda life. Nevertheless, I much appreciated Zhen-Zhen's determined presence. Like other species, she responded to kindness by accepting you. Most animals everywhere remain shy and wild because we have made them so.

We also joined our team in making a survey of the panda's whole range in Sichuan Province. There they survive in about 25 small and fragmented forests. Moving our focus out of Wolong, we set up an additional research base in the Tangjiahe Nature Reserve. There we studied not only pandas but also Himalayan black bears, the two bear species existing in the same forest. And there were herds of takin, a cow-sized, bulbous-nosed, hoofed animal, some of which lingered around our research hut, making a study of their daily habits fairly easy.

By early 1985, having spent four years with pandas, we generally knew what had to be done to offer the species a secure future. Wang Menghu, who coordinated the project for the Ministry of Forestry in Beijing, also felt that things were going quite well. The Chinese team was collecting useful information, and two American researchers, botanist Alan Taylor and zoologist Ken Johnson, had joined the project. Wang Menghu now asked me to do a countrywide snow leopard survey. Somewhat jokingly he also noted that "you will now work in China for the next forty years." With snow leopards found so widely in China's mountains, including the whole Tibetan Plateau, a survey would surely take much time. As I write this in 2020, my compact with China has so far lasted 40 years.

The panda project continued exceptionally well in the years after Kay and I left it because of the dedication of the Chinese staff and the interest of the government. Captive breeding improved and many young were born in zoos. My colleague Pan Wenshi established a new panda research station in the Qinling Mountains of Shaanxi Province. He and his coworkers, among them Lu Zhi, Wang Hao, and Wang Dajun, gained detailed insights into panda biology during their 13 years of research there. All pandas have received full protection in 67 reserves, with many of these now combined in the Giant Panda National Park that covers 27,134 km^2 (10,447 sq mi), and the habitat of these fragmented panda populations is being connected by tree plantations. Censuses show that there may be as many as 2,000 pandas in the wild.

Unlike pandas, snow leopards have a wide distribution in a dozen countries, extending from Afghanistan eastward over the Himalaya to the Pamir and on into Mongolia and the Lake Baikal area of Russia. However, more than half of their 2 million km^2

range lies in China. Though this has not been my experience in some other countries, I readily found coworkers for the field in China, both among young forestry department staff keen to escape an office for a while and among university graduate students. We searched widely for snow leopard spoor by car, on horseback, and on foot. The cats may make a scrape with their hind paws on mountain passes, bases of cliffs, and other conspicuous sites to leave a calling card for others to read. They also spray scent on boulders. Hair in their scats reveals what they have eaten—mostly, for example, marmots, blue sheep, and livestock on the Tibetan Plateau. Such spoor, together with tracks, provides a rough estimate of relative numbers. We were most pleased to note that the cats remained widespread in spite of human antipathy toward them. They kill livestock, though wolves do more such damage. A villager can also get a good price for the soft snow leopard pelt, and for the bones, which are used in Chinese medicine as a substitute for tiger bones. Published estimates for the number of snow leopards in the wild range from 4,500 to 7,000, perhaps half of them in China.

As is evident from this account, I find it difficult to remain focused for long on a limited goal. Soon my mind began to wander, and I wondered about the status of snow leopards and their prey in neighboring countries. Mongolia? There the government was dominated by Russia at the time. Nevertheless I applied for a visa, and to my surprise received permission to come. I left for Mongolia in 1989, the first of 17 trips to do cooperative wildlife studies. Snow leopards are quite common in the sweep of the Altai Mountains, and we decided to do a project there.

I arrived back in Ulaan Baatar, the capital, in late October 1990, and discussed project details with Jachliin Tserendeleg of the Mongolian Society for Environment and Nature. My interpreter Byambaa and I then flew to the town of Altay, where our vehicle full of equipment and biologist Amarsanaa met us. (Mongolians address each other by their last names.) Amarsanaa was the snow leopard biologist for the Mongolian Academy of Sciences. We drove across terrain that looked like an arctic wasteland deep in snow. Near the small town of Beger is the Uert Valley, where we set up *ger*, as yurts are called here, to live in. Several friendly herder families were nearby, and they helped us get established. Soon we had a cozy home, heated by livestock droppings acquired from our neighbors. Later in the month a photographer from the British company Survival Anglia arrived to film the project. And to my delight my son Eric, now a graduate student in biochemistry at Michigan State University, came to assist us.

All was settled and ready on November 11. The following day, as we hiked up the snowbound valley, the herder Amar and Amarsanaa suddenly yelled *irbes*, the Mongolian name for snow leopard, as I described in my book *Into Wild Mongolia*. On the slope, a snow leopard reclined on a boulder. Disturbed by us, it slithered uphill like a wisp of fog and vanished. We checked the site. The snow leopard, a male, had killed a female ibex, her body still warm. We hurried back to camp to get a foot snare and other equipment. I tied one leg of the ibex to a willow shrub and set the snare by the body. The snare was attached by a cable to a chunk of iron we hauled up to serve as a drag. This and a spring on the snare cable reduced the chance that the struggling cat would hurt itself. Once again I had an opportunity to sleep near a snow leopard, and I did so tucked into my warm sleeping bag.

I approached the snare slowly at first light. The snow leopard was there, crouched. I prepared a syringe with tranquilizer and attached it to the end of a special six-foot pole. The cat growled and glared at me as I stepped close to him and injected the tranquilizer with a quick jab. Five minutes later he was asleep. His paw was fine, not injured by the snare. I weighed him: 82.5 pounds. After I fitted him with a radio collar, I covered his eyes so that he could recover slowly and peacefully. We then waited nearby until he recovered and slowly walked uphill. During the following month, he meandered over this and the neighboring valley. Eric and I monitored him for three whole days, recording whether he was active or inactive every 15 minutes. For the first two days, soon after he had eaten, his signal was active 33% of the time, whereas on the third day it is 53%. Joel, the photographer, even obtained footage of the snow leopard as he reclined casually in the sun by a rock cleft. As I prepared to leave the country in late January, I was distressed that no Mongolian biologist was willing to monitor the cat. To capture an animal greatly stresses it, and one should at least get all possible data from it afterward.

Fortuitously, I had received a letter from Tom McCarthy, a wildlife biologist who had worked in Alaska for six years, expressing an interest in studying snow leopards. Tom joined us for our brief time in the Uert Valley in 1992, and then came to Mongolia with his wife and two sons in 1994 to set up a two-year snow leopard study in the Tost Uul, a nearby range, where he radio-collared two males and two females.

Meanwhile I shifted my attention to the Gobi Desert, especially to the Great Gobi National Park. The park comprises two sections, the larger of which extends across 44,000 km². There I was surprised to find snow leopard spoor in low, rocky ranges where summer temperatures often exceed 110 degrees F. This reveals the adaptability of the species. The park was established in 1976 particularly to protect the rare wild Bactrian or two-humped camel, subspecifically distinct from domestic ones. Fewer than 1,000 wild camels persist in Mongolia and the nearby deserts of China. Unfortunately these camels hybridize with the domestic ones, which irresponsibly are allowed to graze in the same areas. One day, as we approached a desert oasis, Mongolian biologists Tulgat and Chuluunbaatar suggested that we stop. Together we crawled onto a low ridge overlooking the oasis. Two wild camels were sucking up water at a seepage, and eight others awaited their turn.

Hovering near the camels were 11 pale-colored khulans or Mongolian wild asses. The camels prevented the khulans access to water by threatening them with raised muzzle. Finally the camels walked off in single file, slowly and stately, and the khulans crowded in for a drink. For nearly five hours we watched this desert spectacle while Kay waited patiently in the car for our return.

We had seen wolf tracks at several oases. Wolves, Tulgat told us, have learned to wait by an oasis until camels come to drink and then prey on the young. Indeed there were no young in the herd that we saw. Concerned for the camel's future, the government is controlling wolf numbers, mainly by killing cubs at dens.

At an oasis, I had also seen the mushy dropping of Gobi bear. This bear is a distinct subspecies of desert-living brown bear with a golden-brown pelage. Only about 40 bears survive, all in the park except the occasional one that wanders into China. In 1990 and 1991, we radio-collared three male bears, but we obtained relatively little information. It was a time of political and economic turmoil, with gasoline and food difficult to obtain. However, we learned that the bears travel from oasis to oasis mostly at night. From their droppings we learned that the bears eat grass, wild rhubarb, and *Nitraria* shrub berries, and scavenge the remains of animals. Park staff also provide the bears with nutritious livestock pellets to supplement their meager diet, and these are avidly eaten.

Fortunately Tom McCarthy collected more data on these bears, and a detailed project was initiated in 2005 by Harry Reynolds from the United States and Mijiddorj Batmunkh of the Gobi Park. One of their radio-collared females had a range of 514 km², and a male an impressive 2,485 km² (957 sq mi). One male traveled a straight-line distance of 200 km between oases, as Douglas Chadwick relates in his 2017 book, *Tracking Gobi Grizzlies*. The bears clearly need much secure space in this spartan environment to survive. The government designated 2013 as "The Year of Protecting the Gobi Bear." Yet they remain in trouble. DNA sampling shows that they are highly inbred. Illegal livestock grazing in the park continues, and gold miners surreptitiously camp at oases, preventing wildlife access to water.

Mongolia's wonderful landscapes and wildlife captivate me. This includes the great eastern steppe, with its vast herds of Mongolian gazelles, but the Tibetan plateau has been described in poetry as "this center of heaven / this core of the earth / the heart of the world." I return to the Tibetan Plateau as often as possible to study the wildlife with my local colleagues and under the auspices of forestry departments and other organizations.

In the southeastern Tibet Autonomous Region, the Yarlung Tsangpo roars down the deepest canyon in the world between two giant Himalayan peaks, both more than 23,000 feet high, on its way into India to join the Brahmaputra River. Just to the east of this canyon is a humid forest, rich with an unrivaled variety of orchids and rhododendrons and the last tigers in Tibet. In 2011, with my keen young Chinese coworkers Zhang Hong, Zhang Endi, and Lu Zhi, I headed up a steep slope toward the 14,000-foot Doxiong Pass, trailed by 18 porters. We were bound for the Medog area, at that time without road access, to look for any sign of the legendary Tibetan tigers. This hidden region is also known as Dechen Pemako, the Lotus of Great Bliss, because in Buddhist tradition it is an earthly paradise.

The year before, the government had designated this area as the 3,600-square-mile Yarlung Tsangpo Great Canyon National Park. The reserve has about 100 villages and 2,000 households in it. The local tribal people, the Lopa and Monpa, practice slash-and-burn agriculture. Our task was to evaluate the habitat in this newly established park. We soon saw that many slopes are denuded, the forest turned into field. Of wildlife we observed little, except for sale in local markets, where black bear body parts, monkey hides, and musk deer pods are openly and illegally displayed. In the Gedang administrative unit, the home of tigers, livestock grazes untended in the forest, with predictable results. There being little wildlife, tigers prey on livestock. We are told that in 1999, Gedang lost 7.8% of its cattle and 1.9% of its horses. Tigers were then killed in retribution, and a decade later the last tiger in Tibet was dead.

This corner of the Tibet Autonomous Region is also within the range of the Tibet red deer or Sikkim stag. It was listed as "probably extinct" in the conservation literature. Yet in the late 1980s, I noted four of these large, gray deer in a Lhasa zoo. I had also seen their distinct antlers in northern Nepal and been told that they had been brought from southern Tibet. When we were doing wildlife surveys in the region during October 1995, we interviewed officials and villagers about this deer. We were told that remnants persisted here and there, informants pointing vaguely at distant hills. Then we had luck. Near the village of Zhenqi, we were told that a high nearby hill covered with alpine meadows and scrub had at this season many deer. And there, at 4,500 m elevation, we found the deer singly and in groups of up to dozen, a total of 110 to 125. There were few stags, but the villagers informed us that more would come later in the season. We admired the Zhenqi community for protecting the deer with goodwill and tolerance, living up to its Buddhist principles. The Tibet Forestry Department later gave protection to the area and appointed guards to prevent poaching, but the community correctly retained its rights to continue grazing their livestock in the reserve.

To participate in the rediscovery of the Tibet red deer pleased me even more than when, earlier in the decade, I had inadvertently taken part in finding a long-missing wild pig in the Annamite Range on the Laos-Vietnam border. A family of Hmong tribal people had invited me for dinner. Pig meat bubbled in a pot over an open fire. I am told that it is wild yellow-colored pig, a *bote lin*. I know only of a black-colored wild pig in Laos. So after prying the boiled meat from the head for dinner, I saved the skull and also a bit of fresh meat. George Amato of the American Museum of Natural History later analyzed the DNA.

Comparing my black and yellow pig samples from Laos, he found that they were distinctly different. A new species? Colin Groves, an ungulate taxonomist at the Australian National University, expertly solved the problem for us. In 1892, a French Jesuit priest bought two skulls near Saigon (now Hoh Chi Minh City) in Vietnam. He recognized them as a new species, though similar to the warty pigs of Indonesia, and gave it the scientific name *Sus bucculentus*. The skulls were sent to a museum in Shanghai. The species then vanished until I ate it for dinner 100 years later, and Colin traced the missing skulls from Shanghai to Beijing.

My rather scattered projects, described in part above, have nevertheless been judged to have scientific and conservation value. I was honored with several prizes, among them the Indianapolis Prize and the Tyler Prize in the United States, the International Cosmos Prize in Japan, and the Baogang Environment Prize in China. I have devoted all award money to fieldwork, especially to help young local naturalists gain the experience of integrating research into conservation planning. Awards such as these also offer tribute to the many persons and organizations who have guided, supported, and offered me hospitality in these countries. And my wife Kay deserves special recognition for her dedicated contributions toward our joint work, both in the field and in the home, for more than six decades.

Below are summaries of six sample projects to which I have devoted effort in recent years.

Arctic National Wildlife Refuge

In 1960, President Eisenhower established what is now called the Arctic National Wildlife Refuge in northeastern Alaska, and in 1980 President Carter enlarged it to extend from the Brooks Range northward to the Arctic Ocean. America's last great wilderness was finally protected, or so I thought. In 1968, oil was discovered at Prudhoe Bay just 95 km west of the refuge. Development was rapid, and by 1977 a large pipeline sent the oil southward. Oil exploration continued, and the great caribou herds that calve on the Arctic Slope, the polar bears, grizzlies, and large migrating bird flocks were all at risk.

Now Big Oil companies, such as BP and Shell, with complete lack of moral vision, have set their sights on drilling in the Arctic Refuge and offshore in spite of a global oil glut. Alaskan politicians and two presidents named Bush encouraged this plunder of a protected area through ignorance and greed, and as of this writing, the current president does too. The Bureau of Land Management (BLM) recently published an environmental impact statement concerning the ecological risks of drilling in the refuge and in the sea. I have witnessed the destructive consequences of oil and gas development, with its roads, pipelines, oil spills, and cesspools of oil on trips there in 2006 and 2008. Reading the BLM report, I found it an utterly depressing statement, subservient and politically motivated, as well as factually superficial. Americans are now speaking up about the sanctity of this precious natural heritage, this symbol of the nation's vision and identity. But many more must do so in the courts and in the voting booths, because the pressure to drill from oil companies and politicians continues unabated.

Marco Polo Sheep Peace Park

In 1974, I found Marco Polo sheep horns at two mountain passes during a wildlife survey in northern Pakistan, and was told that the animals are seasonal visitors from neighboring China. This stimulated me to consider surveys of these sheep elsewhere in Central Asia, though knowing well that an American naturalist may not always be welcome along sensitive border areas. However, on receiving permission to survey the mountains in western China, Aili Kang and I and other local coworkers conducted surveys during which we encountered more than 2,000 Marco Polo sheep. China also established the Taxkorgan Nature Reserve in 1984, about 15,800 km^2 in size, across from Pakistan's Khunjerab National Park. This, in effect, was a trans-frontier reserve or international peace park. Research in adjoining Afghanistan and Tajikistan was a bit problematic. Tajikistan was recovering from its 1992 to 1997 civil war. With the assistance of Abdusattor Saidov of Tajikistan's Academy of Sciences, I was able to join him and others on surveys in 2003 and 2005. The photographer Beth Wald came on the latter and provided us all with photos to publicize the grandeur of these sheep.

Tajikistan has more Marco Polo sheep than the other countries, an estimated 15,000. This is in spite of much hunting by households that naturally prefer to kill and eat wild sheep rather than their own livestock. Marco Polo sheep meat, which is more flavorful than that of domestic sheep, was even served in some restaurants. However, hunting concessions protect the Marco Polo sheep because the large horns are so highly prized by foreign trophy hunters, who pay $15,000 or more to shoot a male. The horns of six- to nine-year-old males may reach a length of 190 cm (75 inches). From a ridge we looked one day into Afghanistan's Wakhan Corridor, which projects between Pakistan and Tajikistan. Marco Polo discovered the species there in 1273, describing it as a "wild sheep of great size, whose horns are a good six palms in length." It was clear that Marco Polo sheep travel readily between countries. If they receive protection in one country but not in the neighboring one, the goal of managing the species is difficult to achieve.

Beth Wald and I were with a small team in the Wakhan during the summer of 2004, where we traveled for nearly two months by yak caravan up and down the corridor. We tallied 625 Marco Polo sheep, and no doubt overlooked some. The Wildlife Conservation Society soon initiated conservation and community projects with the local Kirghiz and Wakhi people in the corridor, and the government established it as a protected area.

Having surveyed Marco Polo sheep widely, I now worked on the concept of establishing a four-country international peace park to encourage friendly relations and cooperation in managing cross-border wildlife and habitat. China hosted a meeting in 2006 during which all four countries agreed in principle to consider a 50,000 km² trans-frontier protected area. But soon Tajikistan backed out, erroneously thinking that its trophy-hunting business would be affected. The other countries are, however, cooperating with each other.

Asiatic Cheetah: The Last of Their Kind

The Asiatic cheetah, a subspecies distinct from African cheetahs, once occurred from the Near East to India. Wantonly shot, the cheetah was exterminated in all countries, leaving only Iran with a small known population of fewer than 100 animals or even fewer than 60 animals. I became interested in this elegant cat after a visit to Iran in 1974, but it was not until 2000 that I joined a team of Iranian biologists to help conduct a status survey of this and other species. Afterward, I made several more visits. On my last day afield in 2016, I saw my first wild Asiatic cheetah in the Miandasht Reserve, a female with two large cubs resting calmly by some desert shrubs. We watched them for more than half an hour before they walked off slowly, having given us the gift of a special memory.

Observations in Iran have revealed that the cheetahs travel so widely that a reserve may not be able to contain them. One reason is that their natural prey, particularly gazelles, have been wiped out over large tracts by hunters. A second reason may be that, with such a low population density, an animal has to roam widely just to find a mate. All this exposes them to various dangers. Without natural prey, cheetahs naturally kill domestic animals such as goats. Aside from herder retribution, large so-called watch dogs roam freely, and these readily kill cheetahs, especially the cubs. Cheetahs are also killed every year by speeding vehicles when they cross highways that even bisect nature reserves. The loss of any animal from such a small population is serious. We have offered the government suggestions for reducing cheetah deaths, such as banning dogs from the center of protected areas and building vehicle speed bumps on certain stretches of road. But Iran's leader, like the one in the United States, seems to have little interest in conservation, only in unbounded development. In late 2017 and early 2018, a dozen Iranian environmentalists were imprisoned, including an American Iranian and a Canadian Iranian; the last-named died in prison. Their "crime" was that they had criticized the government's environmental policies. As of this writing in June 2020, the prisoners have not been released. My cooperative work with Iran is on hold.

Mongolian Gazelles

Mongolia's eastern steppe, about 250,000 km² in extent, was the largest undamaged grassland in the world when I first visited it in 1989. Mongolia was then in transition from Soviet-style socialism to an open-market economy. At the same time the government encouraged intensive livestock production on the steppe, and it promoted unlimited development projects from oil and mineral extraction to road, railroad, and fence construction. My main concern has been how these changes will impact the future of the Mongolian gazelles. About one million gazelles live there, the largest such concentration of a wild ungulate anywhere, except on the Serengeti plains. These gazelles have been studied intensively by the American Kirk Olson and by Mongolian biologists, among them Badamchavin Lhagvasuren and Daaria Odonkhuu. I have helped intermittently, especially during the birth season from late June to early July, when herds concentrate at certain sites. At other times, the gazelles roam widely in search of suitable forage: a gazelle may have a range of more than 70,000 km² (26,910 sq mi), as radio-collared animals have shown. Gazelles occasionally suffer from mass deaths caused by viral and other diseases, but hunting by people is a principal cause of mortality. An estimated 100,000 gazelles are illegally trapped or shot for food annually by households, motorized poachers from towns, and border guards. And the legal take by herder households adds about another 30,000 a year. For some years, the government also shot 30,000 to 50,000 gazelles a year to export the bodies to China and Russia. This, however, was stopped after a meeting in 2003, which I attended.

I revisited the steppe in 2018 with Kirk Olson and Aili Kang, but my delight in being there soon declined somewhat. The changes to the steppe over the last 30 years have been drastic. Most nomadic herders now cluster near communities with their livestock herds, which are larger than ever, and there the rangeland is severely overgrazed. After passing many rows of bulbous-headed oil pumps belonging to PetroChina, we came to an agricultural development of 3,000 km², with tillers slicing up the sod and tractors spreading pesticides. The steppe has no defense against plow and plunder, and it will ultimately turn into desert, as has happened already in neighboring China.

At another site we found large, rotting bales of hay scattered over 300 km². Cut for export to China the previous year, the hay had not been picked up. I'm told that permits to destroy the steppe are easy to obtain from politicians. In my mind I can see a herd of 25,000 gazelles flowing over the steppe in a tawny flood. Will the great herds persist to entrance both Mongolians and visitors in the future? So far there has been too little awareness, too little legal and moral concern, by government departments, development agencies, and corporations concerning their action that may ultimately destroy this great steppe—the Great Father Sky, as Mongolians think of it.

On Brazil's River of Doubt

When Teddy Roosevelt failed to regain the presidency in 1912, he looked for some physical challenge. Someone suggested the descent of an unexplored river in the western Amazon of Brazil, and he eagerly accepted. It was the Rio da Duvida, the River of Doubt, later renamed Rio Roosevelt. On February 27, 1914, a team consisting of 22 persons, including Teddy's son Kermit, began the descent in seven heavy dugout canoes, two of them leaking. Ahead were 600 km of uncharted river. Progress was slow. The river was turbulent, with many rapids and waterfalls around which all the equipment and dugouts had to be portaged though the rain forest. One of the Brazilian canoeists drowned, and another was killed in a dispute with one of his countrymen, who was in turn abandoned, inflicting a loss of three team members. They were worried about poisoned arrows from the Nambiquara Indians, who shadowed the expedition. They ran out of food and were delighted when "Cherrie killed three monkeys and Lyra caught two big piranhas." Both Teddy and Kermit became seriously ill from malaria, and Teddy injured his leg, which became infected. There was concern that they would die. After two months they met a rescue mission, which escorted them to the city of Manaus on the Amazon River. All this is beautifully told by Candice Millard in her 2005 book, *The River of Doubt*.

The great westward expansion by the United States was officially closed in 1890. It continues in the Brazilian Amazon. I was curious to learn what changes had occurred along the River of Doubt in the past hundred years. What might it look like in another 100 years? So, on August 25, 2015, my Brazilian colleague Peter Crawshaw and I flew to the town of Porto Velho in the western Amazon. There we met Ana Rafaela D'Amico who, with her husband Bruno Cambraia, managed the Parque Nacional dos Campos Amazonicos. This park, about 3,700 square miles in size, was established in 2006 to protect the forests along a section of the River of Doubt. Teddy would no doubt be pleased. Now, instead of plodding to the river for 60 days by oxcart and horse, as the team led by Teddy and the Brazilian Candido Rondon had to do, we drove on a dirt track to a tourist lodge, the Fazenda Camaru. A boat, powered by a 40 hp outboard, took us up the River of Doubt over some rapids. Instead of having to carry our boat and gear around a waterfall, a tractor met us, and we ended up at the luxurious Pousada Rio Roosevelt. The hotel had air-conditioned rooms, and it catered to fishermen and to birders who came to see some of the 1,330 bird species inhabiting the Amazon. A local airstrip provided ready access. It felt incongruous and self-indulgent to sit there with a cold beer in a place where the Roosevelt-Rondon expedition camped exhausted, ill, and hungry.

I brought several camera traps to give to the park, and we set these at a natural saltlick. Wild visitors in just two days included two brocket deer, two tapirs, a small herd of white-lipped peccaries, and a jaguar male, which passed by twice. A young, female, black jaguar left me with a lovely memory when one day, while floating on the river, we spotted her sitting by the shore. Instead of fleeing, she calmly reclined and watched us about 50 feet away. She licked her lustrous black chest and shoulder, and her eyes shined like muted gold. After a while she rose and was absorbed by the forest's shadows. Her photo hangs above my desk at home.

I am all too aware that development is rapidly intruding on the River of Doubt. Ana Rafaela told me that two dams are planned along the river. Driving to the area, we saw expanses of black tree stumps, the forest burned and cleared to grow soybeans. After about three years, the soil was exhausted and the fields were turned into cattle pasture.

An Antelope of Fashion

When I began fieldwork in the Chang Tang—meaning "northern plain" in Tibetan—on the Tibetan Plateau, I was captivated by the unique large-mammal community, which includes the bulky, black, long-haired wild yak; the sprightly Tibetan gazelle; the Tibetan wild ass or kiang; and especially the Tibetan antelope. The handsome antelope males have slender, upright horns up to 60 cm long. The species is often seen in herds of thousands. But they are here today and gone tomorrow. Where do they go? It took many visits to learn the answer to this question, and on one of these my son Mark was part of the team. There are five main migratory populations, four of which spend the winter in the southern Chang Tang, where there is grazing at that season and where animals mate in December at specific sites. Then, in late May and June, the females hurry north, traveling some 200 km to remote calving grounds. The males, by contrast, drift here and there. The females with their young return to their wintering grounds in autumn. There are also resident populations, which shift only locally.

Starting in the early 1990s, I discovered something disturbing. Roving Tibetans had piles of skinned antelope carcasses by their tents, and inside were the folded hides neatly stacked. The antelopes had been shot or caught in foot traps. Teams of poachers in vehicles also sought out antelope calving grounds and slaughtered the females as they were giving birth. They took the valuable hides and left the carcasses, which I later saw scattered on the steppe. I also watched Tibetans pluck antelope hair from the hides and stuff them into sacks. For what purpose? Slowly I found the answer.

These antelope have the finest wool of any species in the world, finer than goat cashmere. The wool is smuggled mostly through Nepal to India where, in the Kashmir city of Srinagar, special weavers take the ultrasoft guard hairs of the antelope and spin them into shawls. These shawls are then sold under the name of shahtoosh, meaning "king of wool" in Persian. A simple fawn-colored shawl might sell for $2,000 to $5,000, but a beautiful embroidered one for as much as $15,000. These shawls, so lovely, soft and warm and exotic, became a fashion statement of the wealthy in Europe and North America—even though the trade has been illegal since 1979.

A mass slaughter of the species (also called chiru) for its wool during the 1990s reduced the number of animals from an estimated one million to perhaps 100,000, though a reliable census has never been done. The shahtoosh dealers also pulled the wool over the eyes of their customers for years by claiming that the animals were not being killed, that the shed wool is from wild ibex goats, which local people collect from bushes. It takes the wool from three to five antelope to weave one shawl. It was difficult to curb the sale of shahtoosh. As a woman in America exclaimed, "The shahtoosh thing is all a fiction of the animal rights fanatics." Fortunately many nongovernmental organizations in India, the United States, and elsewhere legally challenged governments to enforce the wildlife laws. Made aware of the chiru slaughter, China's government encouraged me to publicize the problem widely, and it initiated a major effort to reduce the poaching. China noted in 1998 that "17,000 pelts and 1,100 kg of wool have been confiscated, 300 guns and 153 vehicles seized, nearly 3,000 people arrested." In 1999, China also held a workshop, titled Conservation and Control of Trade in Tibetan Antelope, in Qinghai, a province in which there had been much antelope poaching. I participated. The workshop's declaration urged all countries to ban the trade.

The situation has improved. Switzerland and India, the last two legal holdouts, have stopped their shahtoosh trade officially. Chiru are still being killed in western Tibet and the wool smuggled out, and now also woven in Nepal. It remains possible to buy shawls under the counter in Delhi and Dubai. In fact, the Arab countries are at present major consumers, particularly the males making a fashion statement by wearing shahtoosh. I wonder if they realize that they are not wearing a shawl but a shroud of dead antelope. On two positive notes, my recent surveys on the Tibetan Plateau have revealed that at least some antelope populations are increasing with better law enforcement. And China has in recent years placed about one-third of the Tibetan uplands under environmental protection.

As I have related, my initial studies tended to focus on certain species, including their relations with others in the wildlife community, such as the tiger and its prey. One goal was also to establish protected areas for the wildlife and its habitat. But certain species cannot be contained within a limited protected area. Caribou in northern Alaska travel into Canada, and Mongolian gazelles roam over vast distances on the steppe. It's clear that whole ecological systems, whole landscapes, need some form of protection and management. So when China expanded its reserves to cover huge parts of the Tibetan Plateau, I was naturally delighted. Now several antelope populations can, for example, complete their whole annual cycle of migration and remain within protected areas. But a critical issue soon obtruded. Communities of people, with their livestock and even practicing some agriculture, live in certain areas. And commercial development in the form of oil drilling, mining, and others also intrudes. What viable environmental policies and management programs can local governments adopt to ensure long-term economic and ecological sustainability, not only for the human communities but also for those of animals and plants? Now when I travel to Brazil, India, Mongolia, or other countries, I evaluate a region also in terms of landscape protection.

Not that I have abandoned my deep pleasure in meeting a gorilla or jaguar, but my vision is now much broader. My aim is to suggest to communities and governments various measures for integrating ecological values into their livelihood, creating an equitable society that is based on knowledge and compassion for the natural world.

Some conservation organizations have in recent years promoted the integration of conservation and development, calling it "sustainable." Some have even suggested that protected areas should be turned over to local communities to manage. My account here demonstrates that conservation is *not* part of development. Protected areas are the foundation of conservation, in part symbols and in part imperatives, treasures of the natural world for aesthetic and ethical reasons. There are, however, no victories in conservation. Oil corporations insist on invading the Arctic National Wildlife Refuge, and the Tanzanian government wants to build a major highway through the Serengeti, to mention just two such morally corrupt ventures. Conservation, to be effective, clearly

Dr. George Schaller in Tibet.

needs to contribute to the livelihood of communities. In the final analysis, conservation is largely about resolving conflicts among people. I learned years ago that a field biologist does not just study animals, but must also be a social scientist, educator, diplomat, and fundraiser. Every person must in some way become an activist and help promote the survival of nature's beauty. As the poet Ezra Pound exhorted,

Pull down thy vanity, I say pull down.

Learn of the green world what can be thy place.

Further Reading

Chadwick, Douglas. 2016. Tracking Gobi Grizzlies: Surviving Beyond the Back of Beyond. Patagonia.

Darwin, Francis, ed. 1887. The Life and Letters of Charles Darwin. John Murray, Albemare Street.

Millard, Candice. 2005. River of Doubt: Theodore Roosevelt's Darkest Journey. Broadway Books.

Schaller, G. B. 1964. The Year of the Gorilla. University of Chicago Press.

Schaller, G. B. 1967. The Deer and the Tiger: Study of Wild Life in India. University of Chicago Press.

Schaller, G. B. 1973. Golden Shadows, Flying Hooves. A. A. Knopf.

Schaller, G. B. 1980. Stones of Silence: Journeys in the Himalaya. Viking Press.

Schaller, G. B. 1993. The Last Panda. University of Chicago Press.

Schaller, G. B. 1998. Wildlife of the Tibetan Steppe. University of Chicago Press.

Schaller, G. B. 2012. Tibet Wild: A Naturalist's Journeys on the Roof of the World. Island Press.

Schaller, G. B. 2020. Into Wild Mongolia. Yale University Press.

CHAPTER 3

AMONG THE ELEPHANTS

DR. IAIN DOUGLAS-HAMILTON

2010 Recipient of the Indianapolis Prize

African Elephant
Loxodonta africana

Diana—backlit by the setting sun and coming at us full tilt—is etched forever in my mind. I remember that moment in snapshots. She! In all her fury! Towering at full height above me as I sprawled helplessly on the dusty ground. She battered me repeatedly with her forelegs before I, winded, somehow rolled out from beneath her.

I had been walking in the bush with a young Samburu warrior and David Quammen, a writer from *National Geographic*. It was part of my evening ritual, no different from the norm. The sun had dipped low on the horizon, and none of us noticed Diana with her family in the twilight. The warrior only had time to shout "NDOVU!" as Diana was already charging at us with short, shrill trumpets. She chased me around a small bush, then threw me to the ground with a thump of her trunk and tusk. I stared up at her front legs on either side of my head, heart pounding in my chest, as she batted me from side to side with her feet; I was acutely aware that my life depended on what decision she made next. Luckily, she changed her mind—or perhaps had never intended serious harm. Tusks held high, she gradually circled back, retreating a step at a time, while casting ferocious looks in my direction. Then she strode away, leaving me lightly bruised and looking at the deep gouge marks where she had plunged her tusks nine inches into the ground, just above where my head had been.

This was in 2008, many years after I had first come to Africa and 11 years since I'd first come to know her family, the Royals. If she intended only to frighten me, she was highly successful. Or had she wanted to kill me but then decided otherwise? I will never know. The possibility that she changed her mind prompts fascinating questions. We assume that elephants possess an advanced consciousness and that they are sentient beings. It is this sentience—displayed in their complex, multi-tiered social structures; in their ability to learn to avoid beehive fences surrounding farms; in their compassionate behavior toward unrelated elephants, or possibly when deciding in a split second not to hurt a helpless, subdued human—that has driven my passionate interest and research on African elephants over the last half century.

I had been attracted to Africa long before I loved elephants. Originally, I wanted to research lions, but George Schaller got there first, so I moved on and began my journey learning about elephants (*Loxodonta africana*) in 1965, living with them in Tanzania's Lake Manyara National Park throughout the mid-1960s. The elephants were stripping the bark off the trees, and the park managers wanted to know how and why they were doing it. Of course, once I started studying elephants, I was completely hooked.

The 1960s were a golden age for Africa's newly formed national parks. Animals had become tamer when exposed to tourists, and for the first time a window opened where scientists could study wildlife at close quarters without the animals running away. The first behavioral studies began: Jane Goodall with chimpanzees; George Schaller with lions; Hans Kruuk with hyenas; John Goddard with rhinos; and me with elephants. It was a golden age for me, too. I met my soul mate and wife-to-be, Oria, in 1969, and soon we were married parents living in the bush. Becoming a husband and father did not hinder my work; rather, my family and my vocation became deeply intertwined.

Early on it became clear to me that to understand the Manyara elephants' ecology, I would need to study their behavior. The elephants exhibited intelligence and organization, and I realized that their social behavior could be key to understanding their responses to the world they occupy. I spent the 1960s collecting large amounts of data on elephant ecology, population dynamics, and behavior, hoping I would one day begin to understand their thought processes.

Oria and I had to return to Oxford University for a while, and when we came back to Manyara in 1973, we heard new tales of slaughtered elephants. The price of ivory was soaring, and the world's rapidly growing appetite for it seemed insatiable. Indeed, the price of ivory fueled more and more horror. Ivory traders did not see elephants as a symbol of majesty, nor as sentient beings with an elaborate social structure. Instead, they seemed to regard elephants merely as bearers of a commodity to be harvested. Never in our worst nightmares had we imagined that in parts of Africa, men in green uniforms would enter the parks and turn their automatic weapons on elephants, and yet it happened. The ivory wars had begun and would result in the slaughter of nearly half the continent's elephants over the coming two decades. As the next few years provided me with more and more scientific evidence of the threats to their sustainability as a species, I had no choice but to make my behavioral studies secondary to the cause of their survival.

In 1970, a confluence of two powerful forces acted against elephants in Africa. On the one side were conservationists who sincerely thought that culling elephants was necessary in some national parks to maintain ecologic balance and integrity. On the other were people driven by ivory's value. It was a commodity that could be used as a multinational currency. Ivory had become much more important than live elephants, and those who trafficked it were both organized and relentless.

Reaction to the excessive killing for ivory was complicated by a paradox. Although it was accepted that elephants were declining in number across most of their range, in many of the national parks and reserves where they lived at high densities, they were capable of transforming landscapes from woodland to savannah. In the 1960s there was a divisive debate about whether elephants should be culled for their own good and for the preservation of their habitats. If they had to be "harvested," some wondered, why shouldn't money be made from their ivory, meat, and skins? Ethics aside, the root of the conservation problem was that there were many *protected* areas with very high elephant densities, despite a general decline across the *entirety* of their population distribution.

I began to realize that we needed to know much more about elephants, as so much depended on their numbers, range, and trends. How many elephants were there in Africa? Could they sustain the offtake by the ivory trade? How would they interact with humankind's growing footprint on their landscape? What was special about elephant behavior, and how did it relate to the ethics of how to treat them? Those questions and my attempts to reconcile their needs with their relationships with humans—our appetites and our attitudes—would define my family's lives. It was clear to me that we would need to understand all these issues better before we could develop sound policies that would assure the long-term sustainability of elephants. The quest for those data sent us across the elephant's entire range in Africa, and into the skies.

The inclination to fly, as I wrote in Oria's and my 1975 book *Among the Elephants,* is in my family's blood. My father and his brothers all flew, and one of my aunts even had the singular experience of crash-landing in bad weather below Mount Kilimanjaro in the 1930s. In 1933, my eldest uncle was the first to fly over Mount Everest in an open-cockpit biplane. My father flew Spitfires for the Royal Air Force during World War II but was killed when his bullet-damaged de Havilland Mosquito crash-landed after a photo reconnaissance mission over France. So I knew that the joy and freedom of flying also came with risks.

But the sheer exhilaration of flying touched my soul and drew me to combine it with my need to gather as much data as possible about elephants' social groups and movements and their ranging behavior across the remote wildernesses of Africa. Thus began the Pan-African Elephant Census, our first attempt to estimate the number of elephants in Africa. When Peter Scott asked me, along with my colleague Harvey Croze, to form an Elephant Specialist Group for the International Union for Conservation of Nature (IUCN), we had already been collecting data on the status of elephants from game wardens and scientists in East Africa since 1969. The group grew and developed over the years, eventually covering the whole of Africa and changing its name from time to time. As I write, it is called the African Elephant Specialist Group of the IUCN. It is flourishing and includes many distinguished scientists. After 25 years of groundbreaking leadership by Dr. Holly Dublin, the group is now led by Dr. Ben Okita and Dr. Robert Slotow, nationals of Kenya and South Africa, respectively. I am honored to be a member still.

From the mid-1970s into the 1980s, I contacted scientists and park wardens across Africa; accumulated all the available information on elephant numbers, ranges, and trends; and catalyzed and organized counts. Where possible, I counted elephant populations from the air myself. With colleagues, I worked to standardize sampling techniques that would allow large population surveys to be estimated with consistent methods in various locations. At the same time, I continued my studies on the movements and behaviors of individual elephant families in Manyara.

In the air, soaring above the pink flamingos of Lake Manyara, or past a smoking volcano in the Great Rift Valley, I felt a huge sense of freedom. Back then you could fly toward any point of the compass and still find wild country stretching to the horizon. When in counting mode, we flew from treetop height to 400 feet in the air, and from the cockpit I could see the elephant silhouettes beneath the trees. Counting animals from the air was as much an art as it was a science. When we first started our surveys, I flew in a cloth-covered, single-engine four-seater Piper Pacer but later graduated to a Cessna 185. We didn't have any of the high-tech gadgets now used to navigate and maintain precise flight lines and altitude, but we covered the ground thoroughly. Spotting elephants depended on having the right search image in one's mind and the sharp eyes of an experienced crew. Flying was exhilarating and also a vital part of our research. The surveys we made greatly expanded our knowledge of the great elephant populations in Africa, along with the inevitable errors in estimation and how to allow for them.

Support for this research, in the latter half of the 1970s, came from the IUCN, the World Wildlife Fund (WWF), and the New York Zoological Society (now Wildlife Conservation Society). This project was also supplemented by an investigation I directed on the ivory trade for the US Fish and Wildlife Service. Initially, I wanted to see if the ivory trade had either the will or the ability to control itself, going by the rationale that no industry would want to kill the goose that laid the golden eggs. That was idealistic and unrealistic. By the end of 1979, I knew for sure that traders were traders, and they sold ivory without a care for the consequences for elephants. Their actions had brought us to the doorstep of an existential crisis for elephants. My data, combined with those of others, resulted in the African elephant becoming listed as a "threatened species," and agents with the US Fish and Wildlife Service told me that this would allow them to increase their control over ivory in US markets. It remained to be seen whether that would be enough to keep the ivory-harvesting kills within sustainable limits.

In the meanwhile, however, as I gathered and analyzed more data, I saw the beginnings of another concern. The characteristics of the ivory traded that we were recording suggested that the age profile of elephant populations was changing. The mean tusk weight of harvested ivory fell from around ten kilograms to less than five. It appeared that we had already lost most of the big-tuskers, and ivory poachers were now targeting smaller individuals—often breeding females, especially the grand old matriarchs, who would rush out to confront danger while their families escaped, thereby making themselves prime poaching targets. Some herds became grotesquely distorted in their demographics, with all mature females killed and the youngsters left orphaned with no leaders to guide them.

Another worrying statistic soon appeared: in June 1978, I learned that the price of ivory had surpassed $120 per kilo. It seemed that the first effect of the emerging trade restrictions was to increase the value of ivory. How would the lure of high prices affect illegal hunting and the black markets? A tenfold increase in the price of anything over the course of a decade is bound to attract both the desperate and the unscrupulous, and that was certainly the case with ivory. Many of those in the conservation world sincerely, but mistakenly, believed that the high prices paid for ivory could be converted into a regulated ivory trade whose profits could subsidize elephant conservation. But other powerful people took the opportunity to "industrialize" the harvesting of ivory by using modern weaponry and transport and by recruiting bands of hunters. Organized crime and warlords came into our little world of conservation and science.

The devastation was everywhere. In September 1979, I visited Zambia's stunning Luangwa Valley, where 86,000 elephants had been counted in just one section earlier in the decade. After a week of aerial census over the same ground, I reported a loss of 40% of the population since 1973. The situation was worse in Kenya's Tsavo and Uganda's Murchison Falls National Parks, to be followed by the plummeting number of Selous's elephants in Tanzania. My travels and surveys revealed Zaire's corrupt center of ivory exploitation and the ivory trafficking of "Emperor" Jean-Bédel Bokassa and the La Couronne organization in the Central African Republic. The unchecked slaughter in Cameroon and the high-volume smuggling of illicit ivory in Congo meant that the once prolific forest elephants were decimated over the decades. In 1979, I drew up an African Elephant Action Plan that gave the known statistics for that era and suggested courses of action for each country.

The African Elephant Action Plan contained maps and data tables and included specific recommendations. Combined with my report to the US Fish and Wildlife Service, I recommended two governing principles: that we should concentrate on reinforcing the protected areas and that controlling or eliminating the vast illegal ivory trade should be undertaken on every front. I argued for selective trophy-trading bans in Africa, particularly the corrupt collectors' and buyers' permits that gave free rein to whitewashing illegal ivory with claims that it had been collected through natural mortality. I called for complete transparency in all international ivory transactions and forcing open the accounts of all ivory traders. This was seen as a declaration of war by powerful forces that tried to undermine my work.

Nevertheless, my experiences strengthened my resolve, and the data continued to mount. In 1980, when flying over Uganda's Queen Elizabeth National Park with a team of Ugandan and international elephant scientists, we counted just 150 elephants where I had seen more than 1,000 just four years prior. The rest had vanished. South of the Nile, in Murchison Falls National Park, our experience was horrifying. Initially exultant at spotting a big herd of 110 elephants, we realized with horror that those at the rear were wounded, dragging their bodies forward on painfully bullet-shattered limbs. Behind them we found the dead. In the late 1960s this population had numbered over 8,000.

In our efforts to save the African elephant from annihilation, we encountered opposition in almost every form imaginable. We faced militias bent on enriching themselves and their overlords; we and other researchers were shot at in the air and on the ground. We also found that our science was challenged. But behind much of that opposition was the mistaken idea that being friendly and understanding of the ivory trade would lead to positive actions from the ivory traders themselves. I have told the ins and outs of this story in the book I wrote with Oria titled *Battle for the Elephants*. Unfortunately for the elephants, most of the 1980s was wasted before the conservation movement came to grips with tackling the ivory trade.

Early in the 1980s the pendulum of opinion in conservation circles swung in favor of a new ivory quota system. Several earnest conservationists supported this approach, believing that such a system would bring the ivory trade under control by capping annual tusk exports. Each country with an elephant population would establish a yearly limit, and every export would require a permit. It was hoped that imposing a quota would allow for elephant sustainability. I was skeptical about the population estimates and trend projections endorsed by the proponents of the quota system. I feared that a legal trade in ivory would provide cover for a continued illegal trade, and year after year, my opposition hardened. Nevertheless, the appetite for a solution that would grant some degree of victory for all concerned overwhelmed those of us who held absolute views against the trade. The ivory quota system was pushed through at the 1985 conference of CITES, or the Convention on International Trade in Endangered Species, where every three years the world's governments, nongovernmental organizations (NGOs), and intergovernmental organizations come together to discuss controls on international trade in threatened species.

The outcome was as bad as the worst predictions. Somalia scheduled a massive sale of 17,000 tusks; Burundi sold nearly 100 tons of ivory, despite having no elephants; and nearly 300 tons of poached ivory were sold in Singapore. The quota system had become a tool for smugglers and money launderers, and continuing the illegal slaughter of elephants was clearly in their best interests. I came to believe that the only way to move forward from this point was to list the African elephant as a CITES Appendix I species—that is, one threatened with extinction such that trade is only permitted under exceptional circumstances.

That would not happen until 1989.

The violence—against both humans and elephants—and the smuggling and money laundering continued. Opponents to a permanent and complete ban claimed that it would simply drive the trade underground, yet studies showed that 90% of sales had occurred illegally. So at the CITES conference in 1989, everyone knew that all we had spent two decades fighting for was heading for extinction in the wild. The African elephant population was depleted by nearly 50%, down from my initial estimate of 1.3 million elephants in the 1970s to an estimated 600,000.

The tension in the conference hall was tangible. After I presented my report to the assembly, there was a last-ditch attempt to impose voting by secret ballot on the delegates. Fortunately, that desperate measure was resoundingly rejected. There was also a proposed amendment to exempt all the nations of Southern African from a potential ban, and that failed by a vote of 70 to 20, with one abstention. The next vote, for an outright ban, also failed with 53 votes in favor, 36 votes against, and two abstentions. The rules required a two-thirds majority, and the ban supporters tallied only 58%. There was no option other than to push for a compromise that came to be known as the Somali Amendment, which proposed a two-year initial global ban on the ivory trade.

As the hands went up and the votes were counted, one person began to clap. The applause quickly spread, and soon everyone was on his or her feet in an ovation that seemed to come from everywhere. The vote was 76 to 11 in support of the amendment, with four abstentions. An overwhelming majority of the delegates had voted to end the international trade in African elephant ivory.

As I write this in 2020, *Loxodonta africana* is a CITES Appendix I species, except for the elephant populations of Botswana, Namibia, South Africa, and Zimbabwe, which are listed in Appendix II. This classification allows elephant ivory from those nations to be exported as hunting trophies and also some ivory sales, with the proceeds going to support conservation. The 1989 ivory trade ban worked for the elephants in East and Southern Africa, and twenty years of cease-fire had allowed significant recoveries. In Central African countries, however, after an initial lull, the illegal trade grew once again, especially in the vastness of Zaire (now the Democratic Republic of the Congo) and its neighboring countries, where wars, instability, and massive corruption did not allow for stabilization and recovery, and so the secretive forest populations continued to decline.

Sadly, we lost ground again in 2009 as the price of ivory returned to record heights, and a new era of illegal elephant slaughter began, fueled by demand from the increasingly prosperous China. In response, a worldwide coalition formed to counter elephant killing and ivory trading, and to an extent we have been able to contain the new threat. New technology has also enabled far better monitoring, which leads to better understanding of how elephants' needs can be met in the face of expanding human populations and development in their ranges.

The formal ban on the ivory trade gave me enough of a breather to found Save the Elephants and get back to my behavioral research, taking what I'd begun in Manyara in new directions. I have long believed that by understanding how elephants make decisions, we can better understand their needs and try to meet them in a rapidly changing world, while at the same time conserving the habitats on which they and other animals depend. We began tracking elephants in earnest in 1995 with Global Positioning System (GPS) technology; we explored landscapes from their perspective in the vast and arid wilderness of northern Kenya, and with colleagues in the Sahel in Mali, the South African bushveld, and into the deepest forests of Central Africa, we were tracking the elephants' movement on our maps and satellite images. The data we collected helped us stand up for the elephants' right to space, as well as the rights of a host of other species and habitats. Ultimately, it is human beings who will determine wildlife survival or extinction. Through our presence in the field, we have tried to plant an important seed of conservation on the front line, among the people who share the land with elephants.

In 1995, we wanted to track a magnificent elephant in Amboseli National Park. He liked to wander across the border into Tanzania, where he was in danger of being shot by sport hunters. He became the first elephant ever to wear a GPS collar. These collars, the first of their kind, allowed us to follow elephants in all kinds of weather and terrain, by day and night, in and out of forests, and across international borders and man-made boundaries. Remote tracking revealed their intimate lives and problems, and it generated information on a scale never before available to researchers. Nowadays, sophisticated algorithms written by Jake Wall inform us when a radio-tracked elephant is in trouble. Our system enables rangers to respond to specific threats faster than ever before.

The Save the Elephants' Animal Tracking Program, initially supported by Discovery Communications, was a critical step, with each tagged elephant sending text messages every hour of its exact position. This has helped deepen both bull and cow with calf social studies and has identified crucial corridors that elephants use. Such information, which is displayed and analyzed by advanced computer mapping, is vital for wildlife authorities and stakeholders in planning for a secure future for elephants and their habitats.

This project took off in 1997 when we started our long-term monitoring of the 900-plus elephants that used both Samburu and Buffalo Springs National Reserves as part of their range and when we built our Save the Elephants research center. We took on a very able young scientist, George Wittemyer, who for his PhD project had learned the individual identities of more than 500 elephants and began recording births, deaths, estrus, musth, and associations between elephants. Soon David Daballen, who was recruited locally and is now one of Africa's foremost elephant observers, joined him. For ten years we were pleased to discover that births exceeded deaths and that the population was expanding at approximately 4.5% per annum, in contrast to the former years of poaching.

Oria started Elephant Watch Camp, a simple and beautiful eco-camp on the banks of the Ewaso River, after seeking the blessing and protection of the local Samburu elders. Her intention was to employ local young men and women and give them a livelihood and let them benefit from living in proximity to elephants. The camp was a sister organization to Save the Elephants and provided a platform to engage with the community. Oria also set up an educational program for local children. Over the years, many who graduated from the program went on to a university or became involved in professional work that their education had helped make possible. Being closely involved with the community brought a fullness and joy to our work as we shared what we knew with the Samburu, and we benefited greatly from their culture that was so deeply adapted to the rigorously wild landscape. Elephant Watch Camp allowed us to interact with our donors, and it sat just upriver from the Save the Elephants research camp. Our daughter Saba eventually took over from Oria and made a series with the British Broadcasting Corporation called *This Wild Life*, which captured the adventures and challenges of running a camp in the bush, caring for her own small children, and engaging with the Samburu people to find a future for elephants in relation to their culture.

In the same period, we began comprehensive monitoring of elephant deaths in Samburu and northern Kenya as part of a CITES project called Monitoring the Illegal Killing of Elephants (MIKE), which employed Onesmas Kahindi and collaborated with the Kenya Wildlife Service. Onesmas established a valuable network of contacts throughout the local community. This was an innovative participatory project, and the collection of large amounts of data on elephant mortality was meant to serve as an early-warning system that would trigger alarms in the case of a renewed surge in ivory poaching. Our project was part of a network of more than 40 MIKE sites across Africa.

At the same time, we became involved with the last Sahelian elephants that live southeast of Timbuktu in a bend of the Niger

River and survive in extremely arid conditions. We tracked these elephants for two and a half years and, in 2002, charted the longest elephant migration route in Africa, as they moved between Mali and Burkina Faso, eking out an existence between desert lakes and scrubland. Six years later we would radio-collar nine more elephants in Mali and find out that the desert elephants, already constricted by a drying climate, were under new human pressures at the dwindling water holes.

The tracking technology was helping elsewhere, too. We donated some GPS collars to the Wildlife Conservation Society team in Central Africa, who for the first time tracked elephants through the equatorial rain forests. Vital information was gathered on seasonal movements of the forest elephants, whose number had been in sharp decline due to poaching, trading in bushmeat, and logging.

We launched an important transboundary project based in South Africa in the Timbavati private nature reserve, where, happily, neither drought nor poaching prevailed. With an elephant population on the edge of the vast ecosystem of Kruger National Park, and with a new policy of removing elephant fences on all sides, we knew it was important to monitor how the elephants responded. The elephants we radio-collared provided valuable information on the movements of big bull elephants in and out of the Kruger ecosystem, between the park and the adjacent private nature reserve. This project was managed by a subgroup of Save the Elephants in South Africa, which budded off into an independent NGO called Elephants Alive, founded by one of our trustees, Marlene McCay, and run by Michelle Henley. They deployed collars in Kruger National Park, in private nature reserves to the west, and eventually extended farther east across the international border into Mozambique, up to and beyond the Limpopo River. Our aim with these tracking projects was to understand elephant ranging patterns and the complexity of conserving biodiversity in a landscape increasingly dominated by people. This led to extensive collaborations, and all bore fruit in numerous peer-reviewed publications.

A key to our program in northern Kenya has been finding ways to enhance survival and tolerance between humans and wildlife by recruiting local people to participate in wildlife tourism and scientific research on elephants. We recognized that one solution would not fit all areas, as conditions varied from the least-altered habitats of the north to rapidly expanding small-scale agriculture in the south. In the south, elephants and people needed to be separated by fences, but in the north, where elephants still had freedom of movement, coexistence was still possible.

Safe corridors have emerged as one of the most important factors for future conservation, and our software could help define those corridors. We worked with Esri, Google Earth, and later with Vulcan to provide ultra-sharp three-dimensional images of terrain on which we could track elephant movements in close to real time. It was clear that the key would be to lobby for space for elephants. Kenya's land use policy was under review and had reached a critical juncture. In South Africa and Mali, where we were also following individual elephants, policy for land use and for elephant populations was also under the microscope.

For nature to survive, we would need an educated and interested public, people who are aware of conservation needs in their own right. Educating kids was the right place to start, and it is a long-term goal. Oria developed our strategy to give *individual* commitment to the children we sponsored. Our small education program grew fast, and staff formed deep bonds with the children. Few other projects have given more pleasure to our staff.

The year 2008 dawned with intense political unrest following Kenya's elections, but for elephants, this was the last year of respite

before the ivory trade began to stir again. That year CITES decided to allow the sale of South Africa's ivory stockpiles to Japan
and to China. Soon, the resurgence of killing elephants for ivory
that we had long feared became evident in Central and East Africa. Fortunately in Kenya, we had a better early-warning system
than before, but the red lights were flashing: the proportion
of illegally killed elephants in the overall sample of dead ones
was rising. Parallel work by colleagues showed a rising price for
ivory—and an alarming Chinese connection.

The efficacy of our participatory elephant carcass detection
system was such that, out of all the elephant carcasses found in
more than fifty nation-states in Africa and Asia that were monitoring elephants, one-fifth came from our Laikipia Samburu site.
This was not because poaching was worse there but because our
system worked better. Thanks to our wide network of relationships with the local people, started by Onesmas and carried on by
David Daballen, we were able simply to ask, "Where are the dead
elephants?" Because they knew and trusted our team, the nomads
willingly showed us where the carcasses were. Each mortality was
verified, photographed, and its position logged with GPS.

By 2009 the increased Chinese demand for ivory had become
a serious problem. We knew that the only solution would be to
raise awareness for the people of China of the devastating effects
of buying ivory. If their attitudes toward the ivory trade appeared
rapacious, I reasoned that, in the Victorian era, the European
powers had plundered the world's natural resources as though
there were no limits, and kinder behavior to animals had only
came later. We needed to build worldwide awareness that nature's resources can run out and therefore must be safeguarded,
with the overexploited elephants as a symbol of this awareness.

That year the rains failed, and a terrible drought took hold of
northern Kenya. The situation in Samburu and Buffalo Springs
National Reserves was made much worse by the invasion of

countless livestock illegally grazing in the protected areas of the reserves. Hardly a blade of grass remained, and vulnerable species such as waterbuck, buffalo, and warthog were dying. With elephants, it is the young and the old that are vulnerable, and we recorded the passing away of the much-beloved matriarchs Navajo, Mohican, and Rosemary, and many calves died too.

After the drought came the flood. In the early dawn of March 4, 2010, swelled by heavy rains farther upstream, the river crested its banks and a wall of water akin to an inland tsunami washed over the grounds of both Save the Elephants and the Elephant Watch Camp, catching tourists and staff unaware and sweeping away tents and facilities. It was a great pulse of nature. The water came up so quickly that it was only possible to evacuate guests with whatever possessions they could grab with a moment's notice. Some of the staff had to climb trees to get away from the rising water; one was very nearly swept away, and he was saved only when the waves washed him up against another tree that he was able to climb.

The water eventually receded, leaving scenes of devastation in its wake. Beds, tents, and computers were submerged in a thick layer of mud or strung up in the treetops. The relief process began immediately. I flew in blankets and water, and the British Army airlifted people to safety and brought in additional supplies. Through the generosity of our donors and their overwhelming response, we rebuilt the camp and resumed our scientific work, as well as the work of bringing guests to witness this spectacular wilderness. By the simple act of visiting the elephants, they helped to preserve the elephants' home.

It was during this difficult year that I was awarded the Indianapolis Prize, out of the blue! As one of the world's most important awards for wildlife conservation, it was a tremendous boost to all at Save the Elephants to have our labor recognized. I traveled to Indianapolis to receive the Prize at a spectacular gala for a thousand people and was happily joined by family, friends, and colleagues. I received the Prize with deep gratitude and enjoyed a momentary respite from the vicissitudes of drought, ivory poaching, habitat destruction, insecurity, and flood.

We had strong evidence that China was the largest importer of illegal ivory from Africa, fueled by a soaring demand from an affluent middle class, and we surmised that addressing this demand could be the key to lowering the illegal killing of elephants. We had long wanted to build contacts in China and to better understand Chinese views about elephants. The chance came when I met the Fehsenfeld family in Indianapolis. Their company, the Heritage Group, works in China. In October 2010, our team, including Suzie and Courtney Fehsenfeld, Xishun Zhang from Heritage China, Paul Grayson from the Indianapolis Zoological Society, and Oria and I, went to China and were received with great hospitality by the China Wildlife Conservation Association (CWCA). We visited the last 200 wild elephants in the forest of Xishuangbanna, where they are treasured and thrive in the forest. Elephants are strictly protected, and anyone caught with ivory is severely punished.

This was a revelation. We thought that if China treated Africa's elephants as well as it treated its own, we could significantly reduce the demand driving the severe poaching. It seemed that most buyers in China were unaware that elephants had to die for ivory to be available. When a CWCA delegation, organized by Xishun and sponsored by the Heritage Group, paid us a return visit in Kenya, we were able to show them free-roaming African elephants at close quarters and, regrettably, some orphan babies whose mothers were illegally killed for ivory. It was an unprecedented wildlife experience for all, and a deeper level of understanding was achieved. Our Chinese guests were shocked by the facts of poaching, but the living elephants thrilled them. This new awareness laid the ground for further cooperation and harnessed China's influence in Africa to foster better protection.

The breakthrough came when Yao Ming, the famous Chinese basketball player, visited Africa for the first time. We hosted him thanks to WildAid, an NGO that specializes in gut- wrenching videos showing the effects of the illegal wildlife trade. Yao Ming witnessed the joy of sentient, playful, social elephants interacting in Samburu, but we also brought him face to face with elephants freshly killed for their ivory. His words of shock and dismay struck a chord in China and were relayed around the world.

The poaching also reached right into Samburu itself. George Wittemyer, David Daballen, and I wrote a note to *Nature* and pointed out that even in the long-established Samburu National Reserve, poaching had escalated wildly. Poachers had killed so many bull elephants that they had skewed the population into a two-to-one ratio of females to males. With the big bulls gone, large females were being targeted, leaving one in five families with no mature females left and the number of orphans rising rapidly. On the black market, a large bull's ivory was worth the equivalent of 15 years of salary for an unskilled laborer. If poachers were willing to take great risks in a relatively well-protected reserve, we argued that this might be a harbinger of what was to come to protected areas across Africa. And so it proved to be.

By 2012 our warnings about rising ivory poaching had been confirmed by many other parties, from the ongoing body count reported by MIKE, ivory seizures, and investigations into illegal ivory sold on markets in the Far East. Save the Elephants catalyzed a coalition of like-minded individuals, NGOs, and governments to respond. In May 2012 John Kerry held a Senate Foreign Relations Committee hearing, its testimony published as *Ivory and Insecurity: The Global Implications of Poaching in Africa*, where John Scanlon, then director of CITES, and I testified. I reviewed elephant ivory poaching in Africa and concluded that

America should engage with China at the highest diplomatic levels in joint leadership to tackle the crisis. That year the *New York Times* ran a series of hard-hitting newspaper articles by Jeffrey Gettleman about the problem. *National Geographic* came out with an article titled "Blood Ivory." Then secretary of state, Hillary Clinton made an inspiring speech to the diplomatic community on the illegal wildlife trade, centered on elephants. In June 2013, I had the opportunity to brief officials at the White House together with our partners at WWF. In July, former president Barack Obama announced a $10 million wildlife poaching initiative, and during a summit with China's president Xi Jinping, the issue of ivory was raised. The Wildlife Conservation Society then convened a meeting of leading elephant NGOs to meet Hillary Clinton, which seeded a major new coalition to work with the Clinton Global Initiative to stop the killing, stop the trafficking, and stop the demand. The poaching issue even went as far as the United Nations Security Council. These entities, formerly unaware of the extent of the ivory crisis, took note that the world might actually lose elephants in the wild.

All in all, this was a far more robust international reaction to the elephant crisis than we had experienced in the 1970s and 1980s. But the price of ivory was still soaring. The effects of the illegal ivory trade continued to widen and deepen—a tragic echo of what had happened in the 1970s and 1980s, when Africa lost half of its elephants.

The MIKE reports of 2012, backed by good statistics, strongly supported the conclusion that elephants were now declining in all four regions of Africa. This level of decline could not be sustained. Some well-known elephant populations in famous protected areas had suffered high percentages of illegal kills, which pointed to the populations' potential doom. Apart from a few bright spots where more eco-guards had been deployed, the news from Central Africa was unremittingly bad. Never had there been such a storm of opposing forces, organized crime, prolific weapons, and high incentives to participate in the illegal ivory trade, and in many countries there had been an inadequate response and a lack of political will to protect the elephants.

During the 1960s and early 1970s, we believed that elephants still flourished in the vast forests of Central Africa at truly astonishing densities, but by 1979 I concluded that the losses had been dramatic. By 2012 scientists such as John Hart and Fiona Maisels proved that 60% of the forest elephants had been eliminated. Ravaged by bandits and government forces hungry for income, more than three-quarters of Central Africa's elephants were thought to have been lost over two decades.

The global implications of the loss of these elephants were serious. Now that Central Africa had been exhausted as the major source of ivory to the world, I warned that the demand for ivory would fall squarely on East Africa's elephants. If those populations were then depleted, the elephants of Southern Africa, hitherto well protected, would be next. In 2014 I coauthored a paper with George Wittemyer, Joseph Northrup, Julian Blanc, Patrick Omondi, and Kenneth Burnham that analyzed data from the MIKE project and suggested that 100,000 elephants were killed over the three years from 2010 to 2012. This was an astonishing number given a total estimated African population of about 500,000. For our modeling, we drew on our precise monitoring of the deaths of known elephants in Samburu to interpret the continental figures.

Fortunately, awareness of the elephant crisis was spreading from a few conservation-minded people to a broader world consensus. For the first time, scientists—armed with evidence from key indicator populations—were nearly unanimous in determining that elephants were in serious trouble across their range, with exceptions only in Southern Africa. Ultimately it was the facts, given credibility by science, that stimulated united international action.

CITES is the single most powerful forum for deciding the future of elephants, and Save the Elephants was at the 2013 CITES meeting in force. The focus in Bangkok in March 2013 was very much on elephants. Tanzania wisely withdrew a proposal to sell its ivory stockpile, thus leading to a much friendlier atmosphere among delegates who held differing views on the question of such sales. The usual discussion over the theoretical desirability of a controlled ivory trade was postponed, and the ban on international trade in ivory remained in place.

Some major achievements for elephants followed. A new mandate stated that DNA samples should be taken on future ivory seizures weighing more than 500 kilograms, and all parties must report on their ivory stockpiles once a year. The CITES convention also decided that the CITES secretary-general would cooperate with the United Nations Office on Drugs and Crime regarding the illegal killing of elephants, as drug and ivory trafficking often go hand in hand. The CITES convention forcibly acknowledged that world demand for ivory exceeded the available supply from elephants and that the continental population was in serious decline.

In June 2013, the government of the Central African Republic was overthrown. A rebel militia attacked the sacrosanct Dzanga Sangha elephants, made famous by the long-term studies of Dr. Andrea Turkalo. Save the Elephants joined with our long-term allies in America, the Wildlife Conservation Network, to launch a new Elephant Crisis Fund (ECF), which enabled trusted partners to address the three key objectives of ending the poaching, the trafficking, and the demand for ivory. We had no need to invent a new NGO, with so many effective ones already in the field; we just needed to know which was doing the best work for elephants. Within 24 hours of getting the news, we had sent

$100,000 to the Wildlife Conservation Society, which was spearheading a rescue mission to the area in conjunction with WWF.

With the help of the Leonardo DiCaprio Foundation, Tiffany & Co., #KnotOnMyPlanet, and an army of other supporters, the ECF was to become a powerful force for elephant conservation over the next five years, engaging key partners and helping unify efforts across borders and sectors under the strong, strategic leadership of Dr. Chris Thouless. By the end of 2019, the ECF had supported 78 partner organizations to carry out 280 projects across 37 countries in Africa and Asia, with 100% of all donations going to the field.

By 2014, tusks were selling for three times more than they had just four years before. But 2015 marked a real turning point. In May, the Chinese government announced its intention to end the domestic trade in ivory. This pledge was backed by President Xi Jinping, who was working in concert with former president Obama in America. By November 2015, the price of ivory in Beijing had almost halved, although at around $1,000 per kilo, it still remained a strong driver of illegal killing.

With China's commitment to close its legal markets for ivory, the survival chances for elephants distinctly improved. It was research funded by Save the Elephants, and performed by the late Esmond Bradley Martin and Lucy Vigne, that showed for the first time that the price of ivory in China fell by two-thirds from 2013 to 2016, but it still remained too high. Unfortunately, ivory-carving factories mushroomed in Hong Kong, Vietnam, and Laos, from which tourists could smuggle ivory into China. By January 2018, China's ivory ban was in place, and Hong Kong was committed to closing down secondary markets in neighboring nations eventually. The challenge turned to how to help governments enforce the new regulations and how to change the behavior of those few consumers who still wanted to buy ivory.

Sadly, the pressure on the elephants living in Africa's savannahs and forests has yet to let up in response to the ban. Mobile militias have raided across the borders of Cameroon, Chad, and Sudan, while Gabon's forest elephant populations are now facing a huge onslaught. Investigations into the ivory trafficking networks have revealed them to be far more extensive and interconnected than we had previously thought. Criminals from West Africa collaborate with others in East and Southern Africa and try to evade efforts to thwart the trafficking of ivory. The reality is that they are ruthless and dangerous and do not stop short of murder.

However, in Kenya, Uganda, and elsewhere in East Africa, recent counts point to elephant populations recovering. Prosecutions of some high-level traffickers in Tanzania suggest there is a new political will to end the problem. Elsewhere, some areas have seen intense poaching reduced, including Garamba National Park in the Democratic Republic of Congo, Zakouma National Park in Chad, North Luangwa National Park in Zambia, and in much of East Africa and Zimbabwe.

At home in Samburu, rays of sunlight began to break through. Baby elephants began to outnumber the fresh carcasses. The intensive, collaborative enforcement efforts and strong community-led conservation initiated by our close colleagues at the Northern Rangelands Trust had transformed the elephant situation, and it was not so dire as it had been three years earlier, but this sort of response was still rare in the rest of Africa. I hoped that Samburu could once again be the harbinger for Africa, forecasting better times ahead for elephants.

It occurred to me that one of the ways we could measure the danger to elephants was by recording how their behavior changed according to the risk to which they were exposed. I had been greatly impressed by one elephant that we were tracking along the Tana

River, together with Ian Craig. His name was Morgan, after the donor who paid for his collar and the helicopter needed for the darting operation. For the first few months, Morgan lived a sedate life in or around the Tana River Primate National Reserve near the Kenya coast. The reserve was now well protected as a community conservancy under the management of the Northern Rangelands Trust. One day Morgan suddenly decided to move out of safety and headed east toward the Somali border in country where the Al-Shabab were active. His sedate behavior altered, and he became a nocturnal animal, moving into open areas only at night and hiding almost motionless by day in thick bush. It was an extraordinary and striking change. His behavior resembled that of a special forces unit operating deep in enemy territory, where concealment and nocturnal movement are key to survival. Morgan reached the Somali border in a few days and crossed over, spending 24 hours in an ultra-dangerous country. Then he doubled back, and as we tracked him remotely on our tracking app, he suddenly slowed down and started meandering. I had suspected that his motive in leaving the safety of the Tana River might be the allure of finding some receptive females en route. We were able to get an aircraft piloted by our friend Fuzz Dyer, who traveled to the coordinates I sent him, and sure enough he found Morgan in the company of females in a dense patch within the Boni Forest. Morgan consorted with the ladies for the best part of a month and then resumed his nocturnal journey back to the Tana River, where he met up once again with the other elephants and became a diurnal animal spending as much time moving by day as by night.

To investigate responses to danger more generally, we needed to develop a measure of risk across the elephants' range, and we could do so by using a metric from the ongoing body count of the MIKE program. The proportion of dead elephants that had been poached gave us a measure of risk from poachers, a ratio we referred to as the PIKE (proportion of illegally killed elephants). Festus Ihwagi, a promising young Kenyan scientist working for Save the Elephants, took on a project to measure how elephants changed their behavior according to the degree of danger. Using our excellent tracking data of elephant movements, he considered a range of conditions from "very safe," as in Samburu and the private conservancies, to "extremely risky," as in an area just to the south of Samburu where no community conservancy had been set up. It had become a killing field. Festus's work showed marked differences between nocturnal and diurnal behavior. The greater the risk, the more nocturnal the elephants became. He also discovered that when they felt safe, they spent more time meandering, and he confirmed that elephants at risk often moved fast in a single direction at night. He published his findings in a peer-reviewed scientific paper.

Africa is rapidly changing. As the poaching threat recedes in East and Southern Africa, although not in Central and West Africa (at the time of writing), it is evident that elephants are threatened by a tidal wave of human development and encroachment. As economies expand, the once open, unfenced elephant ranges contract. The Kenya elephant range presents a stark example. A century of growing human population and grazing livestock has severely degraded most pastures. When hit by seasonal drought, herders desperate for grazing invade conservation areas, including Samburu National Reserve, where our research center is located. Once the grass is gone, the herders may move on, but little is left for wildlife. Cycles of drought and flood, and the specter of climate change, sweep across landscapes already afflicted by overgrazing. Building and communicating the case for conservation among local people is of vital importance.

Although elephants' rangeland is contracting and fragmenting, we have increased our understanding of elephants, identified important corridors for their migration, and found new ways of conserving habitat that allow humans and elephants to live in harmony. With every passing year, people living on the continent become more concerned about the environment, including elephants and their survival.

We continue to recruit, train, and support the Kenyan people, who will decide the future of Kenya's wildlife, giving them the opportunity to work with some of the world's best-known technology firms and academic institutions. We leverage technology to pioneer new ways to monitor wildlife populations, distinguish among individual elephants, and decipher the movement data that we have collected. Of course, elephant tracking has long been our specialty, and we recognized the value in making our systems available to all. A crack team of software engineers from Vulcan, Paul Allen's innovative company, transformed the architecture into a cutting-edge system for managing protected areas using real-time data. As of mid-2020, the platform was being used in 50 different conservation zones across Africa. We have made a Save the Elephants Tracking App, powered by Vulcan, available to researchers. The elephant movement data collected provide critical information for government planners and stakeholders interested in preserving essential corridors.

In my 50 years of close association with elephants, much more has been learned to support my early belief that they are sentient animals with an advanced consciousness. One of the characteristics that particularly fascinates me is their compassion toward other elephants. One evening in Samburu, we came across an old matriarch, Eleanor, of a family called the First Ladies, who appeared to be extremely weak and stressed, with secretions pouring from her temporal gland. Her trunk was swollen, and our team wondered whether she had been bitten by a snake. Her own family had wandered ahead, but there were unrelated families nearby. Eleanor began wobbling, and almost immediately another matriarch, Grace, from an unrelated family walked up to her. Grace was also streaming from her temporal gland and was highly agitated. Eleanor collapsed in front of Grace. Grace sniffed the fallen Eleanor with her trunk and then touched her with her trunk and foot, evidently using these sensitive tactile organs to perceive what was going on. Then Grace put her tusks under Eleanor and succeeded in heaving her onto her feet again. Unfortunately, Eleanor could not remain standing. After wobbling for a few seconds, Eleanor's back legs buckled and again she fell. This time no amount of pushing and lifting by Grace could get Eleanor back on her feet. Grace would not leave her and started vocalizing with deep rumbles and continued nudging Grace with her feet and tusks. As darkness fell, she was still with her, but Eleanor was too weak to rise again.

The next morning Grace had gone, but other unrelated families came close to Eleanor, who was hardly breathing. A group called the Hawaiian Islands visited her. One female hovered a foot and straddled the collapsed Eleanor, rocking to and fro for a few minutes. The Hawaiian Islands rarely visited Samburu and were absent for most of the year.

Eleanor soon died. The Kenya Wildlife Service came and cut out her tusks. In the week that followed, our Save the Elephants team was there and assembled records of what happened hour by hour, backed up by radio-tracking records of three families and one animal from Eleanor's own family. All in all, five families repeatedly visited the dead elephant, showing a distinct interest in her body.

The reason this behavior surprises me is that there seems to be no advantage for an elephant to care about what happens to another elephant that is not a family relative. Altruism is easy to explain in evolutionary terms when it benefits an organism's own kin, but when displayed toward an unrelated animal, it is mysterious. In our own species there are examples of disinterested altruism, behavior befitting the parable of the Good Samaritan. We all know examples of a human showing kindness to a stranger in distress without any prospect of getting a reward. With elephants, our conclusion is that they are interested in helping sick, dying, or even dead elephants, irrespective of genetic relationship. It would seem that elephants often have a generalized altruism toward the suffering of others of their species, akin to the compassion human beings are capable of showing.

The death of Eleanor and the reactions of surrounding elephants was a rare event, and we were lucky to have detailed knowledge of the family relationships of these elephants so that we could track some of them precisely and plot their positions hour by hour in relation to her carcass. Since the publication of our team's paper on the death of Eleanor in 2006, many more observations of elephant behavior toward their dead were summarized in a comprehensive paper by Shifra Goldenberg and George Wittemyer, who reviewed many reports of their own and others.

The extent to which elephants display behavioral traits in common with human beings, such as their compassion toward others, is relevant to the ethics of how we should treat them.

Along with close colleagues, we have continued to produce scientific publications, including recent papers on how honeybees cause elephants to flee in Sri Lanka; the new crisis in Myanmar, where poachers hunt for elephant skins to be used in traditional medicine; and how animal movements in the Anthropocene are declining globally in response to the increasing human footprint. With our collaborators we have published papers on how elephants move in risky landscapes; how they adapt to the high-speed railway cutting across their range in Tsavo; how they behave in relation to seismic vibrations; how orphaned elephants adapt to life without their mother; and the demography of forest elephants. Our local team grows ever stronger. We have new talent at the PhD and master's levels and many other dedicated team members. Back home in Kenya, our team is focused on human-elephant coexistence. We are working on the challenges of connectivity, while also helping farmers live alongside elephants by using beehive fences and other practical techniques.

Persecuted elephants—like human beings—seek refuge in safe havens, and this can cause problems when they come into conflict with small-scale farmers. Dr. Lucy King's innovative bee project, which used beehives as elephant deterrents in community areas, has now been deployed in 19 countries in Africa and Asia. We need a better scientific understanding of human-elephant conflict to ensure the future well-being of humans and wildlife.

Dynamic partnerships will be essential for forging ecological solutions, just like the coalition of individuals, NGOs, and governments that helped turn the tide against the ivory poaching crisis. Our donors and partners have enabled us to achieve what we have for elephants. The Wildlife Conservation Network has been our main ally in the United States, and we are deeply grateful to all those who have provided Save the Elephants with vital financial and moral support.

In 2017, after more than 50 years of working with elephants, I decided to step back from the day-to-day running of Save the Elephants to concentrate on the science on which our programs are based. I was delighted that our trustees appointed Frank Pope as CEO of Save the Elephants. I am confident that with his leadership, skill, and scientific backing, Save the Elephants will continue to lead the way in securing a future for elephants.

As I look back over the past few decades of conservation work at Save the Elephants, I see that the place in which we now stand is quite different from where we began. International awareness of the plight of elephants has reached new heights, with bold government pledges in 2017 against the ivory trade and grim reminders of the nature of the crime syndicates that profit from it. I continue to be grateful for the quality of those involved in wildlife conservation. I have been very lucky in the people with whom I have worked. They are too numerous to mention, but the mentorship and stimulation of Fritz Vollrath from Oxford has been beyond measure. Marlene McCay has been a wise trustee of Save the Elephants. George Wittemyer has been prodigiously productive as a scientist focused on elephants and has remained a valued colleague throughout the years. The new generation of Kenyan scientists like Festus Ihwagi is steadily rising. In all my endeavors and trials in the bush and in learning about the Samburu, David Daballen has been a vital friend and mentor. Lastly, my wife, Oria, and my daughters, Saba and Dudu, are equally involved with elephants and have been with me through good times and bad, as ever-shining stars in my life.

Dr. Iain Douglas-Hamilton's investigations on African elephants paved the way for today's research on herd dynamics and were instrumental in bringing about the world ivory trade ban. Courtesy: Save the Elephants

Further Reading

Douglas-Hamilton, I. 1987. African Elephants: Population Trends and Their Causes. Oryx 21 (1): 11–24.

Douglas-Hamilton, I., Bhalla, S., Wittemyer, G., and Vollrath, F. 2006. Behavioural Reactions of Elephants towards a Dying and Deceased Matriarch. Applied Animal Behaviour Science 100 (1–2): 87–102.

Douglas-Hamilton, I., and O. Douglas-Hamilton. 1974. Among the Elephants. Viking Press.

Douglas-Hamilton, I., and O. Douglas-Hamilton. 1992. Battle for the Elephants. Viking Press.

Douglas-Hamilton, I., Krink, T., and Vollrath, F. 2005. Movements and Corridors of African Elephants in Relation to Protected Areas. Naturwissenschaften 92: 158–163.

Douglas-Hamilton, O. 1980 Africa's Elephants: Can they Survive? National Geographic. November.

Goldenberg, S. Z., and Wittemyer, G. 2020. Elephant Behavior toward the Dead: A Review and Insights from Field Observations. Primates 61 (1): 119–128.

Hearing on Ivory and Insecurity: The Global Implications of Poaching in Africa, Before the US Senate Committee on Foreign Relations. 2012. 112th Congress.

Ihwagi, F. W., Thouless, C., Wang, T., Skidmore, A. K., Omondi, P., and Douglas-Hamilton, I. 2018. Night-Day Speed Ratio of Elephants as Indicator of Poaching Levels. Ecological Indicators 84: 38–44.

Orenstein, R. 2013. Ivory, Horn, and Blood: Behind the Elephant and Rhinoceros Poaching Crisis. Firefly Books.

Quammen, D. 2008. Family Ties: The Elephants of Samburu, an African Love Story. National Geographic. September.

Wittemyer, G., Daballen, D., and Douglas-Hamilton, I. 2011. Rising Prices Threaten Elephants. Nature 476: 282–283.

Wittemyer, G., Northrup, J. M., Blanc, J., Douglas-Hamilton I., Omondi, P., and Burnham, K. P. 2014. Illegal Killing for Ivory Drives Global Decline in African Elephants. Proceedings of the National Academy of Sciences of the United States of America 111 (36): 13117–13121.

CHAPTER 4

WILD THINGS AND WILD PLACES

JANE ALEXANDER

*2012 Recipient and Namesake of the Jane Alexander Global
Wildlife Ambassador Award*

Wood Thrush
Hylocichla mustelina

We were almost at the top of the world at four o'clock in the morning, and millions of stars helmeted Earth with a glow so deep that spikes of ice in the grass looked like little fallen stars lighting our path. My love for our planet—its place in the universe and our place in it as human beings—couldn't have been more intense.

Phobjikha Valley in central Bhutan has been the wintering home for Black-necked Cranes for millennia. They fly in over the Himalayas from Tibet to raise their young. George Archibald wanted a count of them before they left their roost at dawn for feeding grounds, so we settled on a frost-covered hill, waiting for the birds to stir in the valley below. By 5:30 they were lifting off in family groups of three and four, excitedly honking their departure. George and his Bhutanese colleague Jigme called out the numbers, while fellow traveler Dan and I scribbled them down. They did four counts before they reached a consensus of three hundred adults and thirty-eight chicks, a successful fledge rate. By this time the cold was penetrating our bones, my fingers could barely bend, and intense love was supplanted by a yearning for hot water or, at the very least, thicker socks. Jigme, Dan, and I made our way back the few miles over sunlit streams and fields, passing grazing horses with their colts and a few cranes with *their* "colts," as they are called, picking at wheat chaff. George stayed behind to watch and photograph his beloved birds as he always does, an acolyte at the altar of creation.

In 2006 George Archibald received the first Indianapolis Prize. It was a timely and important award for species conservation. During most of the twentieth century, field biologists and ecologists were dedicated to pure scientific research of an animal or a habitat. Not unlike explorers of prior centuries who mapped the world, these intrepid men and women mapped the behavior of creatures where they lived, expanding knowledge of species. Things had changed by the time I was witnessing their work in the 1980s. Pure research of a species did not ensure it had a future. In fact, the number of species in decline was alarming. One species, however, human beings, had doubled its population in a mere forty years, from two and a half billion people after World War II to five billion by the late 1980s. We are now on course to reach ten billion by 2050. Feeding and housing a global population of people so huge has impacted the lives of all other species on Earth through habitat loss, climate change, poaching, and poisonous chemicals on land and sea, and in the air. The field biologist today is no longer solely a scientist but a juggler of many skills: conservationist, animal advocate, and fundraiser, as well as educator of the public, of politicians and of young scientists on the urgent need for protection.

George Archibald manifests these skills more deftly than anyone I know. He travels many months of every year to save cranes in Asia, Africa, Australia, Europe, and North America. When he is home in Baraboo, Wisconsin, he oversees the International Crane Foundation, which he cofounded in 1973. It is the only place on Earth where one can see all fifteen species of the rare and endangered birds.

It was an auspicious evening for me in 2006 when I was asked to emcee that first Indianapolis Prize Gala. The event was beautifully produced, with remarkable films of scientists and animals projected on huge screens the length of the ballroom. The Indianapolis Zoo's innovative director, Michael Crowther, had conceived of the idea to honor field biologists at a major event in Indianapolis as prestigious as the ones honoring actors in Hollywood. Myrta Pullman was the enthusiastic chairwoman of the prize, and the Lilly family donated the largest monetary award ever given to an animal conservationist. The support of the citizens of Indianapolis was overwhelming.

George and I became friends that night. My husband Ed and I traveled with him to witness the Sandhill Crane migration on the Platte River in Nebraska, one of greatest migrations in the world, and to Wisconsin to see the rarest of all, Whooping Cranes, on their wetland nests, each chick a priceless gift of life, a blow to extinction. Being with George is always a spiritual lesson. His abiding love of fellow human beings allows him to forgive their transgressions and to include one and all in the protection of species by making them aware of the valuable natural resources in their midst. Their desire to safeguard wildlife, not annihilate it, soon follows. There is no conservation without inclusion.

I cherish the hours I have spent with George and others in the field. My thirst for wild encounters has taken me to unique places in the company of these remarkable biologists. I admire their patience and perseverance, their endless wonder, and all they have taught me about tigers in India, jaguars in Brazil, lemurs in Madagascar, and Birds of Paradise in Papua New Guinea.

My biennial trip to the Indianapolis Prize Gala is always on my calendar. It is not to be missed. Who would want to miss being in the presence of the eminent George Schaller, Iain Douglas-Hamilton, Steven Amstrup, Patricia Wright, Carl Jones, or Russell Mittermeier? It would be like missing a nineteenth-century party where you might rub elbows with Charles Darwin, Alfred Russel Wallace, or Thomas Huxley. The gala is even better than the Academy Awards. It is outstanding recognition of real-life heroes, not those in the movies, challenged by precarious situations in order to save wildlife and wild places. These heroes of conservation often make the difference between survival and extinction of a species.

Had I known any of these men and women when I was a youngster I might have tried to follow in their footsteps. It seems I was drawn to the natural world from the beginning. My very earliest memory, as a baby of 20 months, was sitting in the shallow waters of a Nantucket beach picking up sea cucumbers. Huge numbers of the pink animals, headless, limbless, eyeless creatures the size of a large pickle, had washed in with the tide. I remember handling them curiously as they lay there on the sandy bottom all around me. My mother corroborated the scene for me years later. She was not a squeamish woman, being a nurse by profession and the child of a Nova Scotia fishing family. She encouraged engagement with nature. She named the birds for me in our suburban Boston neighborhood, and she quelled an innate terror I had of spiders by plucking one from under the porch eaves and letting it crawl up her bare arm, over her head, and down her back. Then, cradling it in the palm of her hand, she gently set it back up in its corner. I thought she was the bravest person in the world. More than that, spiders never had power over me again. Fear became fascination. And my small backyard became a daily exploration of the fauna that lived there: squirrels, birds, and bugs, for the most part.

Once in a while Dad would take us to the zoo. What child hasn't marveled at her first encounter with an elephant, a giant tortoise, a lion or an eagle? Seeing these animals up close, the variety of creation and the similarities—the eyes, the ears, the feet, what they eat, the fact that they sleep—begins the journey of understanding how unique the world is and how connected we all are. A well-managed zoo—the Indianapolis Zoo being one of them—is often the first conduit to loving wild animals and wanting them to be protected.

Puberty hit with a vengeance. Birds were replaced by boys, and the great outdoors by the equally enchanting world of theater. I did not get back to birds for twenty years. Our careers were well established when Ed and I bought a house in the country backing onto state conservation land. Deer roamed the old orchard eating drop apples, a river otter occasionally splashed in the pool fed by a babbling brook with trout and turtles in it. Flycatchers and bats grabbed insects over the water on summer evenings and opossums played dead in the woodpile when cornered by our dog. It was a bit of paradise. Soon it became clear to me, especially in spring when the same birds returned to nest, that we shared our place with hundreds of species—thousands if insects were included. And all these creatures predated us in the lineage of the land, perhaps for millennia. We were the newcomers, but we would be careful not to interrupt the conditions that allowed them to thrive. After a tree company sprayed the big tree for gypsy moths one day and all the frogs, dragonflies, and fish went belly-up in the lily pond beneath, I threw away all the pesticides and herbicides I had bought. I began planting native species, which drew even more butterflies, birds, and bees to our garden. When the ethereal song of a Wood Thrush emanated from the forest morning and evening, I was in heaven. There was nothing more beautiful. My passion for nature was sealed.

My life has been immersed in the world of make-believe since I began acting. It is a magical world I love and that summons the most imaginative parts of me. But the natural world holds more mystery and beauty than could ever be contained in one life, or vista, or creature. As Hamlet says to his friend, "There are more things in heaven and Earth, Horatio, than are dreamt of in your philosophy." I began to travel with scientists to learn all I could. Each window that was opened to me was a revelation both sublime and terrifying, because one cannot spend time with these heroes of conservation and not understand the crises we are facing with wild things and wild places.

There is no mammal that compares with human beings. We make things: symphonies and clarinets, wheat fields and bread, hospitals and MRIs, rockets and computers. And we make things to kill: pesticides, herbicides, dynamite, guns, and bombs. We are the apex killer, the mammal that kills for revenge, for food, for land, for ideas, and for love. And for fun. No other creature is so versatile in killing. The plummeting numbers of large mammal species, frogs, bats, and insects, and the 30% decline of most species of North American birds since 1970, is directly attributable to us. We have attempted to conquer Earth. But we have succeeded only in subverting the eternal systems that have kept her spinning smoothly, and that have kept species alive.

But Earth is resilient. She has been around for four billion years, adjusting to each new onslaught, adapting to the vicissitudes of space and time, surviving chaos. Earth will survive. It is we humans who will not, and we will take down many living creatures with us. Not all. Some will survive to evolve and begin again. This is the most likely scenario as we continue down the path we are on. None of us today will be alive to see the end, hundreds or thousands of years from now. Extinction takes time. It is a process of loss until the last of a species blinks out. No one knows who shot the last wild Passenger Pigeon more than a hundred years ago. It took a while for everyone to conclude they hadn't seen one anywhere for many years. No one has seen an Ivory-billed Woodpecker for decades but there is still a glimmer of hope it may exist in the swamps of Arkansas, Louisiana, or Cuba. Until then it is not "extinct."

The most promising scenario is that we reduce the amount of carbon emissions that are trapping atmospheric heat; that we remove particulates of plastic and chemicals that are killing plants and animals, ourselves included; and that we enter into a nurturing, not abusive, relationship with our planet. It's like beginning a twelve-step program, changing ourselves for ourselves and for others we depend on. Because for us this is always, and in the end, about people. About ensuring that people have the tools, education, and resources they need to live in cooperation with nature. People will thrive if animals and plants thrive. The earth will take care of them if we take care of the earth.

The earth is in all of us, just as we are the body of the earth. There is not a particle of our flesh and blood that is not of Mother Earth, and the earth is us and the great moving forces we depend on. The great rivers are her arteries, the mountains and soil her limbs and skin, the oceans her blood, while all living things are her cells. We are the collective resonance of Earth's beating heart. She can go on beating without us, but we cannot survive without her.

We must go on faith that everything matters, because we are all connected. Naturalist John Muir said, "When we try to pick out anything by itself, we find it hitched to everything else in the universe." If it sounds mystical, it is. It is a mystery to us, and perhaps the answers are not ours to know, or our reasons for being. Pope Francis, in his eloquent 2015 encyclical on climate, wrote extensively about the connectedness of all living things, and our interdependence. The web of life is so complex that the whole is not possible to grasp, and we must take it on faith that even the lowliest of us, the insects, the microbes, and the fungi of the world have a place and a purpose. This is as much a secular and scientific argument as it is religious. There are things we must keep sacred.

Jane Alexander birding in New Hampshire. Courtesy: Joanna Eldredge Morrissey

Those who study Earth and her living creatures know more than most of us about these connections, but their science is often repudiated, and they struggle to make their voices heard. They are like prophets in the wilderness. We can help these men and women by supporting their work and healing the relations between humans and the natural world. Scientists are our champions. The Indianapolis Prize honors them with unique recognition as protectors of our communal home Earth and of all the miraculous things living in it.

CHAPTER 5

POLAR BEARS, MELTING ICE, AND TURNING CONSERVATION ON ITS HEAD

DR. STEVEN C. AMSTRUP
2012 Recipient of the Indianapolis Prize

Polar Bear
Ursus maritimus

We were tired but energized as we climbed onto the shuttle bus. It was September 7, 2007, the end of several crazy-busy days. In fact, it was the culmination of a crazy-busy summer. My research team, which had been expanded to include government and non-government leaders in ecological research and analysis, had just finished briefing senior officials of the US Department of Interior about the future prospects for polar bears in an ever-warming world. I sat next to Eric DeWeaver, now a program manager at the National Science Foundation, to discuss the presentations and our sense of how they were received. The day before, we had briefed directors and high-level staff. Today, among other things, I had personally briefed Secretary of Interior Dirk Kempthorne, the first in a series of briefings he requested to help him decide whether he should list polar bears as a threatened species under the US Endangered Species Act.

Shortly after we were seated, someone at the front of the bus passed back a printout of a news article describing our briefings of the past couple days. The headline was "Polar Bears Are Doomed, and This Is Irreversible." Eric and I read the copy at the same time. As soon as I saw the headline, I blurted out, "That wasn't our message—that wasn't what we said!" We had predicted that, on our current greenhouse gas (GHG) emissions path, we could lose two-thirds of the world's polar bears by midcentury, and we could lose them all by the end of the century. But we had not reported that polar bears or their habitat had crossed a tipping point and were irreversibly doomed.

When I phoned my wife, Virginia, she had seen the story in the Anchorage paper and was concerned about the headline and my reaction to it. Not only did the public get the wrong message, it was the worst possible message they could hear. The body of the article did include much of the correct information, but when it comes to what the public remembers and, indeed, what policy leaders repeat, an accurate headline is crucial, and this one sent a wrong and dangerous message. Through history we've learned that if people think there is nothing they can do, they will do nothing. And, ever since the late 1970s, when the topic of global warming had reached the level of political discussions, our leaders had done exactly that— nothing. I added, in a too-loud voice for the bus, that we had to do something to counter this incorrect headline! There had been discussions in the public and even in the scientific literature suggesting that we might have already crossed a vital sea ice threshold—a global temperature tipping point that would put sea ice into an unstoppable decline to zero. We did not think that was true and had not suggested that in any of our briefings, but there it was on the front page!

So, what, in fact, had our research shown? Polar bears feed primarily on ringed and bearded seals. These fat-rich seals spend most of their life beneath the frozen skin of ice covering the top surface of the Arctic Ocean and maintain breathing holes by scraping the ice with the large claws on their fore-flippers. Polar bears wait for seals to come up for air at these breathing holes, hunting them from the top surface of the ice. In the spring, the seals give birth to their pups on the sea ice, providing another opportunity for polar bears to catch them. Polar bears cannot outswim seals—the bears depend on the ice surface for access to their prey. Hence, if the ice disappears, so will polar bears. That much was clear from our research. However, with this incorrect but widespread headline, the word in the general public media became, "There is nothing we can do to save sea ice and therefore we cannot save polar bears from extinction."

It was true that greed and shortsightedness had long prevented actions to halt global warming—and the plight of the polar bear, which we had graphically spelled out, provided an apt and poignant message about the threats we all face. Polar bears have long been the universal symbol of the Arctic, and almost everyone knows what a polar bear is and has a conception of the mysterious places where they roam. This popularity and the realization of the threats they face make polar bears a perfect messenger for the climate crisis. But if the public thought it was already too late to save them, polar bears could soon fade into insignificance! Clarifying this erroneous headline suddenly seemed an important step to saving polar bears.

So, how does a kid from the Midwest end up advising the secretary of the interior on whether or not polar bears should be considered for listing under provisions of the Endangered Species Act? First of all, I have to say that Secretary Kempthorne was a perfect gentleman during his discussions with me. Being responsible for personally briefing him was nonetheless a bit nerve-wracking. After all, he was literally my "big boss in the sky," while I was just one of the many employees way down his supervisory chain. The information my team and I developed would normally pass through half a dozen hands before reaching the secretary, but here I was in his office in face-to-face conversation.

My childhood experiences shaped my love for nature; an aspiration for higher education and a commitment to professional achievement ultimately prepared me for these briefings. I was born in Fargo, North Dakota, but my formative years were in Brooklyn Park, Minnesota, a relatively new suburb of Minneapolis at that time. Brooklyn Park much later became known as the home of professional wrestler turned politician and governor Jesse Ventura. But I was there first.

My dad worked for a company that operated grain elevators and provided other farm services over a large swath of the Midwest and West. He traveled frequently, visiting farmers and elevator operators mainly in Minnesota and the Dakotas. When he was home, he took us squirrel or rabbit hunting, or fishing. When he wasn't home, my brother and I would ride our bikes several miles to find a lake that had good fishing. From my earliest days I had a love and a craving for as much of the outdoors as we could fit in. A majority of my outdoor time was spent on the tracts of agricultural land near our Brooklyn Park home. Our house was at the edge of the expanding subdivision, and not far from the back door a tiny creek with trees and shrubs ran through cultivated farm fields and fallowed lands filled with various grasses and forbs. My brother Norman and I spent hours exploring the creek, walking the fields, and climbing trees. We also liked catching minnows, crayfish, and turtles—keeping and observing them for a while before returning them to their rightful homes.

To this day, I remember the awe I felt during special moments in our local outdoors. Rare sightings of birds far beyond their normal range—including a white crane or egret, which I was never able to clearly identify, and a giant "albino" owl that my Dad told me was a snowy owl—provided a sense of the mysteries of nature and stoked my curiosity. One very cold winter day, Norm and I came upon a hen pheasant along the creek. My recollection is that it was between 20 and 30 below zero, and I remember having frost on everything, including my eyelashes. We were not sure what was going on with this bird, but she seemed too cold to move. We were able to pick her up without a struggle and quickly made our way home with her. Surprisingly, she didn't try to escape but rather seemed content to share some of our warmth. We found a large cardboard box and placed her in there with some dry grass, some bird seed, and a small water dish. After a few hours warming up indoors, we took her back to where we had found her. By then she was more energetic and much more of a handful, and upon release she exploded into flight and sailed out of sight over the band of trees that grew along the stream. Norm and I had a real "high five" moment, even though we knew nothing about high fives back then.

My most poignant memory of those days, however, was watching the encroachment of the human footprint on what, as a kid, I had viewed as a relatively natural habitat. "Improvements" including houses, streets, and groomed yards relentlessly replaced the neighboring fields, the stream, and the woodland. I saw the same habitat encroachment wherever we went, and it troubled me. Even in elementary school it seemed clear to me that the relentless growth of the human population was overtaking the world I cherished. I remember thinking, at that young age, "Where will people be able to go hunting and fishing if we continue like this?" By then, my favorite TV program was *Mutual of Omaha's Wild Kingdom*. I remember my mother calling for me when I was outside playing or exploring—*Steven, Wild Kingdom is on!* I knew from that show, corny as it was in many ways, that there were people out there whose profession was to try to "save" wild animals and the wild places they needed. I had determined, by age five or six, that was what I wanted to do when I grew up.

For me, bears were synonymous with "wild country." If there were bears, I thought, there would be everything else too, and I loved bears from my earliest sentient days. I read everything about bears I could get my hands on, from *Field and Stream* magazine adventures to library books. I must have said something in a group of relatives about my career ambitions very early on, as I recall on a later trip to visit distant family, my aunt patted me on top of the head and asked if I still wanted to "go into the woods and study bears?" I thrived on spending time out in the woods and fields. I loved to hunt and fish, and I wanted to work to help ensure future generations could continue to do those activities. My answer to my aunt's question was a simple "yes."

As I grew older, I gained an understanding of what it meant to become a wildlife professional, and I realized the educational path I would need to take to become one. I did my undergraduate work at the University of Washington in Seattle. My degree was in forestry, with a major in wildlife management. I was fortunate as an undergraduate to receive a research participation grant in my second summer. The job was to design and conduct a wildlife survey on the Cedar River watershed that supplies drinking water to the city of Seattle. For me, successfully applying for this grant was the best of possibilities. Not only did I have a summer job but this one kept me in the woods all summer. Other benefits included firsthand exposure to ecosystem monitoring and applied management objectives. I also was able to actually record wildlife indices, like doe/fawn ratios that I'd read about in class. I established "transects" that could be repeatedly sampled, allowing consistency among the observations. And, I tried to figure out ways to mark or otherwise identify individual animals and to develop some kind of survey that might identify preferred habitat areas. My knowledge and skills then were rudimentary, and the project emphasized what I didn't know more than what I did know at that time. My work, however, did prove useful. A few years later a graduate student at UW pored over my observations and developed further studies that ultimately generated data for his PhD in wildlife management.

Although receiving this grant was just about everything I could have wanted in a summer job at that time, human activities on the Cedar River watershed reemphasized concerns I'd developed early on. This area was protected from the encroachment of houses, shopping centers, and the associated land fragmentation, but it was open to logging. I cannot claim that I understood the "management goals" or what the watershed management plan was designed to achieve. I was aware that properly managed forests are a renewable resource, and I assumed the logging plans were sustainable. However, the logging included removal of some of the last old-growth Douglas-fir from the area. I marveled at the sight of loggers felling 300-foot trees and of a logging truck leaving the woods with a load composed of only one log. But I was saddened by the realization that these trees already were giants when Lewis and Clark were making their way to nearby Deception Pass. With the aid of gasoline and diesel fuel, sucked from the ground elsewhere, the wood from these "giants" contributed to the growing human footprint that had been troubling me since I was a kid.

By then, my thoughts had broadened beyond "where will people be able to hunt and fish?" to "how can we balance the ever-enlarging human footprint with the needs other creatures have for the same landscape?" A couple words of wisdom were passed on to me that resonate to this day. Richard Taber, my major professor as an undergraduate at the University of Washington, shared an insight about the importance of being aware of the bigger picture, a benefit we have now that we didn't always have. He pointed out, "When prehistoric people killed the last mastodon, they didn't know it was the last one, they only knew they were hungry." The tools of wildlife science give us the ability to see that bigger picture.

This lesson was reiterated years later by Walt Audi, a long time Arctic resident and charter airplane pilot with whom I flew hundreds of hours in the 1980s and early 1990s. In a private discussion about local knowledge, he told me that the local Eskimo people knew lots of things, and were keen observers, "but their knowledge is limited by how far they can see. Your tools," he said, "allow you to see much farther and fill in the gaps included in traditional on-the-ground observations." Walt's comment carried the same thought Dr. Taber had expressed a couple decades earlier. The value of being able to put human actions beyond the "short term" and into a broader ecological context, and the ever-growing ability of professionals to understand that context, provided current conservationists with the tools to ensure we never again "kill the last one."

With a firm grip on my BS in forestry, I managed to get into my dream master of science program at the University of Idaho—studying black bears. This project gave me a firsthand opportunity to learn about and apply the relatively new tool of radio-telemetry. The experience also gave me a firsthand look at the importance of healthy and contiguous habitat. One of my major discoveries was that black bears in that area made two vertical migrations each year. They used mainly low elevation areas in the early spring, feeding on succulent grasses and forbs, and moving upslope as availability of those plants moved up in elevation behind the melting snow. This first migration culminated with grazing and digging wild onions in the high, moist mountain meadows. When those dried out, however, the bears moved downhill again to feed on the first fruits to ripen in summer. From there, they migrated back up as the fruiting species of higher country came on. My study occurred almost entirely on public land, so the migratory path of these bears was unlikely to be broken up by subdivisions or shopping centers, but still it was clear how breaking up the integrity of this habitat could result in significant conflict situations in which the bears would likely come out on the short end of the stick.

After completing my master's program, I spent a short time with the Utah Division of Wildlife before taking a research project in Wyoming with the US Fish and Wildlife Service (FWS). There I studied pronghorn antelope and sharp-tailed grouse and the anticipated impacts of expanding strip-mining for coal. Whereas my few years there didn't document negative impacts from the mining, I did learn a great lesson about even small obstacles to natural movements. Historically, pronghorns ranged widely in winter searching for forage plants and avoiding too-deep winter snow. My second or third winter there was a snowy one. Pronghorns, which don't jump like deer or elk, were pushed into the fence corners that marked ranch ownership or pasture boundaries. Unable to get over or through drifted fence corners, dozens died and were covered with snow until spring. Before the West was settled and fenced, Wyoming pronghorns may have drifted for many miles as the snow built up and possibly ended up in Nebraska at the end of especially snowy winters. Discovering these mass graves in a couple of fence corners was a grisly reminder of how even seemingly minor obstacles to habitat access can have grave ramifications.

My experience with black bears served me well when the FWS decided to hire someone who could hit the ground running and reactivate a flagging effort to learn about Alaska's polar bears. At the time, much was unknown about these impressive animals, and the chance to work with them exceeded my childhood dreams. What could be more exciting than studying giant white bears roaming around on a habitat that looks more like the surface of the moon than the terrestrial habitats familiar to most of us?

By chance, I came into the polar bear world at just the right time—that is, from the standpoint of providing a clear view of what was soon to happen.

When I first went to Alaska in 1980, the main concern about the future of polar bears was human harvest. Polar bears, like other

wildlife, are a renewable resource if their habitat is sound and harvest levels are kept within the bounds of sustainable yield. Some
folks may not like the idea of shooting polar bears, but the indigenous people of the north have been hunting polar bears for centuries, and it remains culturally important to them. However,
through the 1950s and 1960s, "trophy" hunting polar bears with
aircraft had become popular in Alaska. Two Super Cub aircraft,
equipped with snow skis for landing gear, would fly out over the
pack ice searching for bears. When a bear was spotted, one of the
planes would land and the hunter would get out and ready his rifle,
while the other plane tried to herd the bear toward the hunter. As
you can imagine, this was a pretty effective hunting method, and
the kill grew over the years as the strategy became more popular
and more pilots became "bear guides." Meanwhile, on Svalbard,
north of Norway, polar bears were being trapped in large numbers
and also hunted from large vessels—which allowed unsuspecting
bears to be shot from the relative comfort of a ship's deck. Increasingly evidence suggests that harvests were excessive and that,
without action to curb them, the polar bear's future was at risk.

In 1976, the five polar nations (the United States, Canada, the
Soviet Union, Greenland, and Norway), where polar bears roam,
ratified the International Agreement for the Conservation of Polar Bears. Today this remains the only international wildlife treaty
dedicated to conservation of a single animal species. The Polar
Bear Agreement banned mechanized hunting from planes and
ships. Concerns remained, however, as subsistence harvesting by
Native people living in coastal arctic regions also had become
more mechanized. And a growing concern was hydrocarbon exploration and development, and expanding mineral extraction in
the north. Although land fragmentation in polar bear habitats had
not yet been shown to impact the bears themselves, I knew that
absence of evidence didn't necessarily mean evidence of absence.

Hence, the development of nonrenewable resources seemed at least a looming threat to habitat security.

My early work on polar bears focused on understanding their movements (including where polar bears in Alaska give birth to their cubs), distribution, population boundaries, and population dynamics. Throughout the 1980s and until the mid-1990s, things looked good. I documented population recovery from excessive polar bear harvests, which had ended in the early 1970s. Cub production levels and survival rates were robust, the animals seemed healthy, and an increasing proportion of the population consisted of prime age adults. During the days of aerial trophy hunting, the larger and hence older bears had essentially been wiped out. By the middle of the 1980s, however, we were encountering more giant male bears and increasing proportions of reproductive-age females. The recovery was going so well that, by the late 1980s, my colleagues and I suggested that, if desired, the Native people of northern Alaska and northwest Canada could increase their harvest quota on polar bears in the southern Beaufort Sea population.

In those early days, every talk I gave and every discussion I had about polar bears was fun. The research was exciting, the population had recovered from its earlier decline, and we were breaking barriers in learning about them almost every season. But even then, things were turning. The symptoms were just not yet obvious to us.

Starting with my first year in Alaska, a cornerstone of my polar bear ecology work was my twice-a-year sampling. The small amount of polar bear research that had previously occurred in Alaska always had been in the late winter and spring. Research in Canada and Norway also was limited to those seasons. Immediately after getting my feet on the ground in Alaska, I questioned why researchers weren't looking at the bears at the end of summer—before they faced the harsh arctic winter. By looking at bears in both spring and autumn, I was able to document weight changes over summer. I also was able to observe females as they prepared to enter maternal snow dens in late autumn, and I solved the mystery of where most of Alaska's polar bears went to have their cubs.

During most of those early years, summer sea ice didn't retreat far from the northern Alaska coast. In what proved to be prescient, I observed that, during years when the summer pack ice did retreat north beyond the continental shelf, bears quickly invaded the nearshore ice as soon as it formed in autumn. The shallow waters over the continental shelf are the most productive parts of the Arctic Ocean. In northern Alaska, the "shelf" is limited to a narrow band of productive habitat within 40 miles or so of shore. My research on polar bear movements made it clear that this was preferred habitat for a simple reason: this is where the highest densities of seals are found.

Throughout their range, polar bears feed almost entirely on seals they catch from the surface of the sea ice. Historically, polar bears of the southern Beaufort Sea remained on the ice and were able to continue to hunt for seals through the summer melt season. Our early work indicated they reached their peak body mass by late fall—after the summer foraging season. When ice over shallow productive water is unavailable in summer, polar bears can be forced onto land or far offshore. In those early years, we often observed numerous seal kills dotting the nearshore ice as the bears moved in from the offshore ice where they had spent the late summer. It seemed that this autumn foraging, especially in years of greater-than-average ice retreat, might be critical to the bears. New observations have confirmed that Alaskan polar bears that are now forced to follow drifting ice ever farther offshore are, like those that end up on land, largely food deprived. This terrific nearshore habitat for bears to catch seals in the autumn was also a terrific habitat for us to catch and mark bears for study. Autumn sampling gave us the ability to see polar bears at a very different point in their life cycle than did seeing them only in the spring.

In the mid- to late 1990s, however, the fall freeze-up was occurring ever later, making it more and more difficult to mount a capture effort in autumn. Autumn fieldwork had always been tricky. To catch polar bears in their native habitat, the sea ice has to be thick enough to land a helicopter and do our work, but we also had to have daylight. In northern Alaska the sun sets around Thanksgiving and doesn't rise again until the middle of January. Also, for more than a week before the sun disappears in autumn, the days are too short to make the field effort worthwhile. In the 1980s, I could count on sea ice thick enough to allow safe helicopter work by around October 10 each year, and we could work on the ice until mid-November—the window of time when there was still enough daylight to get our work done. But progressively later freeze-ups resulted in ever-shorter autumn field seasons. Of course, given the natural variation in the climate system, each year was different in terms of the ice quality. Some years were better than others. By the dawn of this millennium, however, we could no longer rely on having ice thick enough to catch bears in the fall because, by the time the ice was good enough to go out, the days were too short to collect enough data to be worthwhile. The year 2001 goes down in history as the last year we conducted autumn field work. The autumn freeze-up, occurring ever closer to operational daylight limitations, meant it was not effective to attempt autumn captures in subsequent years.

Other trouble signs had emerged by the early 2000s. Historically, the ice hadn't moved far from the northern shore of Alaska in summer. In fact, a big concern each year used to be whether the summer ice would pull far enough offshore to allow supply ships to reach the North Slope oil fields and the coastal villages. In those days polar bears were seldom seen onshore. In fact, oil-field workers with whom I spoke in the 1980s commonly said things like,

"I've been here since 1968 and have never seen a polar bear, I don't really believe they are around here." By the late 1990s and 2000s, more bears were spending summer on land instead of staying with the ice as it retreated to the north. This meant progressively more bears posing a threat to human safety.

The retreat of the sea ice also posed an insidious threat to polar bear reproduction. The southern Beaufort Sea had historically been ice-covered for much of the year, and when ice did retreat in summer it usually didn't move far from the coastline. Therefore, there was little "fetch" or open ocean area in which swells and wave action could build. Now, the summer ice is hundreds of miles offshore, and the wave action is far greater. At the same time, warmer temperatures have melted the permafrost that historically hardened the soils of coastal banks where polar bears frequently den. Between more vulnerable soils, greater wave action, and rising sea level, coastlines across much of northern Alaska have been migrating inland—in some areas erasing banks that used to be suitable for maternal denning polar bears. We wondered whether more distant ice retreat would complicate the trip to shore for denning females, and whether coastal erosion might ultimately reduce availability of den sites.

Many processes in nature occur in a nonlinear fashion. Ecosystems like to maintain stable states. As impacts from humans—whether through harvests, grazing pressures, logging, or habitat fragmentation—gradually accumulate, animal species try to maintain, but they ultimately cross thresholds, resulting in what seem like sudden declines. This sort of nonlinearity preceded our "sudden" realization that we could no longer conduct autumn fieldwork on the sea ice, and it was clear that the impacts we already had seen were troubling signs of the polar bear's future in a warming world.

By now, even people who have not paid any attention have heard of human-caused global warming. But most, even many who think we need to take action, don't really understand how CO_2 and other GHGs raise Earth's temperature. Simply put, these gases interfere with the energy balance between the earth and space. Shortwave radiation from the sun warms the earth. Ultimately, this must be balanced by outgoing long-wave radiation emitted from the earth and its atmosphere back into space. This outgoing radiation is the heat you can feel by holding your hand over the surface of a sidewalk or paved street at dusk after a hot summer day. The street, warmed by incoming sunlight during day, reradiates that heat even after the sun has set. CO_2 and other GHGs allow shortwave radiation from the sun to pass through uninhibited, but they are not entirely transparent to long-wave radiation as it tries to move back up through the atmosphere. Higher atmospheric concentrations of GHGs prolong retention of that heat before it escapes back into space and essentially acts like adding an extra blanket to your bed.

Naturally occurring events, like volcanic eruptions or El Niño, result in short-term variation in climate—with some periods cooler than average and some warmer. The important point is that when GHG levels in the atmosphere are stable, the average, or "baseline," around which our temperatures naturally fluctuate, can be represented as a level or horizontal line. When GHG concentrations are steadily increasing as they are now, the natural variation continues, but it occurs over a higher and rising baseline.

Human-caused global warming has been in the news since the 1970s and has been a political hot potato since at least the 1980s. For years, though, the signal of warming, as reflected in the sea ice, had been largely masked by the natural variation or noise in the climate system. That is, despite the long-term rising trend in average temperature and average declining sea ice extent, inter-annual fluctuations at first made it difficult for us to easily detect the trend. Our inability to continue autumn fieldwork was a sign, however, that the "signal" of warming was clearly rising above the "noise" created by the natural variation among years. The whole system was changing before our eyes—in ways increasingly less suitable for polar bears. There is little for polar bears to eat on land, and recent work has shown there is apparently little for them to eat if they follow retreating ice far offshore over the deep unproductive waters of the polar basin. Well-fed polar bears can survive for months without food if they enter the fast in good shape. But ever longer periods when ice is unavailable over their productive foraging habitat mean less time to hunt and fatten up before entering summer fasting periods. We know polar bears cannot fast indefinitely, and that at some point the period of summer ice absence will exceed their fasting tolerance.

The fact that natural variation continues even as the earth's average temperature increases has led to both accidentally and intentionally misleading statements and media presentations. The media and public often focus on an extreme event like a really hot month or a particularly bad sea ice year. People wonder, how bad will *this* year be for the bears? The real problem, however, is the long-term trend ensuring that, with unabated emissions, the number of bad years can only increase—until they are all bad from the polar bear's perspective.

The preoccupation with the short term is a disservice and a distraction with regard to communicating about global warming, because when people are focused on those single bad events they tend to relax if, due to natural variation, the next month or year is not quite so bad. Also, this short-term focus has been purposefully used to distract from the dire trend. Entrenched global warming deniers used the summer sea ice extent in 2008 and 2013 as sirens to attract people away from the long-term trend of sea ice decline. Proclaiming great sea ice recoveries in those years resulted in the incorrect impression that sea ice decline had stopped. The summer sea ice extent in those years was greater than the record-breaking low sea ice extent measurements in 2007 and 2012. But the 2008 and 2013 "recoveries" were both still below the 2005 level, which was the previous record low. Also, both of these "recovery" years were barely above the average long-term trend of decline.

Focusing on the record low sea ice years of 2007 and 2012 enabled the mislabeling of the following years as recoveries, even though all four years in question are merely good examples of the natural variation in the earth's climate system. The media, the public, and the policy makers need to stay focused on the signal evident in the long-term trend. That signal of declining sea ice now stands out very clearly from the interannual variation, with average September sea ice extent declining approximately 13% per decade. The important reality is that, as CO_2 levels continue to rise, bad years, with long periods of ice absence, will be increasingly frequent. At some point, the frequency of these bad ice years, and more prolonged periods of ice absence, will make it impossible for polar bears to survive until another better year comes along. That means that polar bears may disappear from some subpopulations even before summer sea ice disappears every year.

Although I didn't know it then, the trajectory of declining sea ice was taking me steadily toward those meetings with the secretary of the interior. As evidence of the broader problems resulting from global warming and sea ice loss was mounting, my polar bear research team increasingly discussed these risks around the office and in our publications. Year by year, we were pulling together the evidence that ultimately would be a compelling description of the risks polar bears faced. At the same time, we also continued to focus on the traditional shorter term and more tactical issues like on-the-ground threats from hunting and oil and gas development. In the mid-1990s, my job function was transferred to the US Geological Survey (USGS), an esteemed agency that did only research and had no official role in managing the species we studied. As part of a government research agency, our role was to provide information to managers and policy makers on which they could base decisions. Weighing in on those decisions, however, was not part of our mandate as researchers. But the observations were becoming increasingly alarming, and soon, my research team and I would be forced to weigh in—helping to inform decisions that would be made at the policy level.

The increasing impact of global warming on polar bears was, by 2005, capturing the attention of the nation's conservation organizations. These nongovernmental organizations (NGOs) play an important role in assuring our government does indeed promote our general welfare, including that of the environment that sustains us. On February 17, 2005, the nonprofit Center for Biological Diversity (CBD) petitioned the FWS, the government agency responsible for polar bear management, to list polar bears under the Endangered Species Act (ESA).

Although, early in his administration, President George W. Bush talked about global warming, deniers and skeptics were replete in his surroundings, and his administration did not want to list polar bears under the ESA. No species ever had been listed because of the future risks stemming from human-caused global warming, and they apparently felt listing polar bears would be a dangerous precedent. After all, global warming is indeed global, and the administration knew polar bears would not be the only wildlife species affected. My sense was that many of the president's advisers recognized that the polar bear's troubles were an early warning signal—a signal they didn't want to acknowledge— and that listing the bears could be followed by a cascade of petitions for other affected species. The Bush administration bounced the ball around for two years after the CBD petition to list polar bears and pushed past several court-ordered due dates on responses. Finally, though, on January 9, 2007, the FWS announced that listing the polar bear as a threatened species under ESA was "warranted"—and formally proposed such listing.

The "warranted" finding was based on the best available scientific and commercial information and included extensive tracts of language borrowed directly from my previous publications. Whether I wanted to be or not, therefore, I was embroiled in the process of addressing the proposed listing. In response to the FWS finding that listing was warranted, Secretary of Interior Kempthorne ordered the USGS, my research team, to do analyses that could inform him how to respond to that finding. By then, we had documented population decline in the southern Beaufort Sea polar bears of Alaska, and researchers had recognized trouble signs in polar bears in other parts of the world. At that time, however, no one had done a thorough evaluation of global status or projections for the future. My research team, in cooperation with those in other countries, could have provided the evaluation and projections the secretary needed, but under business-as-usual schedules and collaborations, it would have taken two or three years of dedicated focus. Secretary Kempthorne needed us to inform his decision in six months.

Fortunately, USGS director Mark Meyer, and Sue Haseltine, head of wildlife research, backed our task to the hilt. To ensure we could meet the deadline while covering all of the essential bases, we pulled in additional ecologists and analysts from a variety of institutions and localities—American and Canadian. My USGS team of 5 expanded during that summer to 17. As project leader, my job was to provide overall guidance in the process and to synthesize the findings into a comprehensible story the secretary could use to inform his decision. I moved a sleeping pad and hot plate into my office. During that summer I scarcely saw my wife, Virginia—even though I was in town. Occasionally, she brought me a snack or lunch—sometimes at 2 or 3 a.m. when I was working and she also couldn't sleep. Virginia will tell you that our lives have never returned to "normal" since that fateful summer.

By the September 7 deadline, we had assembled nine administrative reports that told a dire story. My synthesis, written with Bruce Marcot of the US Forest Service and Dave Douglas, a long-time colleague at USGS, projected that we could expect to lose approximately two-thirds of the world's polar bears by the middle of this century, and we might lose them all by century's end if societies didn't significantly reduce the global GHG emissions. The briefings we delivered in Washington, DC about those nine reports were the topic Eric and I anticipated discussing on the shuttle bus—before we were handed that "irreversible" headline.

After more months of internal debates, additional briefings, and scientific and legal review, Secretary Kempthorne decided to list polar bears as a threatened species on May 14, 2008. With this act, polar bears became the first species ever to be listed because of future threats from human-caused global warming. With his decision, *conservation as I knew it had been turned on its head*. The challenges I'd seen in my earlier years were those that could be managed by establishing sanctuaries, by enforcing harvest regulations, or by building fences. But we cannot build a fence to save the sea ice from rising temperatures. Saving polar bears, our findings had made clear, depends on changing the ways people, living far from the Arctic, generate and use energy.

The listing of polar bears as a threatened species thrust me into a world where science and logic were confounded by politics and subsidized denial of empirical evidence—and even the basic laws of physics. Our reports in 2007 and the subsequent listing in 2008 elevated polar bears into the role of urgent messengers about global warming's threats to the future of life on Earth. Because they depend on a habitat that literally melts as temperatures rise, polar bears are a great symbol of the threats we all face from a warming world. The reports and subsequent listing, however, also became a new and convenient target for those who wish to mislead the public by denying the world is warming. Their twisted logic goes like this: If polar bears depend on sea ice to make a living, anything that looks like or can be misinterpreted as polar bears doing OK must mean the ice is not melting. And, if the ice is not melting, the world must not be warming, right? This, of course, overlooks the fact that polar bears currently occur over huge expanses of the Arctic at a great range of latitudes. No scientist ever has suggested all polar bears throughout their range would be declining at the same time. Even as evidence shows polar bears in the Beaufort Sea of Alaska already are in poor condition, bears still appear to be doing OK in more northerly areas. Right next door to the Beaufort Sea, polar bears in the Chukchi Sea still seem to be holding their own. The Chukchi Sea has an incredibly broad continental shelf and primary productivity there may be the highest in the Arctic. In contrast, the Beaufort Sea has a very narrow continental shelf and far lower productivity. Although ice is declining rapidly in the Chukchi, it has not yet declined enough to be a detectable problem for the bears.

Global warming deniers choose to ignore great differences in geography and productivity when they suggest "inconsistencies" in the dire projections for polar bears. This is akin to shouts from tobacco companies suggesting, by pointing to a few people who have lived long lives despite years of smoking, that "smoking can't be bad for you." The large geographic range of polar bears doesn't alter the fundamental dependence of polar bears on sea ice, and despite differences in latitude or oceanic productivity that may allow some populations to "hang on" longer, all polar bears ultimately will disappear if warming, and its associated sea ice loss, continues unabated. This great geographic variation in their habitats and the associated differences in sea ice decline, also are reasons for optimism that we still can halt warming in time to save polar bears in parts of their current range. But, for those willing to sacrifice the future for short-term financial gain, and for their messengers, suggesting polar bears are now doing OK in some areas is great fodder for reaching an audience that just doesn't want to believe there is a problem. And if people believe there is not a problem, they will not be concerned about fixing it.

The pledge I made to myself and my coworkers to correct the record regarding polar bears and unavoidable extinction was delayed by new distractions. I found myself increasingly enmeshed in challenging media interviews, where I was called upon to defend the science against intentional misstatements about the current status of polar bears and their future prognosis without sea ice. In 2010, however, we published our paper in the prestigious journal *Nature*. We showed that the world had not crossed a tipping point in Arctic sea ice decline. Rather, we found that Arctic sea ice extent was an inverse linear function of global mean temperature. As the earth's average temperature rises, average sea ice extent declines (albeit with the bumps and dips of interannual variation); it doesn't suddenly cross a threshold beyond which it irreversibly collapses toward zero. If we stabilize temperature, we stabilize the sea ice on which polar bears depend. The cover of the December 16 issue of *Nature* delivered a simple but critical Christmas message based on our paper: *"Cut GHG emissions now and we can still save the polar bear."*

The year 2010 was also a turning point in my thought and the essence of my work. I realized that if I wanted to save polar bears, I needed to change my tactics. I had led the effort that resulted in polar bears being listed under the ESA. My colleagues and I had shown that there is still time to save polar bears and brought new focus on what societies needed to do to accomplish that. There still were many research questions that needed to be answered to fully understand polar bears and how they were responding to human-wrought changes in their habitat. *But* we had already shown the answer to the question, "What do we need to save them?" And that answer didn't require more research. It was clear, at that point, that what I needed to do to help save polar bears from extinction was to push that "answer" to as broad an audience as possible.

I left my research position at the USGS in 2010 and joined the small nonprofit Polar Bears International. PBI is mainly an education and outreach organization. We support research programs of other groups and conduct some of our own research, but our mission is to save polar bears by saving their sea ice habitat. That can be accomplished only by stabilizing atmospheric GHG concentrations. Knowing that too few people understand global warming or just how serious the risks are, a major part of my job is to assure PBI's outreach and education messages are based on the best available science, and to help figure out how to maximize the reach of those messages into the demographic segments that do not understand global warming and/or are not convinced of actions needed to mitigate its threats.

I signed on planning to stay with PBI for about five years—thinking that, by then, societies would have moved toward more sustainable CO_2 emissions pathways and that the future for polar bears by then would look more secure. After all, we had listed the polar bear as a threatened species, our paper in *Nature* showed in dramatic terms the costs to polar bears if we didn't cut emissions, and, more importantly, showed we still have time to save polar bears. The paper made it clear that acting in time to save polar bears would benefit the rest of life on Earth, including humans. In the bigger picture, climate change was increasingly in the news, and the public seemed to be ever more concerned. I thought (with Secretary Kempthorne's bold act to list the polar bear) we had broken the ice of partisan denial among our policy makers. Also, we had a new president who seemed, for the first time, to really take global warming seriously. During his campaign and early in his administration, President Obama vowed to lead the way to the actions needed to change our emissions course and tackle global warming. Shortly after being elected, the Obama administration worked with the 111th Congress to develop the American Clean Energy and Security Act of 2009. Also known as the Waxman-Markey Bill, this measure passed the House of Representatives with some bipartisan support. Although this bill had flaws, it signaled a shift in policy leadership, and seemed to indicate a shift in thinking that could lead to a new emissions path for the United States.

Boy, was I wrong! In 2010, when I felt optimistic about changing our GHG emissions path, I didn't fully appreciate the power of the denial movement. I simply did not imagine how our policy leaders, many of whom are smart people, would choose to literally ruin the world in exchange for the further enrichment of a very few. It has long been understood that rising concentrations of CO_2 and other GHGs must warm the world, and climate models have accurately predicted the rate of global warming. Climate change symptoms, like more frequent and protracted droughts and more erratic and severe precipitation events, are happening just as scientists have, for decades, told us that they would. Yet the denial not only continues but has become more shrill, outlandish, and dangerous.

Ultimately, the Waxman-Markey Bill didn't get through the Senate. The Obama administration was forced to invoke executive actions to try to get the United States onto a less disastrous emissions path, and, with the election of Donald Trump as president, we have seen a step-by-step dismantling of the policy gains made during the Obama years. I can't overemphasize how tragic this is: following the pathway being charted by the Trump administration and its allies in Congress will take us to a climate the world has not seen for more than 3 million years (long before modern humans lived on earth). If they are successful in keeping us on that path, the world will survive but polar bears will not, and "postapocalyptic" probably can't really describe the world our grandchildren will be forced to endure.

Although global temperature projections have thus far been incredibly accurate with regard to the temperature increases we've already seen, they can't account for hidden thresholds, which if crossed could push our climate beyond even the most dire of projections. Throughout the Pleistocene, the last couple million years, the earth has been relatively cool compared to its ancient past. During those "cool" millennia, we have sequestered billions of tons of carbon in soils and cold sea floors. Scientists are not sure what the temperature thresholds are, but if we warm the world enough that that carbon starts "burping" out of the earth's crust, all bets may be off. Likewise, sufficient warming will precipitate wildfires in boreal forests and taiga, where fire historically has been uncommon. The release of carbon long stored in woody material and cold soils of these ecosystems will, along with increased fire frequency in temperate and tropical forests, push us further toward those thresholds. Time, therefore, really is of the essence if we want to save polar bears, and if we want to prevent unimaginable catastrophe.

Society's challenge in dealing with the human-caused climate crisis is to maintain focus on the ultimate certainty that unless we stop the rise of CO_2 and other GHGs, we will exceed all the thresholds we care about—floods, droughts, agricultural failures, sea level rise, immigration crises, and of course, loss of many of the wild species we revere. Secretary Kempthorne understood this and took a bold step that was not popular with the administration for which he worked or his political party. When he announced his decision to list polar bears under ESA, I thought it meant that we had cleared a summit and that information would prevail and drive the societal actions necessary to get on a different emissions path. Yet, at nearly every opportunity, policy and business leaders have steadfastly chosen short-term financial gain over actions that would preserve a climate similar to that in which polar bears (and humans) have flourished.

The campaign to deny global warming and the serious world-wide problems, then predicted and now being observed, had gained full steam by the late 1980s. Researchers employed by fossil fuel companies had, like other scientists at universities or in government agencies, contributed to the understanding of global warming and to the appreciation of the scope of problems that continued reliance on fossil fuels was creating. In the late 1970s, these researchers and their companies seemed poised to help push for reductions in dependence on fossil fuels. Instead, however, they and their minions chose to spend millions of dollars on disinformation programs to prevent policy changes that might reduce short-term financial gains from various aspects of fossil fuel extraction, processing, and combustion.

The resistance to doing anything about global warming somehow became a badge of honor for those who thought of themselves as "conservatives," despite warnings from some prominent conservative voices. Britain's Iron Lady of conservatism, Margaret Thatcher, who was prime minister from 1979 to 1990, admonished the Royal Society that the health of the economy and the health of the environment go hand in hand and warned that global warming could "greatly exceed the capacity of our natural world to cope." Her words in 1990, at the close of her tenure as prime minister, reverberate more strongly today than ever: "Our ability to come together to stop or limit damage to the world's environment will be perhaps the greatest test of how far we can act as a world community. We shall need statesmanship of a rare order." These words suggest she understood that mitigating warming is about the few, while impacts of not doing so are about the many.

Similarly, James Baker, secretary of state under President George H. W. Bush, warned attendees at an Intergovernmental Panel on Climate Change (IPCC) working group meeting in 1989 that "we probably cannot afford to wait until all of the uncertainties have been resolved before we act," "Time" he said, "will not make this problem go away." Baker's early words on the topic were prescient, and in recent years he has been a strong conservative voice pushing for the need to mitigate emissions.

Unfortunately, the words of these conservative policy leaders have been washed aside in a massive disinformation campaign. Following the old adage that politicians know where their bread is buttered, lies and misinformation campaigns backed by millions of dollars from fossil fuel giants seem to have carried the day among politicians who claim to be conservative. The modern conservative movement has wrested the role of government away from the constitutional concept of "promoting the general welfare," by describing any government action as socialism. Yet, the same people and organizations who are most shrill in fearmongering about socialism are happy to enhance their personal riches with government aid at the cost to the general welfare. Those who have been leaders in lying to the world about the dangers and causes of global warming have not spent a penny to lobby for removal of the massive government subsidies that long have benefited the fossil fuel industries. To paraphrase Upton Sinclair, they apparently are happy to take a little socialism, they just don't want to take the name. When not simply lying about the reality of global warming, such organizations distract, confuse, and perhaps most influentially paint a false picture of the "costs" of GHG mitigation while ignoring the benefits.

As we entered the 2000s, the lobbying and disinformation had basically transformed the Republican Party from the party of the Environmental Protection Act (EPA) and the Endangered Species Act (ESA), to the party of science denial. This is a change I take personally. Although I consider myself an independent voter, I grew up in a staunchly Republican family. My parents' philosophy, emphasized at every turn, was to draw conclusions about things you hear or read only after independently verifying the evidence. To them, evidence-based decision making was part and parcel of their "conservative" worldview. How did we get from a philosophy based on verification to a world where evidence based on millions of data points, thousands of scientific publications, and hundreds of scientists could be simply disregarded because someone with a bully pulpit says global warming is a hoax?

My first experience of this disinformation campaign was in 2002. As a researcher seeing the impacts of global warming on the portion of the natural world where I was working, my supervisors told me and my coworkers that our official policy was to stop using the term "global warming." Rather, our new policy was to speak instead of "climate change." I could not see how this change made sense. "Climate change" refers to the cast of symptoms caused by the warming of the world. More frequent and severe droughts, more severe storms, and more radical fluctuations in our weather were predicted climate change consequences, or symptoms, of a warmer world. And the melting of the polar bear's sea ice habitat is caused by warming, not by climate change—it is, in fact, one of the climate change symptoms of a warming world.

I thought this change in the language we were instructed to use seemed misplaced, but initially it did not affect me much, and I thought it was just some misdirected manager trying to put his or her stamp on something. The dictate persisted, however, and I soon learned that the terminology change had come from high levels in the George W. Bush administration. The shift to "climate change" was a deliberate attempt to reduce public fear that we were dangerously altering the world, and was intended to distract people from serious discussions of the causes of warming. Frank Luntz, political adviser to the administration, mapped out talking points to make it sound as if the administration was doing more to protect the environment and our future than it really was. Simultaneously the goal was to mislead about and distract from the dire nature of the challenge. The term "Climate Change," Luntz said, "is less frightening than Global Warming." This policy was followed from the top down. During his first inaugural address, President George W. Bush repeatedly mentioned global warming. But soon thereafter, with advice from Luntz and others, if mentioned at all, "global warming" was replaced by "climate change."

As Luntz and his allies must have hoped, adopting the term "climate change" successfully facilitated a refrain that has become all too common in subsequent years: "The climate is always changing." Discussions of climate change can be derailed when someone simply says, "Oh, the climate has always been changing." The subliminal, but misleading, point is that the current warming and its companion symptoms could be just a reflection of the natural variation that always has been with us. Even among my colleagues who are convinced by the evidence and embrace the need to mitigate GHG rise, there is a reluctance to talk about "global warming" rather than "climate change." Recognizing the politicization of human-caused warming, many believe that it is easier to engage, or at least make overtures regarding the necessary discussions, if we shy away from speaking of "global warming." Most don't know that they are buying into the denialist script when they do so. But many who are providing instruction on how to communicate about this threat have been suggesting that global warming is too scary and that it is less alarming to converse in terms of climate change instead. This, of course, is a trap that was laid down by Luntz and other deniers in 2002. We have to remember that all of the things we lump into the umbrella of climate change are really symptoms of our warming of the world. Sometimes the terms global warming and climate change can be used interchangeably, but we need to clearly differentiate them in communications.

Just as frustrating as the lack of action on the government-policy level has been the relative silence among most wildlife and conservation professionals. They not only buy-in to the denialist script, referring to climate change rather than global warming, when they do speak of the problem, they also simply have not acted in accordance with their purported interests in conservation. The Wildlife Society, for example, has an international climate change group, but they mostly talk to each other. Where, I ask, is the outreach to hunting and fishing groups interested in sustainable wildlife populations?

Colleagues in another major conservation organization told me as recently as 2017 that they just were not ready to take on global warming as one of their issues. This is despite the fact that we have known since 1979 that it is the overarching threat to life on Earth as we know it. Within hunting and fishing groups and other conservation NGOs, global warming and its climate change symptoms mostly have been handled as an afterthought. Most of the energy in the organizations has failed to recognize that humans have turned conservation "on its head," and continue to focus on traditional "on the ground" conservation efforts. Years ago, I attended a kickoff gathering for a World Wildlife Fund initiative to create a Last Ice Area refuge. The concept was to afford on-the-ground protections for the part of the Arctic where the last sea ice would be found as the world continued to warm. This is a nice idea, but it was clear that WWF was pushing this rather than pushing hard-to-halt warming. Conversations with donors to the program who had been invited to the event were even more troubling. At least some of these people either didn't understand or didn't want to recognize that if we allowed the world to continue to warm, *all* sea ice, including within this "last ice area" will ultimately be gone.

Why is the environmental community not paying more attention, and why has it seemingly ignored the impact of warming on its traditional approaches to conservation? The setting aside of parks, preserves, biological hotspots, and marine protected areas, for example, continues to be a high-priority effort throughout the conservationist community—without recognizing that, as the climate continues to warm, the habitats those special designations are supposed to protect will not even be there in a few decades! Without halting GHG rise, huge amounts of money and time will have been spent for nothing as the highly valued habitats disappear from the very areas set aside to protect them. The laws of physics require the world to continue to warm as long as atmospheric GHG concentrations rise, so if we don't stop GHG rise soon, all of our on-the-ground conservation efforts will have been for naught.

Despite conservationists, for years, giving short shrift to the conservation challenges wrought by an ever-warming world, a 2017 article in *Nature* suggested that conservationists were giving *too much* attention to climate change issues—suggesting that the emphasis, instead, should be placed on short-term, on-the-ground measures such as stopping poachers. The *Nature* piece was followed by an article with the same declaration that appeared in the *New Yorker*. The *New Yorker* article was even more damaging because its audience went well beyond the scientists who read *Nature*—instead reaching deep into the general public.

Sure, the poaching of elephants and rhinos must be stopped, or they soon will be gone. And, yes, countless species face imminent threats from wasteful and mismanaged agricultural and logging practices. However, if we don't act soon to stabilize GHG concentrations, global warming will doom any surviving representatives of these cherished species by destroying their habitats. It will be sad indeed if we have to wait until then to realize that our on-the-ground conservation efforts have been for naught. This misguided article in *Nature* closed with an appeal "to all concerned with the sustainability of life on Earth to take stock of the current balance of threats—and refocus their efforts on the enemies of old." This statement falls right into line with the deliberate campaign to distract all of us from the dangers of global warming and is analogous to *turning up the volume on your car's radio so you can't hear the bad sound coming from the engine.* For years, policy makers and conservationists alike have been cranking up the radio's volume instead of paying attention to what is going on under the hood.

The explanation for inaction in the conservation community may stem partly from NGOs' dependence on donations. It is easier to raise funds for traditional conservation measures, like purchasing land for refuges, hiring game wardens, or building fences, than it is to gain funding to pay for educating the public about the consummate threat of global warming. Also, donations often come from organizations with a vested interest in perpetuating use of fossil fuels. In this sense, the environmental community is guilty of the same philosophy as many of our policy and business leaders. That is, valuing short-term gain while overlooking the long-term ramifications.

At PBI, we do both: that is, we recognize global warming as the overarching threat to polar bears, but we also work to reduce more immediate threats, from industry to conflict with humans. Our goal is to keep healthy populations in the short-term so that as many polar bears as possible are still around to repopulate the Arctic once GHG concentrations are stabilized. It is clear, however, that this concept has not received universal recognition in the conservation world.

Fortunately, recent events have led to gains in the battle to inspire social actions. As the long-predicted climate change symptoms of warming have hit us ever harder, new and more poignant language such as "the climate crisis," "the climate emergency," or "global heating" is being adopted. The *Guardian*'s editor-in-chief, Katharine Viner, recently said, "We want to ensure that we are being scientifically precise, while also communicating clearly with readers on this very important issue. The phrase 'climate change,' for example, sounds rather passive and gentle when what scientists are talking about is a catastrophe for humanity." Also, "Increasingly and finally, climate scientists and organizations . . . are changing their terminology and using stronger language to describe the situation we're in." This revised language more directly conveys the urgency of the situation and is not as prone to being easily dismissed with, "Oh the climate is always changing." And, major media is at last clarifying that, yes, the climate may frequently change, but only by ignoring human-caused changes has it become a crisis.

Encouraging actions also increasingly accompany improved communications. The most important global action is represented by the agreements made at the Twenty-First Conference of the Parties to the United Nations Framework Convention on Climate Change, held in Paris in 2015. There, 196 countries agreed to nationally determined contributions (NDCs) toward reducing emissions. They also agreed that, in order to avoid environmental catastrophe, reductions greater than stated NDCs must be made in order to keep global temperature increase below 2.0° Celsius, with a target to hold it to 1.5°C. This nearly global recognition that societies need to individually commit and work together to halt warming demonstrates international understanding and intention that has been missing since the climate crisis was first identified in 1979. Unfortunately actions have, thus far, not followed the verbiage.

The intentions described in Paris are not enforceable or in any way binding, and the Paris Agreement does not specify how countries will achieve their goals. Few countries have codified their NDCs in law, and even if NDCs specified in 2019 are fully implemented, warming will be limited only to about 3.2°C. The last time the global mean temperature was that high was between 3 and 5 million years ago, when sea level may have been more than 20 meters higher than present and the world was a very different place than now. The 2019 Emissions Gap Report of the United Nations Environmental Program concluded that countries must increase their NDC ambitions threefold to achieve the "well below 2°C" goal of Paris and more than fivefold to achieve the 1.5°C goal. This translates into annual decreases in emissions of 2.7% and 7.6% beginning in 2020. Interestingly, had serious climate action begun back in 2010 when I was feeling pretty optimistic about societies getting on the right emissions path, the required cuts would have been only 0.7% and 3.3% per year. With the United States planning to withdraw from the Paris Agreement, and with recent administrative actions virtually assuring US emissions are likely to rise in at least the near term, it is clear global progress toward minimizing temperature increases remains a consummate challenge.

The picture at subnational jurisdictions, however, is more positive. The US Climate Alliance—including 24 states and Puerto Rico and representing 55% of the US population and 40% of emissions—has established ambitious goals to reduce emissions regardless of the federal government's posture. Signatory states must reduce GHG emissions 26%–28% below 2005 levels by 2025, and many are exceeding that requirement. California has set a target of carbon neutrality by 2045. Also by 2045, New Mexico plans to reduce emissions 45% from 2005 levels. In Canada, the Province of British Columbia has had an effective and popular carbon tax and dividend program for several years—presenting a model for the rest of the world. At the business and corporate level, positive steps also are in the works. McDonald's recently announced a virtual-power purchase agreement to support wind and solar projects. Microsoft is increasing its renewable portfolio, and Google plans to purchase a 1.6-gigawatt renewable energy package. Walmart is partnering with environmental groups to cut a billion tons of GHG pollution from its supply chain by 2030 and has been outspoken in opposing the pending US withdrawal from the Paris Agreement. Ford motor company is pushing hard to develop electric vehicles that will be practical for many sectors of our economy.

We can expect more from these and other companies as more and more climate change symptoms of global warming are experienced. Despite great progress at the state, local, and business levels, the need for federal-level action is still omnipresent. In 2019 General Motors, Fiat Chrysler, and Toyota joined the Trump administration's effort to hold back motor vehicle pollution standards, citizens of Washington State again voted down a statewide carbon tax, and a Canadian national climate tax was being resisted by several of the provinces. Clearly, the world has a long way to go in getting onto the path agreed to in Paris, and national and international commitment is still lacking.

In 2007, I told the secretary of the interior that, if we stayed on our current GHG emissions path, we could lose two-thirds of the world's polar bears by midcentury, and by the end of the century we could lose them all. In the intervening 12 years little has changed to alter that projection, and because we have not mitigated GHG rise, the challenge is greater now than it was then. If we are serious about saving habitat that will maintain polar bear populations, we need to begin dramatic emissions reductions within the next decade and stabilize atmospheric GHG concentrations by midcentury. Achieving this will require total societal commitment at the global level. In 2008 I gave a talk suggesting that what we needed was to think that the way to beat global warming is something akin to the Apollo Project that took Americans to the moon—an endeavor the whole nation got behind. I was gratified to see this terminology adopted in a 2019 *Forbes* editorial by Steve Denning. Although years overdue, the recognition of the serious nature of the climate crisis and the need to unite to tackle it is welcome.

Estimates suggest that if we can hold global temperature rise to under 2° Celsius, the climate future our grandchildren face will at least overlap with the climate to which humans have become accustomed. That is, at least some years will be somewhat familiar with what we used to have. Halting GHG rise in time to hold global temperature to that level will require a full-court press including reducing consumption, switching to renewables, taking advantage of every possible sequestration sink, and boosting research and development. The full list of areas requiring action and focused communication is long. It ranges from elimination of subsidies for fossil fuel exploration and development to modernizing of electric grids to increases in renewable electric generation and electrified transport to more sustainable agriculture and forest and range-land management to different and more thoughtful relationships with human food.

In asking how we can help society make headway on these big items, we need to recognize all of us have an opportunity to help save polar bears and secure a climate future that will preserve the other species we love. We now recognize that conservation is not something done only in the field by professionals, but rather something to which we all need to commit in our daily lives. Traditional actions, like sending a donation to hire game wardens or build a fence, are no longer enough to allow us to sleep well at night, thinking we've done our conservation duty.

Many in the public and policy arena simply have not made the effort to understand the evidence. They don't know what is at stake or don't want to believe. The more people understand the problem and the required solution, the more likely we are to fix it. All of us can play a role in reaching these folks. Being willing and prepared to engage with and try to motivate sections of our society that are currently not engaged may now be the single biggest part of our personal responsibility! This means doing enough homework to be able to engage with our friends and relatives and coworkers over shared values—such as leaving a livable planet for our grandchildren. Each of us comes from a different background and has our own knowledge, connections, motivations, and passions. These differences mean that we all can find a niche within the broad range of things we need to change, and about which our passions can drive us to help in this battle.

Taking advantage of naturally occurring teaching moments is important. Because people identify most strongly with the environment around them, bring local or regional issues into conversations rather than talking about the plight of people in a far-off land. The failure of outdoor ice-skating rinks to freeze in winter, crop failures caused by ever-more-common heavy rains and flooding, and greater fluctuations in temperature and precipitation all provide talking points for engagement with our friends. Where Virginia and I live, home air conditioner use has been increasing, and people are noticing. During the early and mid-1900s, we had about 20 days each summer over 90° Fahrenheit. During the last decade we've seen approximately 30 days over 90°F each summer. On the emissions path being pushed by the Trump administration, we will see 90 days above 90°F each summer during the latter part of this century. This statistic got my attention, and I'm using it to get the attention of our friends and neighbors.

Where appropriate, we must not shy away from laying shame on the leaders of the denial movement. They have known for decades what is at stake and have chosen their short-term financial gain over the future of the rest of life on Earth. It is time to point out this complicity at every opportunity.

Outreach efforts to reduce emissions and halt global warming have historically focused on individual actions like encouraging people to drive less, take public transit, or turn the thermostat down. Such efforts are important in showing we are walking the talk, and many of us already are doing so. But these "personal" actions will not save polar bears. Years ago I remember an outreach campaign based on the calculation that if all Americans did whatever they could in the way of living more efficiently (e.g., driving and otherwise traveling less, recycling, turning off lights, and adjusting thermostats), we could save the equivalent of all of the CO_2 emissions of France. The problem in this calculation is the "if." The required national level of commitment (to get everyone to act) could happen only with inspiration from top policy leaders. William Nordhaus, the 2018 Nobel Prize recipient in economics, and others have emphasized the need for coordinated national and international action and shown that government policies such as a carbon tax and rebate program can set a national path that allows our free markets to make the changes necessary to save the world. Without such policy leadership, we are unlikely to head off our looming disaster. Communication with policy leaders is more critical than ever. We must aggressively support proposed legislation that shows promise of moving us onto a better GHG pathway. And, we need to take every opportunity to call and write and otherwise point this out to our elected representatives.

Most importantly, we must maintain hope that we can convince world societies to make the right changes in time. And, we need to realize that hope doesn't just come from our thoughts or desires—our actions must justify it. Many people, even those who seem to have their minds made up—including our policy leaders—can change their minds if we present the right information in the right way. But they will not change their minds on their own. If we all pick our battles and persist until we make changes, our hopes will be justified.

Most of our policy leaders who deny global warming don't disdain future generations. Rather, they have somehow been convinced—by those who are focused entirely on short-term financial gain—that the dire consequences of continued global warming are not real, or they don't recognize that the severity of the climate change symptoms will be so great we will be largely unable to deal with them when the time comes. Often, this "convincing" resulted from something as simple as political donations to election campaigns. These people increasingly will realize the error of their ways and/or realize they are on the wrong side of history. In his epic movie role as General Patton, George C. Scott gave a compelling speech in which he told his soldiers they should be proud of their service because, when their children ask, "What did you do in the great war Daddy?," "you won't have to say, well I shoveled shit in Louisiana." When asked, "Grandpa, when you were in office what did you do to prevent the disaster we are now struggling to live through?" few political leaders will want to have to admit that they fought to prevent the actions that would have saved us from this tragedy.

If we strategically use examples close to home and connect people with things we all care about, we can engage even those who may not want to believe in global warming. One event that keeps my hope alive goes back to that crazy 2007 summer, and my personal experience in briefing Secretary Kempthorne. We'd seen the Bush administration scrub the term global warming from the federal vernacular. We'd seen them stall on any action to reduce emissions, and we'd witnessed pushback and delays in responding to the petition to consider listing polar bears under ESA. There was much uncertainty regarding how the administration ultimately would respond to that petition. Many feared that the decision would simply be "warranted but precluded," a convenient political escape from the evidence. Yet, when I was speaking one-on-one with Secretary Kempthorne, I could tell he was listening and thinking. And, in the end, the findings in our reports led him to list polar bears under protections of the ESA. Coinciding with the announcement of his decision, Secretary Kempthorne held a conference call with my entire research team. He thanked us for our efforts and acknowledged candidly that the Bush administration did not want to list polar bears. But, he told us, the evidence in our reports convinced him that listing was his only choice and that it was the right thing to do. Despite efforts of many in the George W. Bush administration to deny global warming, Secretary of Interior Dirk Kempthorne remained open-minded, demonstrating that scientific evidence and rational thought can sway policy leaders to forsake partisan loyalty and short-term personal gain and work to secure a future we all might choose.

My hope is that a critical mass of our citizens will buckle down and keep information flowing. Also, that the same critical mass will vote in the marketplace and the polling place to support businesses and policy leaders who have shown they care about a sustainable future for polar bears and for all of life on Earth. Doing so will ensure the needed policy changes take place and convert hope to reality.

Acknowledgments

The list of those who helped me along my professional path is long, but several deserve special mention. First my wife, Virginia, whose steadfast love and support has encouraged me through even the most challenging times. She is always free with a critique or advice and most importantly provides me a consistent reminder to appreciate the joys of life even with the challenges we face. My parents, Carl and Pat Amstrup, guided my evidence-based decision making and consistently told me I could do anything I wanted to do. George Durner worked with me for 18 years at the USGS, contributing many essential components of our polar bear knowledge. Dave Douglas has been a source of advice, knowledge, and critical analytical skill through all my years with polar bears. Dave and Bruce Marcot were essential in helping me develop a cogent synthesis of our 2007 studies for the secretary of the interior.

The current understanding of polar bears would not have been possible without the contributions of George, Dave, Eric Regehr, Geoff York, Tom Smith, Tony Fischbach, and Kristin Simac, longtime coworkers and confidants on the USGS polar bear team. I am grateful to Trent McDonald for years of idea exchange and statistical advice. I could not have reached my current understanding of polar bears without the four decades of consultation and advice from Ian Stirling. Eric DeWeaver introduced me to the climate sci-

Dr. Steven Amstrup carries polar bear cubs back to their mother
Courtesy: Daniel Cox

ence world and is the greatest philosopher I know. Cecilia Bitz and
Flavio Lehner are critical in helping me understand climate science and sea ice dynamics and ways to think and communicate
about both. I am grateful to Krista Wright, Geoff York, BJ Kirschof-
fer, and Barbara Nielsen for their ideas, collaboration, and support,
and the rest of the PBI team for giving me opportunity to make the
career leap from research to conservation. Finally, I thank Mike
Lockhart, the best field biologist I know, who has for 44 years provided a sounding board and is my best and oldest friend.

Further Reading

Amstrup, S. C. 2003. Polar Bear, *Ursus maritimus*. Pages 587–610 in G. A. Feldhamer, B. C. Thompson, and J. A. Chapman, eds., Wild Mammals of North America: Biology, Management, and Conservation. Johns Hopkins University Press.

Amstrup, S. C., et al. 2010. Greenhouse Gas Mitigation Can Reduce Sea-Ice Loss and Increase Polar Bear Persistence. Nature 468: 955–958.

Amstrup, S. C., and F. Lehner. 2017. Anthropogenic Ocean Change: The Consummate Threat to Marine Mammal Welfare. Pages 9–26 in A. Butterworth, ed., Marine Mammal Welfare, Animal Welfare, vol. 17. Springer International.

Durner, G. M., et al. 2009. Predicting 21st Century Polar Bear Habitat Distribution from Global Climate Models. Ecological Monographs 79:25–58.

Harvey, J. A., et al. 2018. Internet Blogs, Polar Bears, and Climate-Change Denial by Proxy. BioScience 68 (4): 281–287.

Lenton, T. M., et al. 2019. Climate Tipping Points—Too Risky to Bet Against. Nature 575:592–595.

National Research Council. 1979. Carbon Dioxide and Climate: A Scientific Assessment. National Academies Press. https://doi.org/10.17226/12181.

Post, E., et al. 2019. The Polar Regions in a 2°C Warmer World. Science Advances 5 (12):eaaw9883.

United Nations Environment Programme. 2019. Emissions Gap Report 2019. UNEP.

CHAPTER 6

DEEP IN TIME, BROAD IN SCOPE

Conservation Science Empowers Communities
and Saves Species in Madagascar

DR. PATRICIA CHAPPLE WRIGHT

2014 Recipient of the Indianapolis Prize

Sifaka
Propithecus sp.

When I was growing up, I didn't know anything about tropical biology or conservation. All I knew was that I loved animals. And I felt happiest when I was walking in the woods, in nature. I remember the series of pets, from raccoons, wild kittens, baby rabbits, snakes, turtles, and tropical fish, to seven chickens, cocoons that became moths and tadpoles that became frogs. My family of both parents and six children lived in the countryside of western New York State near Lake Ontario. My dad, a supervisor in a factory, loved natural history and had spent his early years in Ontario, Canada. My mom was a city girl, raised in Buffalo, New York, who, before I arrived, had a life in science as a chemistry teacher. But three kids in four years ended that career.

In addition to a love of animals, I was born with a keen curiosity. By the time I reached high school in the tiny rural village of Lyndonville, New York, I knew I loved biology. The winters were long and cold, and I read books by Gerald Durrell and Ivan Sanderson, books that took me to exotic places and told animal stories. I was awestruck to read about the diversity of tropical animals, their wonderful antics and lifestyles. This interest in animals guided me to a biology major at Hood College in Maryland, and my favorite moments were doing estuary ecology research along the Patuxent River. After graduation, I moved to Boston to take a laboratory assistant job at Harvard Medical School, in an immunology lab, where I performed experiments on white mice. They were animals, but not very happy ones, and I decided laboratory work was not for me. In the meantime, I had fallen in love with Jamie Wright, a tall artist with a similar love of animals and travel, who was finishing an English major at Brown University. We married that summer, and he began a master's in fine arts in New York at Pratt Institute.

When I reached New York, a newlywed with aspirations to support my husband, I found out that, with only a bachelor's degree, jobs in biology didn't pay enough for us to survive in New York City. So I took a higher-paying job as a social worker for the Department of Social Services in Brownsville, a section of Brooklyn. There were no animals involved, but I was fascinated by the prospect of learning about the people of Brooklyn. They were poor. Not the kind of countryside poor I had grown up knowing (farmers seldom had many extras, but always had food on the table and pride in growing it), but a "city" kind of poor, blighted with malnutrition, poor schools, unemployment, and what seemed to me like a pervasive kind of hopelessness. My job was to help these city poor get out of poverty. The Great Society program offered training and opportunities, and I was the ambassador between president LBJ and these Brooklyn residents who had landed on the unfortunate side of life. I had a caseload of 120 people and visited them all. Those were the days when New York was dangerous, especially Brownsville and Bedford-Stuyvesant, but I was young, naïve, and lucky. I learned about the lives of the residents through careful listening, and then tried to help solve their problems with my portfolio of government assistance. It was a challenge, and I embraced the challenge.

But it was the 1960s, and by night Jamie and I went to rock concerts. In the Village, the Fillmore East was alive with rock and roll. Janis Joplin, Cream, Led Zeppelin, the Doors, Dylan, and Jimi Hendrix. Every weekend the shows were electric. It was just before a Jimi Hendrix concert that we had an experience that changed our lives. Arriving early at the Fillmore East, we went across the street to a pet shop called Fish and Cheeps.

Amazing how one day can change a life and jump-start a career. There in a cage, curled up asleep, was a monkey who had just arrived from the Amazon. The little primate awakened, and reached out for my outstretched finger in a gesture of friendship. I looked into his eyes and I was hooked. "What does he eat and how much does he cost?" I asked the shop owner, but he just replied, "He sleeps all day and his food is gone in the morning." It was then that I realized he was a night active monkey. Jamie thought it was a good idea to have a companion at night while he was painting his art projects.

I returned to the pet store on Monday, bought the monkey, and we named him Herbie. He ate mostly fruits, was well behaved, and stayed up nights with Jim as he painted. It wasn't until he began to object to our going to rock concerts on weekends without him that I realized we should get him a companion of his own species. But none of the New York pet stores I called had even heard of a night monkey, so I went to my boss and quit my job, explaining I was going to the Amazon to find my monkey a mate. My boss and I settled on my taking a leave of absence. I chose the country of Colombia as our destination because, according to a book I borrowed from the New York Public Library, it was the closest destination to New York that had night monkeys. We packed Herbie into a cat carrier and took him with us to help find his mate.

I remember that moment of first being in the rain forest. The smell of life. The orchestra of sounds, the richness of the wild jungle. Even though it was my first time, I immediately felt at home. Deep down I felt I never wanted to leave. In Leticia, Colombia, along the Amazon River, we observed the dark side of pet stores and northern laboratories. Local people were filling their dugout canoes with wild animals—monkeys, macaws, ocelots, jaguars—and selling them to dealers who were shipping them off to distant destinations in Florida. I was horrified by the thought of most of these beautiful animals dying en route, and my opinion of pet stores changed. One of the dealers had a young, female owl monkey and we hesitated to buy her, but when I imagined this pretty little monkey being shipped to Florida in a cramped cage without food and water and probably not surviving, I shuddered. I couldn't allow that. We purchased Kendra, a red-chested female owl monkey, for a dollar. Although Herbie was jealous of her at first, within a few weeks the two became an inseparable couple, and we returned to New York.

Back in New York City, Kendra loved the city life. Sleeping on soft pillows and being fed the finest fruits the city had to offer suited her. But my curiosity returned when I read in another book at the public library that the northern border of the geographic range of night monkeys was Panama. Yet on the map I could see that the rain forest was continuous into Costa Rica. Surely there were night monkeys in Costa Rica, and I wanted to find them. I asked my boss for another leave of absence and Jamie, Herbie, Kendra, and I arrived in San Jose and then Limon, on the Caribbean coast of Costa Rica. We were heading up the canal to Tortuguero when I got sick. Vomiting, diarrhea—I thought it was something I ate. But I kept getting sicker and eventually flew back home and was admitted to

New York Hospital. They put me on an IV and gave me all the tests for tropical diseases. I was just relieved to be alive. The next day the doctor came in to give me the diagnosis. "The good news is that you don't have any tropical diseases." He hesitated for a moment. "Mrs. Wright, you are pregnant." I was quite surprised.

Amanda Elizabeth Wright was born seven months later. And I quit my job. Jamie had his master of fine arts and a job with the O'Henry photography business. I became a mother and housewife, cooking, cleaning, and taking care of the baby. Jamie would come home late, say hello to Amanda and me, and I would put her to bed. Two weeks into this routine, Kendra had a baby girl too. We were stunned and elated. But the monkey family had a totally different approach to child care. Herbie was the primary caretaker. Kendra would nurse the baby, give it a nip, the baby would squeak, and then Herbie would run over to take the baby on his back. He carried her, introduced new foods, and played with her. I was observing extreme father care in our primate cousin. I had read Jane Goodall's account of maternal-infant relationships in chimps, and Irv DeVore's descriptions of male dominance and aggression in baboons, but I had never dreamed that there were primate infants that were cared for by dads. The time was the early 1970s, and the sexual revolution was in full swing. I knew this news was important and that this was a primate model that we had to know more about. How had this paternal behavior evolved? I had to go to the rain forest and find out.

But in those days, before internet, how did one get to do this kind of research? I wrote to National Geographic, but the secretary wrote me back a letter stating I did not have a PhD, and they didn't give grants to people without PhDs. I wrote to Jane Goodall, but her letter must have gotten lost, as she never replied. I called my mother, who suggested I speak to our neighbor, Mrs. Nancy Mulligan, who had taken a chance on a crazy idea once before. The risk of investing in George Eastman's Kodak

Company had paid off for her, and maybe she would be interested in this crazy idea about paternal care. Nancy Mulligan was 81 by this time, and indeed she gave me my first funds. My mom was also a "clipper," which meant that she read the *Buffalo Evening News* and sent to all her children articles that might interest them. She sent me an article about a professor from City College, Dr. Warren Kinzey, who studied monkeys in the Amazon. I called up the Department of Anthropology. "Dr. Kinzey, I am a Brooklyn housewife, and I want to study *Aotus* in the wild. Can you tell me how to take data and what equipment I should buy?" There was a long pause at the other end of the line. Then he said "You do know that *Aotus* is nocturnal, don't you?" I said yes, that I had three as pets. Again the silence. Then he said he could see me next Monday.

After that meeting at City College, I wrote down every word that Professor Kinzey told me about equipment and methods and sent the project proposal to Nancy Mulligan. Within months, Amanda, Jamie, and I were off to Peru to study father care in monkeys. Six months later I was back with the first description of the life of night monkeys in the wild, and that scientific paper, "Home Range, Activity Patterns and Agonistic Encounters of a Group of Night Monkeys (*Aotus trivirgatus*) in Peru," was published in 1978. Dr. Kinzey insisted that I go to graduate school, only, I didn't really want to go back to school. I wasn't confident that I was smart anymore. But I took the GREs and was accepted at all the places I applied. I chose to work with Dr. Kinzey.

I was so involved with analyzing data and getting into grad school, I didn't realize my marriage was falling apart. The young girl who had enjoyed rock concerts and recreational drugs had evolved into a single-minded field biologist. As focused as a laser—on questions and hypotheses. On testing those hypotheses. Day and night all I could think about was science and the science of studying monkeys. Jamie wanted to take a different path. Suddenly, not only was I in graduate school but Amanda, four years old, and I were also on our own in New York City. I had no funds for a babysitter, so she attended all my classes with me.

When it came time for doing my dissertation research, what was I going to do with Amanda? A proper primatology dissertation, answering the questions I had about night monkeys, would require following them in all seasons—more than a year of fieldwork in the rain forest. Then one evening in Greenwich Village, I had dinner with Professor John Terborgh from Princeton. He suggested that I do my dissertation research at Cocha Cashu Research Station in Peru. I knew that site was remote, located in Manu National Park, five to 10 days by boat into the unexplored Amazon.

"John, I would like to do my research at your site, but I have a child, Amanda, who is six years old." Professor Terborgh looked me in the eye, took my hand, and proclaimed, "I can't think of a better place to raise a child than the rain forest at Cocha Cashu." I blinked. Professor Terborgh had just given me and Amanda permission to go to his field site.

Cocha Cashu is over the Andes, on the other side of Cuzco. After bumping in the back of a truck for ten hours, we boarded canoes with all our field equipment and supplies and journeyed another three days down the rivers into the wild. Cocha Cashu was indeed a pristine paradise, filled with macaws, tanagers, woodpeckers, a thousand species of birds, giant river otters, tapirs, giant anteaters, jaguars, pumas, bush masters, fer de lance, boa constrictor snakes, harpy eagles, and 15 kinds of monkeys. The canopy reached 35–40 meters, and we humans were just a small speck in the midst of the power of nature.

Amanda thrived, helping ornithologists untangle birds from mist nets, paddling along with the river otter researchers, collecting flowers and plants with the botanists, and I completed my dissertation on monkey behavior and ecology. A year later I returned to New York City to analyze my data. My brother, Ted, a building contractor, always generous with supporting my projects, kindly offered to take me in to the home he was building out of a silo, and my parents welcomed Amanda into their house a few miles away. I wanted to be isolated to concentrate on my behavior and ecology data about night monkeys.

But one evening at dinner, Mom said that a very insistent gentleman had called me and wanted me to call him back as soon as possible. When I called back, a voice with hint of a Texas drawl answered, "This is Elwyn Simons, director of the Duke University Primate Center, and I need you." The voice had the authority of Uncle Sam recruiting for the army.

"I have an NSF grant to study tarsiers in the wild and bring back 12 to Duke to start a breeding colony. There are no tarsiers in the USA right now. Do you know what a tarsier is?"

"Yes sir, a small, nocturnal primate from Asia," I answered timidly.

"Great, I want you to go catch some in Borneo, and I need you to come to Duke soon."

"But Professor Simons, I have just returned from the Amazon, and I don't have my dissertation finished—in fact I haven't even begun to analyze my data."

Dr. Simons called my adviser, and within three months I was in Sabah, the northwest corner of the island of Borneo.

Tarsiers are an enigmatic species. They sit at the foot of our primate ancestor trees with characteristics that make them both like monkeys—with substantial brain size and notable dexterity in their hands—and like lemurs, lorises, and bushbabies, a primitive group of primates with smaller brain size relative to body size and less dexterity. Tarsiers exist as ancient relics on a variety of islands in Asia. All living tarsiers are small-bodied, weighing about 4 ounces, and are distinguished by being the only primates that eat nothing but live animal prey, usually large grasshoppers or small lizards. Their brain size is akin to that of prosimians, but their reproductive organs and genetics display evidence that they are also monkey-like.

I learned a lot about conservation from the tarsiers. First, cooperation and collaboration are important ingredients. Duke had no connections in Borneo, but by a collaboration with colleagues at the US National Zoo, including Devra Kleiman, research director; Ed Gould, head of mammals; and scientist Miles Roberts, I met Patrick Andau, head ranger of the Sabah National Parks. Patrick Andau hosted me in Sabah and gave me access to 10 rangers and mist nets to set out in the night where unsuspecting tarsier pairs became entangled. As a guest of the Sabah Park Service, I lived at Sepilok, a rain forest park and rehabilitation center for young orangutans confiscated by the Park Service from the pet trade or from burned forests. The free-ranging juvenile orangutans were curious, by day peering into the windows of the small cabin where I slept and often strolling with me around the grounds. Each morning they were taken out into the rain forest by the rangers to learn to maneuver in the trees. The forestry station was a temporary home until they were released. The efforts were well intended, but when I asked where the released animals went, the rangers just shrugged, and I realized the released orangutans were not followed into the forest to understand how they fared in the wild. Conservation is a process, and follow-up is an important part of that process.

During those three months in Sabah, I learned for the first time that one of the main enemies of rain forests is fire. In 1982, because of the droughts, massive fires had raged across Borneo. Slash-and-burn agriculture and selective logging had made the dry rain forest particularly vulnerable to fire. By 1983, when I arrived, many areas that had been populated by tarsiers the year before were barren of animals. Rain forests, as large and wet as they are, are much more vulnerable to human impact than I had ever suspected.

That expedition taught me about export and import permits, and the importance of paperwork to conservation. We captured 12 tarsiers (six males and six females), and the stamped documents weighed almost as much as they did. The tarsiers flew back with me in two cat transportation boxes carried onboard Swiss Air and stored under my seat and my neighbor's seat. Every four hours I would bring a carrier to the rest room, feed each tarsier a lizard from a box in my pocket, and give each water from an eye dropper. With such constant care, all the tarsiers arrived safe and healthy to the Duke Primate Center in Durham North Carolina. The pampering didn't end there. Cages were handcrafted to accommodate the tarsiers' vertical clinging and leaping locomotion and their need to catch live animals.

Our next hurdle was an attack from the animal rights front. The Primate Protection League challenged Duke's right to keep such endangered animals in captivity to do research. I confronted the attack directly: I met with President Shirley McGreal's assistant and showed her the good conditions under which we were going to do our observational research on tarsiers. Dr. Simons and I explained that we needed to understand the husbandry of such rare animals in order to have a "second line of defense" for keeping the endangered primates from going extinct. Shirley McGreal was eventually convinced, and we ended up being good friends and allies. Good conservation requires a diverse network of members, each with their own expertise and resources working together to save wildlife. We are all basically on the same team against the greater forces of the depletion of nature.

Tarsiers also taught me that captive conservation is not easy, and although the tarsiers thrived, my goal of having a successful reproductive colony was a challenge. Infants were born, but did not survive. David Haring, my Duke Primate Center collaborator, and I succeeded in hand-rearing one infant, Mandarin, to more than one year of age, but that was the only success. The tarsiers lived long lives, more than 12 years, but our breeding colony failed. Rescue centers and rehabilitation areas, and keeping a stock of endangered animals in captivity are all important, but I was convinced that saving habitat and the wild places where endangered animals live is the most effective way to practice conservation.

Dr. Simons had a strategic plan for making a haven for the rare and critically endangered lemurs, as part of the second line of defense for extinction at Duke. Madagascar had been under socialist rule for over a decade, with trade and contact with all Western countries forbidden. Many of our primatologist friends had been arrested and extradited from Madagascar during the revolution of 1972. But, beginning in the 1980s, rumors circulated that the country was becoming more open to Western ideas, and the president of Madagascar seemed to trust research scientists. Taking advantage of this window in time, Dr. Simons planned his rescue missions. He suggested that I go to Madagascar to search for the greater bamboo lemur, *Hapalemur simus*, which was once abundant throughout northern Madagascar, according to the fossils, but had been last seen decades ago, and was probably extinct.

Therefore, in 1986 I launched an expedition to the world's fourth-largest island to find out whether the greater bamboo lemur still existed. Arriving on Madagascar, the reality was shocking. I was not prepared for the fact that 90% of Madagascar's natural habitat was gone, totally destroyed. The island looked like a Martian landscape with gaping red wounds called *lavakas* or erosion gullies. There were nine million people on Madagascar in 1986, in an area the size of France or California. There were few paved roads, almost no cars or machine-made clothing, and the poverty of the people was Paleolithic. Dr. Simons shipped an ancient Land Cruiser from his Egyptian field site, and David Meyers and Deborah Overdorff (graduate students), Patrick Daniels (a research assistant), Bedo (a famed young Malagasy guide), and I began our search visiting the places in southeast Madagascar where the greater bamboo lemur was last seen. What we found were muddy, rutted roads, deforested landscapes, and a few brown lemurs.

Discouraged after months of camping and finding no bamboo lemurs, we looped back from the Indian Ocean coast to Ranomafana village in hopes of taking a soothing bath in the hot mineral springs. After the much-needed soak, I noticed that there was gorgeous rain forest in back of the Hotel Thermal. I asked for a local guide, and I was introduced to Emile and Loret. Crossing a treacherous, rickety bridge, we found the most beautiful forest I had seen in Madagascar. We camped across the river and searched daily for our lemur. One chilly, misty morning at dawn, Deborah and I sparked a fire, heated a pot of coffee, and began our forest search. Suddenly, out of the fog, I was confronted by a golden lemur clinging to a bamboo stalk, menacing me with a guttural growl. Then he and his companions leaped off into the bamboo away from us. Was it true? Had we seen *Hapalemur simus*? I knew I had never seen a lemur like that. But I was puzzled by its orange color, as *H. simus* was gray with white ear tufts in the drawings. Perhaps these differences were only color variations? I was so excited by seeing this lemur in the bamboo, I pushed those doubts aside and assumed the animal was *H. simus*, the greater bamboo lemur.

Not until weeks later did I realize I was wrong—that golden-orange bamboo eater was not *Hapalemur simus*. David Haring, a photographer from Duke Primate Center, had joined our team, and stayed out late one night. When he appeared at camp out of the darkness, I began to scold him, as we had been preparing to launch a search for him. At that time, no trails were marked, and a person could be lost for days in the vast wilderness. But David explained he had been photographing the lesser bamboo lemur (*H. griseus*), the more common species, which was at Duke already. "But it was bigger than those at Duke, and it made a deep growling noise I never heard before, and there were 11 of them."

"David, *H. griseus* is monogamous, and doesn't come in groups over five or six. Did you count some twice?" He added, "And they had white ear tufts." Then it dawned on me: the animals that he saw couldn't have been *H. griseus*. They must have been *H. simus*, the species we were searching for! "Are you sure, David, about those white ear tufts?" I was breathless. David pointed to his camera and said, "I took two rolls of film." And at that moment I realized, that first bamboo lemur I had seen, the orange one, was a species new to science. There were three species of bamboo-eating lemur in this rain forest! Amazing!

First, we had to catch all three species to describe the new ones. With the help of Ken Glander and a National Geographic grant, we found they had different gland locations and different weights, as well as different coat colors. When we followed them, we realized that they had different vocalizations and different social systems.

My next research question was, how do those three species co-exist in one rain forest? Answering that required following the three species and describing dietary differences. We watched as *Hapalemur simus* opened up bamboo stalks with their specialized teeth and scraped out the inner pith. *Hapalemur aureus* (the golden bamboo lemur) feasted on young shoots coming out of the ground; the smallest species ate the petioles of the young bamboo leaves. When we looked at the nutrition of the bamboo shoots, we found that each shoot was filled with cyanide. That daily dose of cyanide would kill a human. How could this five-pound lemur survive this poison?

But before I had time to write my next grant, more than 200 lumberjacks moved into the forest and we heard the chilling tonk-tonk of the axe at work. Next we heard the crack and crash as a 35-meter-tall tree fell, taking down another eight trees in its path. I was horrified and rushed to the local villagers, explaining that this was too important a forest to chop down. They didn't understand my bad French. Coming to my senses, I went to Antananarivo, the biggest city, and capital of Madagascar, to the office of the head of the Department of Water and Forests to explain about the importance of keeping this forest to save these endangered species of bamboo lemurs. The Water and Forests director watched me attentively as I explained about the new species and the rediscovered species. When I was finished, he sighed deeply and explained, "Yes, I agree that this Ranomafana forest is important. However, this is Madagascar. We have no money to make a protected area. It takes funding for maps, boundary marking, park infrastructure, staff salaries. It takes big money, and Madagascar does not have the funds for that. But . . ." He hesitated, and then looked deeply into my eyes, "but if you find the money, Madame Patricia, we will do everything possible to help make that park a reality." And he rose, shook my hand, and ushered me out of his office.

I stood outside the forestry director's office shaking my head, "Oh, no, no, no. I cannot do it." I was an assistant professor at Duke and had never raised big money. How could I raise millions? No. No. No. I had never learned anything in graduate school even close to how to make a national park. No. No. No! If I made this park, I would never get tenure, and my academic career would go out the window.

And then the resolve came from someplace deep inside me. If I let the greater bamboo lemur go extinct . . . If I let this species, entirely new to science, this golden bamboo lemur, go extinct, I could never live with myself. It was a big responsibility, and I had no choice but to take it on. During that moment it became crystal clear to me that I had to save those lemurs. And in that "eureka" moment, I became a conservationist.

I took a year sabbatical from Duke University, and 12 eager Duke undergraduates came with me to help. Amanda, my daughter, moved to Madagascar for her senior year in high school. We all worked together to create the fourth national park in Madagascar.

The first step was to figure out the boundaries of the park. One road bisected the forest on its way to the Indian Ocean. More than 50 villages surrounded the forest, and each village housed from 200 to 300 people. These were very poor people, who lived by growing everything they ate and using firewood and wood for construction from the 20-mile-wide continuous rain forest that covered the mountain range from northern to southern Madagascar. To define the park boundaries, we had to negotiate with those 50 villages, walking for days to reach them. And we had to carry all our food and cooking pots, because the villagers had no food to share. Having been totally ignored by the national government for decades, those village residents were really surprised to see us arrive. My field assistant Patrick Daniels, my two local guides Loret and Emile, Edmond from the local forestry department, and I would meet with the village elders and explain what a national park was. Some villagers were afraid, and some just laughed, but by the third visit a year later the majority of farmers were on board, and with their authorization, we could start establishing the park. It was three years of hard work. The forestry department and our Duke team marked the boundaries, built trails, and accomplished biodiversity surveys.

Funding? Although I wrote the first draft of the proposal in 1987, funding to establish the decree and the park infrastructure, totaling $4,387,000, was awarded to Duke from the United States Agency for International Development (USAID) on August 10, 1990. But that money didn't cover the health and education programs that the villagers had asked for. The village residents had been very clear that they would obey the park rules, but they needed education for their children and health clinics for all. I had to do more fundraising.

To my surprise, the John D. and Catherine T. MacArthur Foundation awarded me a fellowship (the Genius Grant), which provided enough money for the education component. Liz Claiborne and Art

Ortenberg funded a grant for the health team. Then a Man and the Biosphere grant from UNESCO as well as awards from the Brookfield Zoo and National Geographic came through. We had the big funding not only to establish a park but also to honor our agreements with the peripheral zone village residents. We secured a law requiring that half the tourist entrance fee to the park would be set aside to sustain village projects. Surely someday tourists would pay to see the lemurs. In May 1991, the Ranomafana National Park (RNP) was inaugurated—43,500 ha of beautiful rain forest.

Management of the park transitioned from Duke to Stony Brook University (SBU) when I moved there in 1991. In 1998, while retaining management of research in RNP, SBU handed park management over to the Madagascar national park system. Until 1989, researchers lived in tents; the first research structure, a small one-story log cabin, had been built in 1989 near the river inside the forest. With all the research activity, we needed to expand our facilities.

In 1993 I married Jukka Jernvall, a Finnish evolutionary biologist. Discussing the constraints of available facilities, Jukka and Jari Neimela, dean of biology at University of Helsinki, suggested I approach the president of the University of Helsinki with the architectural plans for expansion. The president loved the idea of a research station in Madagascar and contributed a hefty sum. In 2003, thanks to funding from the University of Helsinki, the US National Science Foundation, and UNESCO World Heritage, the station was upgraded to a three-story cement and brick facility adjacent to the park and overlooking the rain forest.

The new research station, named the International Centre for Research and Training for the Valorization of Biodiversity (Centre ValBio, or CVB), is located on Route 25 approximately 50 meters from the park entrance. This hub of scientific research and education is managed by SBU. Founding institutions include SBU and the Universities of Antananarivo (at the capital city), Fianarantsoa (a city an hour from the RNP), and the University of Helsinki. The first building was completed in 2003 and houses administrative offices, a small drone laboratory, and a dining hall that serves more than a hundred people. But even with the completion of our first building, our researchers were still sleeping in tents.

While discussing our needs with my building-contractor brother, Ted Chapple, he suggested an architect, originally from Cyprus, named Ali Yapicioglu. Ali and his firm, INsite Architecture, created plans for a four-story-tall sustainable building, with a balcony overlooking the river, a green roof, and a central atrium, looking out to the rain forest. Funding to make that dream a reality happened when Ali introduced us to his other clients, Jim and Robin Herrnstein. Jim and Robin were astrophysicists trained at Harvard; now Jim worked for Renaissance Technologies. After Jim and Robin saw the energy, motivation, and accomplishments in Madagascar, they generously provided the funds and have remained our enthusiastic supporters. NamanaBe Hall, a four-story building (15,676 sq ft), opened in 2012 and is equipped with high-speed internet; a modern hormone, parasite, and genetics laboratory; an infectious disease laboratory; an audio/visual/computer center; and living accommodations for 48 students and researchers. The third building is the SOS/IUCN Multipurpose Education and Communication Pavilion. In 2020 the SOS (Saving Our Species) IUCN Biodiversity Research Center will house the CVB herbarium, CVB insect collections, research office space, and a conference room.

Everything we have accomplished at CVB, we have managed by working closely with every level of government. The CVB has authorization to do research from the Madagascar Ministry of Environment, Ecology and Forests; as well as the regional governments of the central highlands Haute Matsiatra region, the southeast Indian Ocean coast, Vatovavy-Fitovinany region, and the village communes in the peripheral zone of Ranomafana National Park. CVB works closely with the Madagascar National

Park Service, especially on conservation management. In 1991, I partnered with Benjamin Andriamihaja who especially helped with governmental liaisons and permits, and is Country Director for our operations today. His wisdom and diplomatic skills have contributed significantly to our success through many Madagascar government administrations.

From the very beginning we have believed in an integrated program of village assistance and biodiversity science. One hundred thirty-two full-time local staff with health care and retirement benefits have been trained as lemur technicians, Malagasy biodiversity experts, health workers, or teachers. The staff work at CVB and live in the villages surrounding the park. The CVB health and education teams provide training and outreach programs to 50 nearby villages and our CVB primary education team is active in 30 villages, providing school lunches from school gardens and innovative programs such as developing Lemur Radio shows, participatory learning, and question-driven science. CVB Conservation Clubs include those youth who drop out of school early. Reforestation with native species and medicinal plant gardens managed by traditional healers are two important components of CVB's outreach efforts, and a cooperative of artisanal women weavers is a sustainable contributor to village economics.

CVB is primarily a research center, and the work of more than 60 PhD dissertations and 226 master's theses has been completed there since the park's initiation. The major foci of these long-term studies are lemurs, including behavioral ecology, demography, life history, reproductive biology, stress and reproductive hormones, parasites, feeding and nutritional ecology, morphometrics, predation, communication, genetics, and cognition. Ongoing research includes studies on ecosystem dynamics and conservation, with emphasis on lemur seed dispersal, climate, and lemur and tree phenology.

Beginning in 1987, we began individual health records of lemurs, capturing individual lemurs to obtain morphometric and health data for all seven diurnal lemur species. These baseline data are important for tracking changes not only in individuals but also in populations.

In addition, we track lemur fruits through time. Since 1987 we have been monitoring fruiting and flowering of more than 100 endemic tree species, as well as collecting daily rainfall and temperature data. Camera-trap data are taken in distant regions of the park to monitor carnivores and terrestrial vertebrates. The Tropical Ecological Assessment and Monitoring team also monitors botanical plots and surveys birds and primates throughout the park. Cameras in drones assist in surveying the forest at a landscape scale. The Participatory Ecological Monitoring team trains village residents to participate in wildlife surveys. In all of Madagascar, only CVB has these kinds of integrated long-term data, which are deeply useful for understanding climate change.

Because of the continuous deforestation outside the park for slash-and-burn agriculture, and the selective logging of part of the forest before it was declared a protected area, we began to study the wildlife's response to human disturbance. We compared life histories of lemurs at sites within the park that display high levels of disturbance with those that have experienced low levels of disturbance. The strictest frugivore, *Varecia variegata*, black-and-white ruffed lemurs, did not occur in the high-disturbance-level site where the big canopied fruit trees were removed. The first decades after selective logging, the impacts of habitat disturbance affected the rarest and most undisturbed forest species. However, 35 years after the selective logging, the forest is regenerating, trees are taller again, and rare species such as the Short-legged Ground Roller bird and the black-and-white ruffed lemur have not only been sighted but are also breeding in the regenerated selectively logged forest. Although forest recovery has been slow, the good news is that the rain forest can regenerate.

Ranomafana National Park was designated a conservation priority, and in 2007 was declared a UNESCO World Heritage Site. RNP is a good example of successful conservation, and hunting and deforestation have been stopped there since 1990. We have successfully integrated education, health, and economic assistant programs with biodiversity research and habitat protection goals. An evaluation of the educational impact has shown that local people have experienced a change in attitude. Villages that are the farthest from the road tend to encroach farther into the park than do the on-road villages. Moreover, the park itself has maintained edges with minimum invasion by exotic plants. Ecotourism has added more than the equivalent of $3 million a year to the local economy through environmental jobs (rangers, research technicians) and hotel/restaurant industry work. The 35,000 tourists that visit each year, however, do have some negative consequences for the habitat. Better management of tourism is in process. Satellite photos suggest that there has been minimum forest destruction since 1991, when the park was established.

Conservation is possible only with strong partnerships and allies. The research success at RNP has attracted other nongovernmental organizations (NGOs) to work in this region, such as PIVOT, an NGO that upgrades health infrastructure. Catholic Relief Services has offered expertise in sustainable development and malnutrition. USAID and the US embassy have been close allies from the very beginning. Joining with researchers from across the globe we are beginning to understand the value of this rain forest and its wildlife. Particularly engaged institutions include: Stanford University (California), especially Dr. Mark Krasnow; Rice University (Texas), especially Dr. Amy Dunham; Sussex University (UK), especially Daniella Rabino and Malread Dunne; University of Calgary (Canada), especially Steig Johnson;

University of Helsinki (Finland), especially Jukka Jernvall; Hunter College (New York), especially Andrea Baden; University of Florida (Gainesville), especially Brett Scheffers; University of Utrecht (Netherlands), especially Iris de Winter; Emory University (Georgia), especially Tom Gillespie; and the Smithsonian Institution (Washington, DC), especially Tom Snyder. Zoos such as the Seneca Park Zoo, Woodland Park Zoo, Indianapolis Zoo, and Oakland Park Zoo have contributed educators, ideas, grants, and equipment. Earthwatch Institute assisted in data collection and, twenty years ago, introduced me to a great friend of Ranomafana, Susan Cummings Findel. In addition, the hundreds of study abroad undergraduates and nearly 100 graduate students, with their energy and caring for both wildlife and people, have been an important component of the conservation success. With this research information, and global and widespread communication, we can better increase the funding base and manage the conservation.

But conservation is a process, and constant vigilance against the destruction of nature is necessary. After a period of political instability in 2009, artisanal gold mining began to be observed inside the park. The police arrested gold miners each year, but they came back. By 2018 the goldmining had increased, and the goldminers—outsiders from a different region—began to hide in the forests and attack and steal money from villages closest to the RNP. During a bandit attack in July 2018, one of our CVB research technicians from Ambatolahy village was murdered, shot in the back, by a robber. Soon afterward the commandant of the brigade was shot and killed when he was defending the village of Bevohazo. A collaboration among conservation NGOs, the CVB research station, the Madagascar National Parks, the gendarmes, the army, and the local residents launched a major attack against the bandits and, for the moment, the banditry and goldmining within the park has stopped.

• •

What have we learned? Having long-term data enables better understanding of the effects of climate change and human disturbance on rain forest ecology and lemur populations. Indeed, lemur observers with long-term research projects were among the first to gain evidence of the effect of climate fluctuations on mammal populations. Using Madagascar climate data and the CVB long-term rainfall and temperature database, we discovered that dry seasons have become longer, and cyclones more frequent.

Most of the lemur species in Ranomafana had never been studied before, and there was no scientific information available about them before we initiated our first studies in 1986. The virtue and vice of long-term research is that it is never complete. Thus, over the years, we established the number of species residing in Ranomafana National Park through the rediscovery of *P. simus* (the greater bamboo lemur), and the discovery of *Hapalemur aureus* (the golden bamboo lemur), *Cheirogaleus grovesii* (Groves' dwarf lemur), and *Cheirogaleus sibreei* (Sibree's dwarf lemur). We have established demographic changes through time including life history events, mortality, lifespan, and dispersal patterns for *Propithecus edwardsi* (the Milne-Edwards's sifaka), *Eulemur rufifrons* (the red-fronted brown lemur), *E. rubriventer* (the red-bellied lemur), *V. variegata* (the black-and-white ruffed lemur), *H. aureus* (the golden bamboo lemur), *H. griseus* (the gray gentle bamboo lemur), *P. simus* (the greater bamboo lemur), and, to a lesser extent, *Microcebus rufus* (the brown mouse lemur). We have documented variability of social organization in each species, and we have described how populations recover after cyclones and droughts.

We have confirmed that lemur population densities vary over time, and predation by raptors and mammalian carnivores can have a major impact on local lemur populations. But we have also learned that populations in a big enough protected area bounce back. We know that many lemur species are important to seed dispersal and thus to forest dynamics. Monitoring and measuring the long-term effects of habitat disturbance on lemur populations, we have evidence that selective logging may negatively impact population densities of *E. rufifrons, V. variegata,* and *P. edwardsi,* even a decade after the last logging disturbance. We have determined that fertility of *P. edwardsi* females decreased during El Niño phases, and infants of older *P. edwardsi* females died in years with extended dry months.

But are these facts alone reflecting the true value of this long-term integrated conservation project? The trust we have built up with both the communities and the lemur groups is an added value that enables us to obtain nearly 100% compliance for any research or development project we do. With communities, we work together as true partners, collaborating with our different sets of expertise to improve livelihoods, while protecting nature.

We build trust by investing in Malagasy people and improving their skill sets. In the 1990s we hired and trained local residents with only three years' primary education, which has now resulted in a generational change. The next generation is going to high school and university, and a few have even obtained doctorates. These people are coming back to work with us as adults. They are now leaders of conservation agencies, working high in the ministries or in other ways to improve the environment or communities. My Stony Brook graduate students are returning as professors and bringing their graduate students to do research in Madagascar. Our fame as a center for learning, where Malagasies gather and generate new ideas, is growing. Whether it is a workshop on new sources of energy, new farming techniques, or new ways to use drones, innovation and transformation is happening at the research center. CVB continues to grow as an institution and as a conservation force.

Despite these victories, when you look at a map and see that 90% of the rain forest and natural habitats of Madagascar have been destroyed and continue to be ravaged by fires, it is discouraging. Instead of giving up, we have decided to go on the offensive.

As everyone knows, the best vanilla comes from Madagascar. What most people don't know is that Madagascar also produces the finest peppercorns in the world, especially the newly discovered "wild pepper from the Ranomafana rain forest," with the highest oil values ever tested. And these spices need trees to survive: vanilla is an orchid that grows on trunks and needs shade, and wild pepper is a vine that uses rain forest trees as structure on which to grow. Vanilla is worth more than silver now, and pepper is approaching that value. But traditionally the spice business is run by one or two companies based in northern Madagascar.

Beginning in the 1990s, when a research project demonstrated that forest tree seeds that had passed through the guts of lemurs grew faster, with less seed mortality, than the seeds from the same tree that hadn't been eaten by lemurs, we knew lemurs were important seed dispersers in Madagascar. When the project forester, Dan Turk, planted those saplings grown from "lemur-treated" seeds into land previously slashed and burned. I feared the shade-loving trees would perish once exposed to bright sun. But they didn't. They grew quickly, and within 15 years these deep rain forest tree species were fruiting and flowering. That development was revolutionary. The information that Malagasy rain forest trees can grow relatively quickly when released from the shade of other trees meant we could use them as structure for the vanilla orchids and wild pepper vines.

Partnering with Catholic Relief Services and Seneca Park Zoo, we have planned a major offensive to take back the damaged land with an eco-agriculture project that extends from the Ranomafana National Park east to the Indian Ocean. The business plan involves building warehouses and developing marketing strategies and security defenses, in addition to working with thousands of village associations to do agro-farming, with the rural village associations making a good deal of the profits. We will be restoring a new kind of Malagasy rain forest: a rain forest that features high-value crops within it. The high value of these crops could potentially produce prosperous humans, and therefore this system could stop the culture of burning. Success depends on simultaneously ensuring that the local residents have a love of nature and a desire to preserve their wilderness. We have already succeeded in a pilot study and hope that the project will be expanded soon.

Part of our conservation challenge is to bring media attention to Madagascar. Most of the world does not know the value of Madagascar and its wildlife and products. We increase Madagascar's profile by obtaining widespread media coverage, such as the IMAX film, *Island of Lemurs: Madagascar,* narrated by Morgan Freeman; coverage by ABC news, the BBC, and CNN; Anthony Bourdain's *Parts Unknown*; and by me winning the Indianapolis Prize for Animal Conservation. Media can never be underestimated when conservation action is needed. CVB is doing well, but it's no time to sit on our laurels. There is so much more to do and to discover.

Discoveries are often serendipitous. The biggest joys of working in Madagascar have been the surprises. After all the exploration we had accomplished throughout the years, I never would have dreamed that a "lost rain forest" had yet to be revealed in Madagascar, bursting with secrets of the past. But in 2016 I received a phone call from Leona, a Malagasy woman telling me about a giant cave to which she hoped to guide tourists. The caller was from Ihosy, not a place known for its tourist attractions. In fact, the region of Horombe had been so devastated by fire, barren except for invasive grassland, that there was not one environmental or tourist project in the whole region, which is a little bigger than the US state of Maryland. So with seemingly good reason, I ignored the phone call from the woman who wanted to be a tour operator.

But as luck would have it, I had invited a young photographer and biologist named Peter Houlihan to Ranomafana National Park to photograph our star orchid, the orchid that Darwin had predicted the existence of when he observed the 10-inch-long tongue of the hawk moth that pollinates it. Peter had found more than a hundred of these plants in the far south of the park. He was returning from an expedition there with Ian Segebarth, a lepidopterist. The two of them had hoped to film the pollination event. However, it had rained every day, and not one of the hundred flowers had bloomed. They had waited in the canopy through 16 days of rain, and no flowers, no pollination. They were not happy, and I hate to see tropical biologists defeated.

"You can climb up in the canopy, but can you climb down into caves?" I asked. And when they both said they loved spelunking, I suggested we go investigate the giant cave with 7 chambers south of Ihosy. They eagerly said yes, and the next day we met Leona at the Jovena gas station on the road going west to Tulear. Leona said that to reach the cave we must take the road south for about 2 hours. We jumped back into the car and after 5 hours along a very bumpy, slippery road we arrived at the tiny village of Baratratra. Nearly 100 people, mostly children, greeted us. We met the elders and asked them if we could see their cave, and they said they would ask the ancestors. After marching up a steep, grassy hill for an hour, we reached the tiny cave entrance, covered by a bush. At the entrance we proceeded with the ritual calling of the ancestors and sharing the *tokagasy* (local rum, which we had been smart enough to bring with us). The ancestors acquiesced, and Peter, Leona, and Ian descended into the cave with ropes and big lamps. We organized our camp near the cave. They returned after an hour and exclaimed that the cave was immense and beautiful, and after dinner they would explore it thoroughly. It was an ice-cold mountain night, and after dinner I nestled into my sleeping bag in my tent while they explored the cave.

In the morning they emerged with the news. First of all, it was hot inside the cave, a consequence of some kind of thermal condition. However, there were no longer 7 chambers, as a cave collapse had blocked the entrance to all but the first chamber. There were bats, but none had been caught. The photos Peter showed us were eerie and mysterious, with stalagmites and stalactites and giant red boulders. I sighed when I heard the 6 chambers were blocked and then inquired about a forest that Leona had suggested was nearby. I couldn't believe there was any kind of greenery in this wasteland that looked like the surface of Mars.

We took off in two groups. The elders, me, Pascal, and our CVB lemur team moved up the mountain to the west, while Leona, Peter, and Ian charged up the mountain in a more southerly direction. After about twenty minutes we heard lemurs. The sound was unmistakable, and our CVB sifaka techs were off in a flash. Ahead was a rain forest, and when we arrived we were stunned. We couldn't catch the fleeing lemurs, but we saw species of trees that we knew from Ranomafana National Park. In the middle of this barren, mountainous region were rain forest trees and lemurs. The local elders knew about the forest, but explained that they rarely entered it. The elders were clearly bewildered and pleased that we were so excited about this forest. Then we called Peter (cell phones work in even the most remote places in Madagascar). Peter, Leona, and Ian were standing on the top of the mountain ridge, gazing down on miles and miles of nearly pristine rain forest. We had discovered a Shangri-la in the middle of the Horombe Plateau! It was located in an area that bridged between the rain forest of the east and the dry deciduous forest of the west. The plant and animal species of these two halves of Madagascar are quite discrete, including the lemurs. The center of Madagascar has been burned and destroyed for millennia, and theories of what existed here before the first humans arrived are controversial. Would this forest answer some of the questions about the region's past?

Back at CVB I contacted Peter Raven, chair of the National Geographic Committee for Research and Exploration, and three months later we were back at the site with an NGS grant and a team of biodiversity experts. As we approached the forest, it looked like there was snow ahead. But of course it doesn't snow in Madagascar. Across the mountain it looked as though there were rivers of milk tumbling down the mountain. Upon closer examination, the ground was covered with sparkling white quartzite, the tiny diamond-like crystals glittering on the stream bottoms. It was a beautiful wonderland of green shades and sparkles.

We pitched our tents and started to investigate the flora and fauna. The first animals we saw were ring-tailed lemurs eating fruits at the edge of the forest. Ring-tailed lemurs are not found in rain forest anywhere—they are a dry-forest species—and I couldn't believe my eyes. But ring-tails they were, and we found they were acting quite differently from those that lived in the spiny desert of Madagascar, one of the driest places on Earth. The lemurs shouted a warning and then disappeared into the canopy. Our cook, digging the garbage pit, came running up with a "snake" that looked to me like a giant earthworm. It was a *Typhlops* sand snake, known only from the far southern beaches of Madagascar, in the sand dunes. And here it was in the center of Madagascar. What was going on in this rain forest?

Our next surprise was finding two species of giant chameleons together—the bright green Parson's chameleon, the largest chameleon in the eastern rain forest, and the gray bark-colored Oustalet's chameleon, the largest from the western dry forest. And then we observed a blue-nosed chameleon, which could have been related to a northern species. Although the birds were all rain forest birds, the "unexpected" rain forest seemed to be a jigsaw puzzle made up of animals from all regions of Madagascar. We couldn't find any day-active lemurs except the dry-forest ring-tails. Maybe the rain forest species had been shot out long ago. But then night came, and again there was a big surprise. Zaka, our CVB technician, set out 40 live traps and we captured dwarf lemurs, but the CVB techs said there were two species that looked like they could be entirely new discoveries! One had a white tip on its tail. Later genetic analysis determined that there were indeed two species of dwarf lemurs. The mouse lemurs that we captured had a reddish coat and green eyes. One of the dwarf lemur taxa and one of the mouse lemur species were closely related to a far southern mouse lemur species. The paper describing these new species is in process. Is this a relict forest, where an ancient community of animals survive together, or a refuge forest, where species have fled from both east (wet forest) and west (dry forest) to escape the fires? Our studies should shed some light on these questions.

The more we explored the forest, the more surprises we found. The Missouri Botanical Garden botanists found a new species of ebony tree. The lichen specialists are still describing new species of mosses and lichens. We found 11 species of tardigrade (water bears), the toughest animals on Earth and in space, and nine are new to science. The mammologists found a new species of bat. This "unexpected rain forest" was a treasure trove of wildlife.

How did this forest remain in this pristine state without being burned like the remainder of the landscape? The forest was protected from the fires by being sunken into a sharp valley protected by a steep cliff, and the roaring fires in October only lap at the canopy. This protective cliff gave us observation advantages. As we walked around the periphery of the forest, we saw lemurs at eye level as they foraged on figs. When we walked the trails at night, a giant tenrec nearly ran into me. Tenrecs are a group of insectivores only found in Madagascar. They can look like hedgehogs or shrews or tiny porcupines, but this species of tenrec weighs more than 2 kilograms (5 pounds), resembles a small pig, and had been hunted to extinction in Ranomafana forest before it became a park. The Crested Ibis, the largest rain forest bird, another hunting target, also was seen. The lack of trails and the abundance of tall, wide trees were other unmistakable indications that the area was quite undisturbed by humans.

When we talked to the elders, they explained that they were afraid of the forest. They were Bara, the Malagasy ethnic group that valued cattle. There was only one trail through the forest, used for herding cattle on the way to a distant market. The Bara are also known for cattle rustling, and a young man cannot be married without stealing cattle for his prospective bride, showing he is clever and tough enough to be worthy of her. This is Madagascar's wild west, and lawlessness is common. Would we be able to work with these people to establish a protected area?

Upon my return to RNP, James Lewis, the International Union for Conservation of Nature (IUCN) coordinator, called me to discuss an invasive species of very toxic toad recently arrived into the port of Tamatave that was wreaking havoc on the Malagasy wildlife. We discussed the next steps, and then James revealed that he was leaving IUCN to take a new job with Rainforest Trust. I had not heard of Rainforest Trust, as this NGO had never worked in Madagascar. "Not yet," declared James. Rainforest Trust was looking for new forested areas to protect, forests that were of special importance but had not yet been declared protected areas. I told James about our unexpected rain forest, and he suggested to Rainforest Trust that it begin operations in Madagascar. James helped shepherd a conservation plan to make Ivoriboro Forest an official community-managed protected area with funds from Rainforest Trust. Once again, networking assisted in making conservation happen. On January 29, 2020 the official documentation to make the Lost Rainforest a protected area was signed by the Ministry of the Interior, Ministry of Mines, Ministry of Environment and Sustainable Development, and the Ministry of Culture. The name of the protected area in Ihorombe is Ivohiboro and it is managed by MICET/ICTE/SBU.

I have learned a lot from spearheading the establishment of Ranomafana National Park. I have learned that only by working with local communities, regional governments, national governments, and outside funding bodies is it possible to create a successful protected area. I learned that you need a loyal, hardworking team you can trust. For me that was Dede Randriarisata, Pascal Rabeson, Jean Claude Razafimaihaimodison and Benjamin Andriamihaja.

Over these 35 years, what have we learned about conservation of rain forests? After 4 decades of international development and conservation in developing countries, large conservation organizations and bilateral international aid have resulted in nothing but success, or so all the reports say. The general pattern is to fund a project from three to five years, declare it a success, and then move on geographically to the next project and challenge. Nobody seems to notice that what remained onsite was frustration and the crushed dreams of the abandoned local people. Without providing any preparation for sustaining a project, the endeavor dies quickly when the project (and funding) ends, and the situation returns back to what it was before, or worse, because of the bitterness left behind. As a rule, we hate to admit failures; we don't want to disappoint our donors. But I have learned as much from our RNP and CVB failures as I have from our successes. The truth is, if we examine and dissect those things that didn't work, we can move on to do better. "Failure is the fertilizer to success," I once said in a film called *Me and Isaac Newton*. Conservation is long term. It takes one decade, two decades, or a generation or even two to change things, so why not try to sustain these projects?

Capacity-building and training are crucial for sustaining real economic development. Skill training and inspiring young people to take on the challenges will make a difference. When they feel invested in a project that could improve their children's future, people are motivated to work hard. We have the funds to make their dreams come true, but we need to convince them of the importance of the effort with more than words and lectures. Working side-by-side with students learning participatory science and development can jumpstart a deep understanding of the issues and the challenges. Another key to changing people's lifestyles is to appeal to their hearts and their emotions with music, dance, and the arts. Celebrations bring people together, and we all feel a part of a family, a team. Songs in the local languages, talent contests that are open to everyone, may also help.

Conservation is complicated. It can't be about just protecting nature without considering the humans that live near wild places. It can't happen quickly. Putting Band-Aids on deforestation wounds isn't enough. Tweeting about the insults of plastic isn't enough. Being a vegetarian isn't enough. We have nearly eight million people on our planet—needy people, and also greedy people. Humans are taking more than our share, pushing all other species to extinction, making climate change an issue that affects all species and even the future of our planet.

Can we wake up in time? Can we heal the devastation, and adopt a new approach to saving natural resources? Humans are smart, and nature is resilient. Our Earth will never be the same as before the industrial revolution and incredible assault of the last three decades, but we can save enough of the species and habitats so that our grandchildren and great-grandchildren can survive in a world with nature and wild places. If we prioritize stabilizing the human population; if we proceed slowly and thoroughly, deep in time; if we work in an integrated fashion, broad in scope; if we keep conservation science at the core, and empower communities and citizens to assist in saving species and wild places everywhere in the world, we will be able to save a kind of nature, transformed, but still diverse.

I love the tropics, the wildness of it, the animals in it, the way everything is linked together in a giant ecosystem, the diversity of plants and animals. I also love people and their brains, laughter, creativity, and empathy. I am optimistic that with technology, common sense, and a strong political will and purpose, people and

Dr. Patricia Wright's efforts create collaboration among scientists, local communities, and the government to save lemurs, like this Milne-Edward's sifaka (*Propithecus edwardsi*), and sustain their unique ecosystem on the island of Madagascar.

nature can survive together. I am encouraged and hopeful, but it will require a tremendous changing of gears throughout the whole world. It will require a huge shift in the media and its approach to sharing news, and a reversal of the culture of greed. The Indianapolis Prize is an example of how change can happen, and I thank Mike Crowther and his team for initiating a movement toward conserving our natural world and the diversity of animals within it. We need more bold champions to lead our planet to a harmonious future.

Further Reading

Wright, P. C. 1999. Lemur Traits and Madagascar Ecology: Coping with an Island Environment. Yearbook of Physical Anthropology 42:31–72.

Wright, P. C., E. L. Simons, and S. Gursky, eds. 2003. Tarsiers: Past, Present, and Future. Rutgers University Press.

Wright P. C., F. Larrey, C. Girard. 2010. Madagascar: The Forest of Our Ancestors. Regard du Vivant.

Wright, P. C., et al. 2012. Long-Term Lemur Research at Centre Valbio, Ranomafana National Park, Madagascar. Pages 67–100 in P. M. Kappeler and D. P. Watts, eds., Long-Term Field Studies of Primates. Springer.

Wright, P. C. 2013. High Moon over the Amazon: My Quest to Understand the Monkeys of the Night. Lantern Books.

Wright, P. C. 2014. For the Love of Lemurs: My Life in the Wilds of Madagascar. Lantern Books.

CHALLENGING BOUNDARIES

The Legacy of Dian Fossey

SIGOURNEY WEAVER

2016 Recipient of the Jane Alexander Global Wildlife Ambassador Award

Mountain Gorilla
Gorilla beringei beringei

Dr. Dian Fossey was a legendary hero of conservation who never really received the honor or respect she deserved during her lifetime. Sadly, that also meant that she never achieved the influence that is necessary for today's conservationists. You see, conservation scientists need to do more than conduct science; they also need to change hearts, minds, and behaviors. Therefore, Dian's story is both an inspiration and a cautionary tale.

Dian Fossey was certainly a genius and a pioneer. As a woman who understood that protecting gorillas meant understanding their psychology and sociology even more deeply than their physiology, Dian unashamedly brought something to science that is too often overlooked: *love*. I think that we need to ensure that love never disappears from the conservation equation again, because without it we simply won't care enough to take the radical action we need to save our shared future.

Dian's personal challenge was that the wonder, majesty, and sentience of her beloved mountain gorillas was so obvious to her that she could neither comprehend nor accept that others could feel differently. She was more attuned to the way gorillas thought and acted than of how humans behaved, and it ultimately cost her life.

The day after Christmas in 1985, Dian Fossey was murdered, her body discovered the next day in her cabin in the Virunga Mountains of Rwanda, in east-central Africa. She had been killed with a machete.

Playing Dian Fossey in the movie *Gorillas in the Mist*—and spending two months with her Study Group 5—transformed how I see everything. I'll tell you how it all began . . .

I didn't have the opportunity to meet Dian, but I'd read her book and I was intrigued when I was asked to portray her on screen a couple months after her death. I'd never played a real person before, and I knew that Dian was a complex personality, so I began to research everything about her in earnest.

It was challenging. Every time I interviewed people who knew Dian and had worked with her, I got a lot of contradictory information. It seemed that Dian could be gentle and fierce, coldly scientific and warmly human, melancholy and exuberant, depending on circumstances and who she was dealing with. When I read that the great Farley Mowat, another one of my conservation heroes, had written a biography of Dian, I called him for help. He very kindly invited me to come up and read his manuscript at his home in Nova Scotia but it was one simple piece of paper that told me the most pivotal thing I needed to know in order to see the world through Dian's eyes.

The sheet of paper was a letter from Dian to a friend named Cindy. The letter began by talking about how extraordinary Cindy's parents were, and as I read on, it became clear that it was written to Cindy after her death. But it wasn't until the end of the letter that I realized that Cindy was Dian's dog. For Dian, an absolutely basic tenet of her existence was that animals and humans had the same value in the world and deserved the same rights and consideration.

The rest of my education about Dr. Dian Fossey came from Ziz and Maggie and Effie and Cantsbe and all the other gorillas in the group I became immersed in. It was, at first, surreal to be sitting on the side of a green volcano in Rwanda, surrounded by these extraordinary beings, with three or four gorilla youngsters playing around me very much the same as human toddlers would. But then it became the most natural thing in the world, and I began to see how those walls we humans put up between us and other species could quietly and beautifully crumble.

The film became what Dian had hoped it would be. It became an ambassador for her beloved mountain gorillas. And I became one too.

I could never have realized that a film would lead to my working for 30 years with the Dian Fossey Gorilla Fund International and with the many incredible people who have carried on Dian's work saving gorillas. But playing Dian brought me into her world and the world of gorillas, and made it clear what a difference we can make.

In 1990, the Dian Fossey Gorilla Fund International asked me to serve as honorary chairperson, and I've been in that role ever since. It has given me a chance to be part of one of the most remarkable conservation success stories ever. Mountain gorillas are the only great ape subspecies in the world that is increasing in number. With only around 1,000 individuals in existence, their sustainability is still fragile, but the research, anti-poaching, and other techniques pioneered by Dian Fossey herself have been refined and expanded over the years, resulting in huge gains in knowledge and a critical population rebound for the gorillas.

In 2020, the Fossey Fund celebrates its fiftieth anniversary, and now our mission has expanded to include saving Grauer's gorillas in Congo, which are critically endangered after years of conflict in the region. We're also working with other components of gorilla ecosystems—ranging from golden monkeys to amphibians and plants—because it's clear that their elegant efficiency and aesthetics result from countless parts working together.

However, to me the most forward-reaching thing we did at the Fossey Fund was to focus on the local people at the base of the Virunga Mountains. Focusing on their health, their education, their economic well-being, and their culture has made all the difference. As brilliant as Dr. Dian Fossey was, this was an area that she left to those who came after her.

"Little did I know then that by setting up two small tents in the wilderness of the Virungas I had launched the beginnings of what was to become an internationally renowned research station eventually to be utilized by students and scientists from many countries," wrote Dian. She named her research center Karisoke, combining the names of nearby Mount Karisimbi and Mount Bisoke. The Dian Fossey Gorilla Fund International expanded Karisoke over the years, adding laboratories and libraries and employing more than 100 local people. Today, the Karisoke Research Center is led by a Rwandan scientist, Felix Ndagijimana. Hundreds of local college students study at Karisoke each year; and thousands of young children are reached through its conservation programs in primary and secondary schools. The next generation of conservationists is being created in the mountains where Dian walked. And soon the Ellen DeGeneres Campus will be built to house a new Karisoke Research Center with an Education Center, a Conservation Gallery, and housing for conservation students and professionals from all around the world.

Indeed, in Rwanda, the whole nation has embraced gorilla conservation, as demonstrated by the gorilla-naming ceremony, called Kwita Izina, that is now a major event held annually, with the country's president attending.

A local health clinic now has a first-ever maternity ward, built by the Fossey Fund and its donors. And at a nearby school, a library and computer center now serve a community of 20,000 people who have never had access to basic services.

The Fossey Fund has shown that when conservation includes community, everyone is lifted. When people thrive, gorillas and other wildlife will, as well.

The legendary Senegalese environmentalist Baba Dioum wrote, "In the end we will conserve only what we love; we will love only what we understand; and we will understand only what we are taught." We need teaching to evolve into understanding, and understanding to allow love to blossom. That's the best hope for our planet.

The Indianapolis Prize exists for the purpose of taking the understanding of the most accomplished conservationists in the world and teaching it to the rest of us. When we share that understanding, we can be transformed, just as I was by my time living in Dian Fossey's world.

Jane Alexander and her husband Ed Sherin have lived this process of transformation for many years. Ed was a brilliant stage, television, and film writer, director, and producer who knew how to craft a journey that would enthrall, nurture, challenge, and goad audiences to travel to imaginary destinations most could never have imagined. Jane is not only one of our most accomplished national treasures as an award-winning actor but is also a committed and knowledgeable conservationist who has served many important environmental organizations. Both have been a part of the Indianapolis Prize since its inception.

In 2012, the Indianapolis Prize created a new award and named it in Jane's honor. The Jane Alexander Global Wildlife Ambassador Award is presented to someone who has served as a trustworthy, consistent, and influential voice for wild things and wild places.

As Mike Crowther, founder of the Prize, said, "We can have all the scientists in the world working for all its species, but unless we can help people, organizations, and governments care about sustainability, all their efforts will go to waste." Jane Alexander has spent decades helping people learn to care, and she was the first person selected to receive the award named for her.

I was deeply honored and humbled to accept the second Jane Alexander Global Wildlife Ambassador Award. I feel fortunate to stand with many of the world's real conservation heroes—to be included in their discoveries and discussions, and to help tell their stories. It has been a privilege to add my voice and support to all of those who do so much.

Dian Fossey loved the gorillas. She passed that love on to many of us as well, along with the responsibility to do everything we can. The Dian Fossey Gorilla Fund has provided me with an opportunity to help, and I am grateful that I have the chance to serve our world and its inhabitants.

Sigourney Weaver has been an advocate for the mountain gorillas of Rwanda since her starring role in the 1988 film *Gorillas in the Mist,* and serves as honorary chair of the Dian Fossey Gorilla Fund International. Courtesy: Dian Fossey Gorilla Fund International

Our children and our fellow creatures deserve to live on a peaceful and verdant planet. If countries and politicians can focus attention on the great apes and their habitats, and on all the species that together create this glorious home we share, then there is hope that Dian Fossey's beloved mountain gorillas, and all of our precious wild friends, will be with us for generations to come.

CHAPTER 8

LESSONS FROM THE DODO

Saving the Endangered Wildlife of Mauritius

DR. CARL JONES

2016 Recipient of the Indianapolis Prize

Mauritius Kestrel
Falco punctatus

During those quiet moments when one's mind drifts, I often think of what it would be like to go back in time to see the world before we modified it so dramatically. I would like to travel to the sixteenth century, to the island of Mauritius, to see the Dodo and many of the other remarkable birds and other animals that lived there, but are now extinct. The Dodo was last seen in 1662 and has become the iconic lost species. I have visited museums all over the world to examine the mounted specimens and skeletons of these vanished animals. To hold a skin of an extinct Mauritius Blue Pigeon *Alectroenas nitidissima* or the bones of a Dodo is a powerful experience, touching the past and stirring deep emotions of wonder and despair, lamenting their loss. Being so close to these past lives has been a strong and potent motivator for me to nurture those species that still survive.

I was a keen, driven, and somewhat arrogant 24-year-old when I arrived on Mauritius in 1979. It was my dream job: I would be working with some of the world's most endangered species, including the Mauritius Kestrel *Falco punctatus*, then the world's rarest bird, as well as the rarest pigeon, parrot, fruit bat, and snake. I was told I would be there for one or two years, developing a conservation program, after which the international funders would pull out gracefully, handing the project over to the locals. My bosses told me time and again that there was not enough money in the international conservation pot to try to save these critically endangered species. I was soon to learn that Mauritius did not have the resources to carry on this conservation work either; it seemed to me that the conservation community was going to turn its back on the kestrel, and all the other species, consigning them to certain oblivion.

Mauritius is a beautiful tropical island, multicultural and verdant, surrounded by a lagoon of clear blues, turquoise and indigo. It is a popular tourist and honeymoon destination, yet behind this veneer lies a disrupted and impoverished native ecosystem, damaged by habitat destruction and introduced species. The native wildlife has been unable to cope with the onslaught wrought by people and their attendant cats, dogs, rats, mice, goats, and rabbits. What little indigenous forest remains has been invaded by plants from elsewhere, weeds that are swamping out the natives: guava from Brazil, privet from India, and traveller's tree from Madagascar. It is clear why there have been so many extinctions, and why the remaining wildlife is so imperiled.

I was thrilled to be working on the conservation of such interesting, rare species, on a friendly island, where I felt I could make a difference. I lived in a small wooden house, with a tin roof, next to a small captive breeding center in the village of Black River. Here we kept Mauritius Kestrels, Pink Pigeons *Nesoenas mayeri*,

Rodrigues fruit bats *Pteropus rodricensis,* and occasionally other species as well. In addition to running the breeding program, I conducted fieldwork on the wild populations and also visited some of the other nearby islands to survey the species there and formulate plans for their care. I was in my element—I could not have been happier—what more could a young conservation biologist want? However, at the back of my mind was always the nagging feeling that there was not a workable long-term plan that would secure the species that were beginning to become so important to me.

At the breeding center we had six Mauritius Kestrels: some had been harvested from the wild, and one had been bred there, the first breeding in captivity. The plan was to establish them in captivity and then use the young captive-bred birds to reintroduce the species into suitable areas of Mauritius. I loved the kestrels, small neat falcons with a spotted front. Their shape was different from the kestrels I was used to in Europe and America: they had more rounded wings, longish legs, and a typical kestrel long tail. At the time, only two pairs of kestrels were known in the wild in Mauritius and a few others were suspected. It was my job to study the kestrels and find out as much about them as I could.

The remaining kestrels lived in the Black River Gorges, an area of deep gorges, sheer cliffs, forested slopes, and clear, turbulent rivers and streams with dark, deep pools. This area became my playground; at any opportunity I would cycle up a stony track into the gorges for the day and hike around looking for kestrels. There the paths and tracks had been kept open by introduced deer and wild pigs. Or, I would wander along streambeds to get to some of the more remote areas. During these hikes I would always learn something new. Kestrels were initially elusive, and all I got were fleeting glimpses of birds racing across the sky or weaving among the canopy. I saw deer and found wild pigs living among large boulders, where they rested and farrowed under overhangs. On every trip, monkeys—the long-tailed macaques *Macaca fascicularis*—crossed my path. These monkeys had been introduced by sailors and had a reputation as being egg thieves. Some felt it was the monkeys that had caused the decline in the kestrels.

After a few trips into the gorges, I started to understand the kestrels and where I was likely to find them. In addition to the two pairs, I occasionally saw others; these were probably nonbreeding birds. The kestrels liked the good areas of forest and the cliffs, where they nested. I soon learned why their bodies were the shape they were: the kestrels were adapted to life in the forests and could maneuver in and out of the trees with great agility. I watched them flying into the tree canopy, turning on a dime, weaving in and out among the branches. At first, I was not sure what they were doing, but soon discovered they were hunting the bright green day geckos *Phelsuma* spp., chasing them among the branches and grabbing them. I was to discover that the kestrel was a specialist gecko catcher—these were its main food.

Slowly I was beginning to get to know the kestrels. I had also settled into life in Mauritius; I loved the country and its people and felt very much at home there, even though it was so different from the life I was used to in Wales. It was much simpler and more focused. I developed my routines, working with my Mauritian colleagues, feeding the captive birds in the morning, making regular field trips, and feeding the bats in the evening. At night, before going to bed, I spent an hour or two writing up my notes, reading anything I could get on the natural history of Mauritius and about the animals I was looking after. I read Victorian texts and recent scientific papers. I was developing a broad impressionistic picture in my imagination about the Mauritius that once was, how it had changed, and how the changes were challenging the surviving wildlife. Embedded in my thoughts was the genesis of a vision of what could be, and how we were going to develop the project. I wanted to make the conservation of Mauritius' wildlife my life's work.

Running the captive breeding project took up a great deal of my time; there was always a lot to do. The Pink Pigeons were breeding well, although there were always issues to sort out: new pairings to be put together and old pairings to sort, since Pink Pigeons suffered high rates of divorce. Most of my effort was going into trying to breed the kestrels. The six kestrels we had were the pair and the young male they had produced, plus two other unpaired males and a female. I had to get a second pair together. The unpaired female was proving problematic—she did not like the males we had. I tried the female with all of the different males, leaving her with the most compatible. The breeding season was approaching, and I felt excited and apprehensive. This was my big chance to show I could breed the kestrels, and I hoped that it would be enough to encourage further funding for the project. The birds were showing signs of breeding: they started to court, call enthusiastically, and enter the nest boxes. However, they looked a bit under the weather, and the closer we got to the breeding season, the sicker they looked. I consulted vets; there was nothing we could identify as being wrong. Then one died, followed by a second, and a third, and then a fourth. I was devastated—the birds I had invested so much in were dying, and I was sad, helpless, and wracked with guilt. I felt that it was my fault.

I had been in Mauritius for nearly a year, and it would soon be Christmas. My friend Richard Lewis was staying to help, so at least we could enjoy a tropical Christmas that would take our minds off the kestrel problems. The run-up to Christmas was hectic; Mauritius virtually closes down over Christmas and the New Year, as everyone is in party mood and takes a long holiday. There was a buzz in the air, the weather was hot and humid, and, just before Christmas, the weather deteriorated. A cyclone was heading our way. On the night of December 22–23, the cyclone hit. Richard and I were safely sheltering in my hut, which had been through many tropical storms. It was reinforced with impressive hardwood diagonal braces, both along every wall and joining the roof joists. The cyclone came after dark, building up slowly. As the wind increased to 221 kph, it became a load roar, made worse by the pounding rain on the tin roof. My small house shuddered and shook, and rain oozed through the walls. Sleep was impossible, as flying objects crashed against the hut. Richard and I could communicate only by shouting, and the candles we had for light were continually snuffed out by drafts. The cyclone left at dawn and we crept out of the hut in the early morning gloom to a scene of devastation.

Many of the houses in Black River had been smashed, there were fallen trees across the roads, and broken branches and debris were strewn about. Every tree had been defoliated, so they looked like bare skeletons. We worried about all of our captive animals in the breeding center and checked on them with some trepidation. Fortunately, the captive animals, which had secure enclosures with cyclone shelters, all came through the storm with no problems. The two remaining Mauritius Kestrels looked fine. The wild birds, however, had been affected by the storm, and the exotic (nonnative) birds that nested in the bushes around my home had all gone. We found the carcasses of doves and other nonnative species hurled to the ground by the high winds. In the weeks afterward we saw no Waxbills *Estrilda astrild*, few Spice Finches *Lonchura punctulata*, and fewer Red-whiskered Bulbuls *Pycnonotus jocosus* and doves. The bird population of Black River had been decimated by the cyclone.

I became anxious to check on the last pairs of wild Mauritius Kestrels. One pair we had been watching were breeding and we wanted to get up to their nest, on a cliff deep in the Black River Gorges, to see if they had survived. They could be extinct, wiped out by the cyclone. The river was flooding and the road had been washed away. We could not get up the gorge for several days. As soon as the floodwaters had died away, Yousoof Mungroo, my right-hand man, friend, and Mauritian counterpart, and our other

Mauritian colleagues were left in charge of the captive animals, and Richard and I hiked into the Black River Gorges, where we camped for three days. I had come to know the gorges intimately. All along the valley bottom, large trees had been knocked down, and the Black River had changed its course in several places. When we got to the heart of the gorges, to where the kestrels lived, we hiked up along the streambed to their nesting site. The stream that I had come to know so well—with gin-clear pools where crayfish lived and fern-covered boulders on the banks—was gone. The comfortably familiar landmarks no longer existed. Large boulders had been thrown down the stream.

Within the Black River Gorges, all the exotic trees were badly damaged, but the native trees were largely intact. We climbed up to the base of the waterfall, where the stream tumbled over the cliff where the kestrels nested. Halfway up the cliff was a wide vegetated ledge that we could reach by some careful climbing and scrambling over and around huge boulders and fallen trees. The ledge was the nearest we could get to the nest and, after an hour of climbing, we were there—hot, sweaty, and exhausted. Within minutes we found the two young Mauritius Kestrels, on a beautiful black ebony tree, which had come through the cyclone intact. It seemed like a scene from pristine Mauritius, the young birds in their fresh plumage contrasting with the black branches and dark green leaves of the ebony. Here we watched the parents returning every hour or so with geckos to feed the young that were perched just feet away. They had survived.

The exotic birds may have been decimated by the cyclone, but I subsequently learned that the native Mauritian birds knew how to cope with these storms. The kestrels had sheltered deep in their nest crevices in the cliffs to survive. In the following weeks the island slowly returned to normal. The damaged trees burst into leaf and the few remaining wild birds living in my garden, the Spice Finches and doves, started breeding.

The feeling of rebirth was short-lived: the last two captive kestrels lost condition and expired. I had now been in Mauritius for a year, and the captive Mauritius Kestrels that I had so wanted to breed had all died. My dream job had become a nightmare. The loss of the kestrels hit me hard; I did not at the time appreciate just how profoundly I had been affected. Richard, who had been so supportive during this difficult time, left to go home. I took stock and refocused my efforts. I worked closely with Yousoof and my other Mauritian colleagues, doing fieldwork and breeding captive Pink Pigeons and Rodrigues fruit bats. At least this work was going well.

The death of the kestrels weighed heavily. Why had they died? Could I have done anything to save them? The initial postmortems were largely inconclusive. I had a sneaking suspicion the birds had died of some form of poisoning, since before dying some had showed neurological problems. It took several years for us to get to the bottom of why they perished; detailed tests suggested that the kestrels had been carrying high levels of pesticides, although how they had become contaminated was initially unclear. Later I was to discover that the building in which we had been breeding the mice to feed the kestrels had, in its previous role as a forestry office, been regularly sprayed with DDT to control malaria-carrying mosquitoes.

The fieldwork slowed down as the southern winter approached. I had been on Mauritius for a year and a half and needed a break; I was physically and emotionally drained. I traveled home to Wales to spend some time with my parents. It was a Welsh summer, and I was able to slowly reenergize in my old home and think about the future. My bosses were uncertain how long they could keep supporting the project—there was just not enough money. I made it clear that I wanted to stay in Mauritius and continue the work. The project funders were far from encouraged: the kestrels seemed to be a write-off, and they were skeptical—in their eyes, the project was failing. I, however, was not defeated. Being in Wales, away from the day-to-day demands of Mauritius, gave me the space to think, plan, and study. I made sorties all over Britain to visit museums and libraries, looking at specimens, trying to piece together a picture of what Mauritius was like, and researching how we could look after the dwindling populations of plants and animals. I visited captive-breeding experts, vets, and scientists, trying to glean any information I could that would help me in my quest to turn the project around.

Gerald Durrell, a writer, naturalist, and zoo owner, had a long-term interest in Mauritius, and in his Jersey Zoo he had several Mauritian species. I had an invitation from Gerry to visit Jersey, in the British Channel Islands, to meet him and see the captive-breeding efforts. Gerry had been my hero since I was a boy; he had revolutionized zoos and had shown the world the importance of captive breeding as a means of conserving the most endangered animals. The Jersey Zoo was arguably the world's first conservation zoo. I traveled to Jersey and met Gerry, who was all I had hoped for: charming and intelligent, with a wicked, irreverent sense of humor. We got on well. Here was a kindred spirit—we both loved Mauritius, its people, and wildlife. I found him to be understanding; he could clearly see I was bruised by the loss of the kestrels. Gerry reassured me that losses were common early on in a breeding program, and he was encouraged by the progress I had made breeding Pink Pigeons and Rodrigues fruit bats. When I told him I wanted to stay on in Mauritius to continue the work, he was delighted and vowed to help support me. True to his word, his Durrell Wildlife Conservation Trust provided a grant to the project and later I was to work for them full time as their man in Mauritius.

I returned to Mauritius energized, with some guarantees of money to keep me and the project afloat and some ideas about how we were going to progress. I had formulated a plan to save the kestrel and I was developing a big vision. At first, I had some hazy ideas that I fed with new information as I learned more and more about the ecology of Mauritius. I imagined how we could rebuild lost ecosystems or perhaps, if that was not possible, build new ones. That, however, was way in the future.

My research had shown that the Mauritius Kestrel's decline was probably caused by the widespread use of DDT in the 1940s and 1950s. Even before this period, the kestrel was rare and it had shown a decline in the early twentieth century, although no one understood why. By the 1980s, DDT use had been abandoned, and suitable habitat was available for a reintroduction. The plan was to closely monitor the last breeding wild pairs and, when they had completed laying a clutch of eggs, to take the eggs to hatch and rear in captivity. Work with other falcons had shown that if this is done early in incubation, the birds will recycle and lay a second clutch that can then be left with the birds to rear. Potentially this technique could double the annual productivity. Those young reared in captivity would be retained for captive breeding. I also suggested that we should feed some of the wild kestrels, since this would encourage them to lay bigger clutches and rear extra young. If we were successful in breeding kestrels in captivity, we could release them, provide them with nest boxes, feed them, and double-clutch them also, to rapidly increase the population. I wanted to apply all the management techniques that had been used on birds of prey elsewhere to the Mauritius Kestrel, to boost productivity, enhance survival, and, hopefully, recover the population.

I discussed these ideas with Yousoof and other Mauritian colleagues, who were enthusiastic that we should try something. Together we developed these ideas into a discussion document that I circulated both to the main people involved and to falcon conservation biologists. We soon started to get responses to our proposals: a few were noncommittal, others skeptical, feeling the plan was too high risk. The falcon biologists all liked our ideas and urged us to push ahead and implement them. Professor Tom Cade, from the Peregrine Fund, was fulsome with his praise; he supported our ideas and wanted to sponsor the kestrel work. The Peregrine Fund could help with advice and a grant. It was Tom and the Peregrine Fund who had worked out how to breed falcons in captivity, release them back into the wild, and how to nurture the wild populations. I was thrilled that I had the support of the world's most prominent falcon biologist and geared up for the next breeding season, when we would take the eggs from the last pairs of Mauritius Kestrels.

Our work was being recognized and we were attracting help from prominent conservationists. To support this work and to provide some long-term security, we set up a local conservation organization, which eventually would grow into the Mauritian Wildlife Foundation. There was now some stability and we could move forward with our ambitious plans for the kestrels. We were prepared for the breeding season, finding two pairs of kestrels and harvesting the eggs. From these we were able to rear three healthy chicks. The season stretched me: I quickly realized that I was not as good at it as I thought, and needed help for both the fieldwork and the captive breeding. I approached the Peregrine Fund and together we came up with a solution: they would provide us with seasonal help. They sent over one of their most experienced captive-breeding technicians, Willard Heck, and we hired my friend Richard Lewis, who would do the fieldwork. Over the next decade, the three of us, working with Yousoof and our other Mauritian colleagues and volunteers, would become a dream team, restoring the kestrels.

Tom Cade visited us frequently and gave advice and encouragement. He had become a cherished mentor. He was a man of few words, although when he did have something to say it was always worth listening to. A formidable academic, Tom had forged a sparkling career working in several fields of biology, although falcons were his favored subjects. Like all good friends, he was always prepared to offer support and did not hold back when he felt that I was screwing up.

Richard did most of the fieldwork, monitoring the wild birds, finding the nests, and harvesting the eggs. Willard hatched and reared the young, and Yousoof helped look after the captive birds and had the critical role of getting permissions and steering us through the labyrinth of government bureaucracy. For the first few years we were building up the captive population and learning how we could best look after the kestrels, both in the wild and in captivity. Within two years we were breeding kestrels, and soon we had enough to start reintroductions. I carried out various studies and developed some of the management techniques that would help us increase the numbers in the wild.

One pair of kestrels was nesting in an accessible nest site near the mouth of the Black River Gorges, at a site called Montagne Zaco (Monkey Mountain). This became my study pair, and every day for a decade I cycled up the track to the gorges, to their territory, to learn as much as I could. I spent countless hours with them and got to know them well, their personalities and quirks. Slowly I entered their world and began to think like them. I trained them to fly to me and take food, and when I arrived at the site they would fly down and greet me, wanting to be fed. These kestrels became a major focus of my life. They were used to develop and test a range of management techniques—they were our guinea pigs. We took their eggs to encourage them to lay more, and used them as foster parents to rear birds hatched at the breeding center.

Like Tom, Willard was a man of few words and extraordinary abilities. He was amazing with the kestrels and blessed with common sense. Soon he became a major stabilizing influence on the project. I would come up with harebrained plans, or aim to do too much, and Willard would gently inject a dose of reality. He had considerable experience, and state-of-the-art falcon breeding skills, and applied them to our kestrels. If the females were laying infertile eggs, he would artificially inseminate them, incubate the eggs in an incubator, and the great majority would hatch. He hand-reared the chicks and rarely did he lose any; some years he reared them all. After a few years we became a production line for kestrels.

In the first few years we built up the captive population and fostered others to the Montagne Zaco pair. We released some in lowland areas of dry forest around the Black River Gorges where there were plenty of geckos. Tom Cade came to Mauritius for a season with his wife Renetta, and they looked after a group of kestrels being released. Tom and Renetta were a wonderful help. They would spend the day in the field and, in the evening, Tom would visit to debrief. Normally very reserved and taciturn, he would bubble with interesting observations on the kestrels, full of enthusiastic ideas for how we could improve our release technique, or better manage the free-living birds. Slowly, we were developing the skills and knowledge to restore the population.

The young kestrels were all banded with color rings so we could identify them easily, and we trained them to come when I whistled, to be rewarded with a mouse. Years later, they would still respond when called, making the monitoring of their survival quite straightforward. These releases in lowland areas taught us a lot: we had transmitters on the birds and followed them. They could find plenty of food and we were optimistic that these areas would support kestrels. However, some of our birds disappeared and we found that they had been killed by mongooses *Herpestes javanicus*. We started trapping mongooses and found that in the dry forest they were very common, making these areas largely unsuitable. This finding gave us a great insight as to why the kestrels had been common in the nineteenth century but had declined in the twentieth, after the introduction of the mongoose.

Other release sites for our captive-bred birds were needed. Mauritius has some separated mountain ranges, and sometime around the 1950s the kestrels had disappeared from the Bambous Mountains, in the east of Mauritius. The mountains had ample good habitat and few mongooses. The kestrels had died out there during the pesticide era and, now that pesticides were banned, it seemed a perfect place to release kestrels. The Bambous Mountains became one of our main release sites. Young kestrels were reintroduced, and survival was good; when only a year old they started to breed. They were nesting in the nest boxes we had provided, and we looked after them carefully, as if they were captive birds. We wanted to ensure that the maximum number of eggs hatched and that the young were reared. The first clutches of eggs were removed for captive rearing, and the birds laid another set of eggs. It is important that young pairs successfully rear young—it strengthens their bond. Since young pairs often struggle feeding tiny newly hatched chicks, we replaced their own eggs with strong, part-grown young from the captive breeding center, which they could more easily rear. From 1984 to 1994, 333 young kestrels, either captive bred or from harvested eggs, were reintroduced. The population soared.

The success with the kestrel gave us the confidence to tackle the conservation of some of the other species. The Pink Pigeon had been rare for at least two centuries, and we were not sure why. The pigeons were breeding successfully in captivity and there were enough birds for a reintroduction program. I suggested that we set up a pilot release into the 62-acre Pamplemousses Botanical Garden until we had a better idea of the limiting factors in the wild. Here we could closely monitor the birds and find out more about their biology. Twenty-two birds were released, and these did well for a while and started breeding. The birds were tame and trusting, and we hoped they would become an attraction. All was going well until suddenly some disappeared and others were found with injuries—the local children were shooting them with slingshots. Our missing birds had probably ended up in a curry. The release there was not going to work, so we caught the remaining birds and set up a plan to release some into a suitable area of native forest.

The great rarity of the Pink Pigeon had been attributed to the introduced monkeys, which were known nest predators, although this explanation remained unproven. I felt that pigeons may suffer seasonal food shortages, brought on by competition with several introduced bird and mammal species, including the monkeys, which also ate the flowers and fruit of the native trees. To try to understand the Pink Pigeon and its problems, I suggested that we release birds in an area of good native forest, and monitor them carefully to find out what was limiting the population.

Something needed to be done, and quickly—the wild population of Pink Pigeons was slipping toward extinction. In 1991, only 9 or 10 birds were left, found in a small area called Pigeon Wood. This was in the wettest part of Mauritius, where conditions could be grim: wet, cold, and muddy in the winter months, and oppressively hot, humid, and mosquito-infested in the summer. At the same time that we were setting up our release program, we started to provide food for the last wild birds—no mean feat. We knew from our captive work that the pigeons readily ate grain, so we fed the birds on wheat and maize. We did this with a dedicated group of international volunteers led by talented young biologist Kirsty Swinnerton. Feeding worked dramatically; the pigeons bred and produced multiple broods. The population started to grow quickly, and then it crashed. Pigeons disappeared, and we found remains of our birds cached under logs and bushes. Something was killing our birds.

In addition to the work on the wild birds, we released birds into the native forest, surrounded by a mosaic of other habitats, in an area where there were no wild birds. This would give us information on which areas they preferred. These had a slow start while we worked out how best to look after them. To really understand the pigeons, we wanted to get as close to them as we could. We built a campsite in the forest, so that the fieldworkers could live with their birds. By living intimately with the pigeons, they could start to enter their world and begin to understand their needs and challenges. It was Kirsty who drove the early work on the pigeons; she lived in the forest for five years and eventually wrote up her pigeon work for her doctorate.

The released birds were fed, and we put transmitters on them so we could follow them and find out how they lived, where they went, and their needs and challenges. The pigeons spent much time high up in the canopy, feeding on flowers and fruit, as well as leaves. They spent some time on the ground, flicking over dead leaves and broken twigs with their beaks to look for fallen seeds. They started to breed, building nests high up in the trees, well hidden by the vegetation. The released Pink Pigeons were doing well, and slowly their numbers increased. We were beginning to understand the pigeons. Our confidence grew; we felt we could easily increase the pigeon population. The numbers then crashed and, as we had seen in Pigeon Wood, we found remains stashed under bushes. What was killing our pigeons? Was it mongooses, which had been such a problem with the kestrels? Or perhaps monkeys, which many had labeled as the major enemy of the birds?

This crushing setback was telling us there was a major predator in the forest that we had underestimated. I was in touch with others working on endangered species, and one of my most important advisers was Don Merton, who was working on a range of endangered species in New Zealand. Don and our other New Zealand friends told us to be aware of feral cats, which had proven to be a great problem on islands elsewhere. We had never considered cats to be an issue, since they were rarely seen deep in the forest. Heeding their advice, we set traps around the feeding stations and close to where the birds were breeding. It was not long before we caught our first cat, an impressive animal, a beautiful tabby with long legs. A few days later we caught a second, then soon after, a third—all very similar animals. They were not like the domestic cats we had seen around the villages—these were sleek athletic animals. They showed the proportions and characteristics of African wild cats *Felis lybica*, the wild ancestor of our domestics. Skins and skulls were sent to a museum cat expert, who confirmed that they were feral cats, although they did bear a resemblance to African wild cats. We surmise that they were descended from cats that reached Mauritius with the sailors in the sixteenth century. Those early cats were probably closer to wild cats than our modern domesticated felines, and by living independent of humans, these feral cats had reverted back to wild type.

Observations on the wild and released birds were giving us good evidence: there were shortages of food in the forest and there was a problem with feral cats that were proficient pigeon predators. Mongooses could also be an issue, although not to the same extent as the cats, and rats would rob nests of eggs and young. The released pigeons needed nurturing to help them with these challenges; we fed them and controlled predators. With the help and advice of Don Merton, we put in trapping grids around foraging and breeding areas and set up feeding stations. It was clear that if the Pink Pigeons were going to survive, we would have to have a team of fieldworkers living on-site to look after them; the government's National Parks and Conservation Service, our partners, built field stations that would allow us to do our job more effectively.

We released 294 captive-bred birds between 1987 and 1999, fed them, trapped cats and mongooses, and controlled rats. The Pink Pigeon populations grew rapidly. By 1993, with the released birds, we had 72; only 2 years later, we had 207; and by 1998, we were hovering around 300 birds. During the period from 2000 to 2015, the pigeon population fluctuated between 300 to 400 free-living birds. Since 2015, the Pink Pigeons have been established in new areas, so that in 2019 we have more than 450 Pink Pigeons at 8 sites, including the original wild population. We now plan to establish additional subpopulations to increase the numbers to 600.

This work with the pigeons brought home just how important it is to look after them, to provide food and control predators. Just releasing birds into apparently suitable forest was not enough—in damaged habitats some extra care is necessary. The approach we were developing, and embracing, was to get to know the birds and learn about both their problems and what was limiting their populations. Our mantra was "know your species and understand its problems." This had served us well with the kestrel and pigeon. Once we could identify what was restricting the populations, we could then put in place corrective actions.

The pigeon population was recovering, and now I wanted to tackle the Echo Parakeet *Psittacula eques*, which, with only about a dozen or so known birds, was the world's rarest parrot. My colleagues were reticent and felt it was too difficult. At an international conference on endangered species conservation, I told the story of the kestrels and pigeons and said that we wanted to apply the same approach to try to save the Echo Parakeet. I explained that we were unable to raise any funds, since most felt that the species was too high risk; no one wanted to support a project with a high chance of failing.

After my talk I was approached by a tall, distinguished-looking gentleman, Mike Reynolds, who had just started the World Parrot Trust. He wanted to help with the Echo Parakeet. I was to learn that Mike owned his own bird gardens in Cornwall, England, and specialized in parrots. He was so moved by the plight of parrots worldwide, and had had such a rich life enhanced by his parrots, that he wanted to do what he could to help them. This was the start of a relationship with the World Parrot Trust, and the Reynolds family, that has lasted nearly three decades.

The Echo Parakeet is the last endemic parrot in the Mascarene Islands, which once had a wonderful radiation of six to eight different parrot species. This parakeet is a beautiful emerald green; the adult males have a coral-red bill and a crescent of pink on either side of neck, making an incomplete collar. The females are all green, of various hues, with a black beak. They had once likely existed in the thousands and had declined in distribution and numbers as the forest was destroyed. Very little was known about their biology; we did not even know how many eggs they laid. The priority was to get to know the species: how many were there, where did they go, what did they eat, and when and where did they breed? Most importantly, why was the population so rare and what could we do to help it?

With funding from the World Parrot Trust, we started to conduct surveys, follow the birds, collect information on their biology, and, most importantly, try to understand their challenges. They nested in hollows in large forest trees, of which there were few, and when they did nest, most failed. The nest sites were often in poor condition and flooded when it rained, or were accessible to predators and competitors like rats, monkeys, and mynah birds. The parakeets laid three or four eggs, but only ever reared one young, or two if they were lucky. Young were dying in the nest from starvation; there was insufficient food (native fruits) for the parents to rear all their chicks. The forests had become degraded, many of the native trees had been displaced by introduced ones and the exotic rats, monkeys, and birds ate much of the food. In nests that did succeed in rearing nestlings, they were often attacked by parasitic flies, whose maggots sucked their blood.

There was no time to stand back, watch, and document the outcomes like objective scientists; without intervention, the prognosis was terminal. We were conservation clinicians and reacted immediately. Don Merton came to help and advised on how we could look after the wild population. He also sent over fieldworkers from their endangered parrot project on the Kakapo *Strigops habroptila*, and for the next decade there was a regular exchange of staff and ideas between New Zealand and Mauritius.

Nest sites were made more secure and protected from the extremes of the weather. The nest substrate was treated with insecticide to kill parasites, and young were rescued from failing nests and reared in captivity. As we learned more about what was restricting their breeding, we became proactive and never left the young to progress to where they would need rescuing; we harvested the "surplus" young, which we hand-reared. They became our captive-breeding stock.

The captive breeding of the parakeets was initially led by Kirsty, who had moved across from fieldwork to running the captive-breeding center. Kirsty was assisted by a young Mauritian, Frederique de Ravel. Freddie was a neighbor in Black River who, as a young girl, had frequently visited to see the captive animals and was now working for us. When Kirsty left to write up her doctorate, Freddie became the manager of the Captive Breeding Centre and drove the complex job of keeping and rearing parakeets

The Echo Parakeets proved difficult to keep in captivity; they became obese and some died. They were also prone to infections. By working closely with experienced technicians and the specialist vet Andrew Greenwood, we solved these problems. Since the wild parrots ate fibrous native fruits and leaves, they became fat when fed on refined captive diets. The diet was modified—plenty of high-fiber foods, lots of fruit and vegetables, and specially formulated low-protein parrot pellets. Some of the parakeets had died of bacterial infections; we checked the local water supply and found it was badly contaminated. A filtration system that purified the water was installed. The birds responded to the improved diet and water supply; they now flourished and bred.

The captive-bred birds were intended for release to boost the small wild population. We soon had surplus captive-bred birds and also young that we had rescued/harvested from wild nests. The first release was a trial so we could work out the best techniques. When released, the parakeets had to learn a range of survival techniques. They perfected flying and landing as well as foraging and climbing. They learned vocalizations and followed and copied each other. Our observations showed us that the sooner after the normal fledging age they were released, the happier and better adapted to the wild they became. In all, 139 birds—captive-bred and rescued young—were reintroduced from 1997 to 2005. They were provided with additional food and nest boxes. The wild birds, initially reluctant to take supplemental food or use our nest boxes, learned from the younger birds. The parakeets responded rapidly— most now nest in boxes, and about half take supplemental food. In 2015, we started a second population in the Bambous Mountains, where they had been absent for almost a century. The population is still growing (as of early 2020), and is about 750 birds.

Important lessons have been learned from this work. We can recover the populations of even the most endangered animals; however, it may be necessary to look after them long-term and artificially provide for some of their needs until their habitats recover. The most important lesson is that working with species long-term can drive a much bigger conservation agenda. Lessons learned with one species can be applied to others, and often this approach grows into the conservation and rebuilding of entire ecosystems. To help support our birds in Mauritius, we have worked with the government to restore degraded forest. I have often taken politicians and other decision makers to see our conservation work. I took the prime minister and his family to feed the kestrels at Montagne Zaco and also showed them the captive-breeding work. Some years later, when debating in parliament whether Mauritius needed a national park, the prime minister argued that, since we had restored the populations of the kestrel, pigeon, and parakeet, they now needed a national park where they could live.

The Black River Gorges was turned into Mauritius' first national park in 1994, and my friend and colleague Yousoof Mungroo became its first director.

In the early years of the project, we were often criticized for putting valuable resources into species conservation, when perhaps they could have been more effectively used restoring habitats, thereby benefiting a whole range of species. This argument often surfaces, although my experiences show it is redundant. Working on the conservation of species is a powerful driver of habitat protection and repair and, I suspect, more effective than if we started with the goal of habitat restoration. The main island of Mauritius has been seriously altered by the impacts of introduced species; the best that can be done is to control them in small areas, since the island is just too big ($2,040$ km^2) to be able to eradicate the offending aliens. Our colleagues in New Zealand had successfully removed exotic mammals from small islands and then used the islands as homes for some of their most endangered species. Don Merton was urging us to find suitable islands around Mauritius that could be restored and used to support populations of the endangered animals and plants.

By great fortune, in 1995, the small island nature reserve of Ile aux Aigrettes (27 ha) was offered to the Mauritian Wildlife Foundation on a long-term lease. This island is in the middle of the lagoon, only 600 m from the mainland. Although it had been a nature reserve for many years, it had been badly neglected, overrun by rats and feral cats. The island had important coastal vegetation but was badly invaded with exotic plants and regularly visited by locals who were systematically cutting down the trees for firewood.

A respected local fishing family was hired to help look after the island; they became the guardians, and kept off woodcutters. We got help from local organizations to rebuild some abandoned buildings, which became the warden's home and a bunkhouse for volunteer fieldworkers. Don Merton helped us get rid of the rats and cats: he set up a rat poison grid across the island and we trapped the cats. The sugar estates provided labor during their off season to weed the island. Wendy Strahm supervised the restoration and set up a small native-plant nursery and, as the invasive weeds were removed by the sugarcane laborers, we filled the gaps with our nursery-grown plants. A warden was hired and we built a team of volunteers; together, an ambitious plan for the island was developed, with a list of all the plants and animals that we wanted to restore. With huge energy and enthusiasm we embraced the project; we were going to rebuild our island. As soon as the rats had been eradicated, the island started to bounce back into life. The endemic ebony trees that had been badly damaged by woodcutters slowly recovered and burst into flower and fruit. Seeds of native plants that had been dormant in the soil began germinating. We were now ready for the next step.

The first species we reintroduced to the island was the Pink Pigeon. The island was large enough to hold a small population that we could keep a close eye on. The pigeons were hesitant about crossing water, so remained resident, and we fed and monitored them closely. The trees on the island were all quite short, since they had been pollarded by the illegal woodcutters, and all the nests were accessible. This was a huge boon for our research, since we could gather accurate information on the breeding success of the pigeons. The island was ideal, since it had no major predators, and soon the pigeons were breeding. It was suspected that they would be very productive, but this was not the case: we found there was high squab (chick) mortality. The squabs were dying from a parasitic disease called trichomonosis, which was being spread by exotic doves that were also found on the island. The doves flew across to the island from the mainland and were so numerous that we could not control them. The infected squabs were treated, but those that survived became reinfected. The disease could not be eradicated and we had to learn how to control it. By keeping the doves away from the supplemental feeding sites, we were able to reduce cross-infection rates, and the pigeons became successful in rearing some young.

The Pink Pigeons have been on Ile aux Aigrettes since 1994. The island is open to visitors and is an accessible site where people can see the pigeons. They have become our most important study population, from which we have learned how to look after free-living birds. In common with all the other Pink Pigeon populations, they do need some care with feeding and the occasional translocation of individuals, to and from the population, to maintain gene flow and genetic fitness.

Mauritius has several endangered songbirds, and we had long been thinking about how we could help them. Putting them on suitable predator-free islands was always considered a priority, and now, with Ile aux Aigrettes, this became a reality. The first species to consider was the Mauritius Fody *Foudia rubra*, a sparrow-sized critically endangered weaverbird. The males in breeding plumage are spectacular, with a vivid scarlet breast and head, and a black highwayman's mask; the females are greenish-brown and sparrow-like. The fodies were limited to small pockets of upland forest, where their population had declined to about 200–250 birds. They fed on nectar, insects, and spiders, and some biologists felt they would be unable to survive on a small island, since the climate and habitat would be so very different. I felt confident that they would do well on Ile aux Aigrettes, since other species of fodies on other Indian Ocean islands have proven to be adaptable and can, when there is enough food, occur at high densities. It seemed likely the last wild birds were restricted to small, wet areas of upland forest, since the introduced mammals, such as monkeys and rats, which are such effective nest predators, were less common there.

For this experiment of putting fodies on our island, catching wild birds was not an option, since they were so rare. Also, I suspected wild birds would not have done well in such a different area.

I felt the answer was to release some hand-reared birds, which would be tame and tractable, easily followed, and would take supplementary food, which would boost their chances of surviving. We harvested eggs and young from wild nests, hatched the eggs, and reared the young at the captive-breeding center. The young were reared on a mix of boiled egg, minced baby mice, bee larvae, and papaya, and grew well. As soon as the young could fly we put them in an aviary on the island and, after a few days, let them out. Far from disappearing into the forested parts of the island, they hung around the warden's house and raided the kitchen for scraps of food left lying around. Many were surprised by how personable and tame they were. I was delighted, since this is how some fodies behave elsewhere; one seventeenth-century account describes how some of the early colonizers to Mauritius complained that "sparrows" entered their homes looking for food. They were probably describing Mauritius Fodies.

The fodies soon settled on the island and, when only a year old, started breeding. As I expected, they proved to be highly adaptable and prolific. In common with other species of fodies, they eat all types of food—fruits, insects, nectar—and scavenge around the house picking up crumbs of food dropped on the floor. We also recorded some previously undescribed foraging behaviors; one was seen feeding on dove eggs, piercing the shells and eating the contents. While in the house, a young male searched among some cables running up the wall, and probed behind them with the aid of a thin stick about 2 cm long that it held in its beak, presumably trying to dislodge spiders and cockroaches that lived there.

We provide them with some additional food to boost the population on such a small island. Breeding has been recorded in every month of the year, although with a peak breeding season in the southern spring and summer, and a pair may produce several broods of young. Not surprisingly, the population has grown: by 2020 we had 350–400 birds on the island.

This spectacular success motivated us to try to do something for Mauritius' most threatened bird, the Olive White-eye *Zosterops chloronothos*. This small (weight 8 gm) olive-green bird, with a longish curved bill and white spectacles of feathers around the eyes, feeds on nectar and insects. The wild population is probably in the region of 150–250 birds and steadily declining. We realized that this would be a real challenge, since they have such a specialized diet and are territorial and aggressive to one another. Hence, we could never have the numbers of them on Ile aux Aigrettes that we could with the fodies. Nevertheless, we felt we could use the island as an experimental site to learn the techniques to better look after them in the wild. We did some rough calculations, based on how much area they required and the amount of habitat on the island. If we were lucky, the island would hold 50 birds.

Our approach was similar to what had worked so well with the fodies. We harvested eggs and young from wild nests and hatched and reared them. When we take the eggs or young, the adult birds re-cycle and lay replacement eggs, therefore we do not have a negative impact on the wild population. The Olive White-eyes were more problematic to rear since, when they hatched, they were only about 0.8 g and needed intense care, with regular feeding, using a diet similar to that used to rear the fodies. Our hand-reared White-eyes were released on the island, and we fed them on a nectar mix and a formulation made for insectivorous birds. The birds settled in the best areas of forest, where we built feeding stations so they could top up if they could not find enough food by natural foraging. The following year they started breeding. Slowly the population has grown, and the island is nearing its holding capacity. We have exceeded our original estimate that the island would hold 50 birds, and have, by 2019, about 55–65 birds. The island is once again gaining a community of native birds

Ile aux Aigrettes used to have colonies of seabirds: the bones of White-tailed Tropicbirds *Phaethon lepturus* and Wedge-tailed

Shearwaters *Puffinus pacificus* have been found on the island, and several of the other islands in the region are named after the seabirds that once occurred there. Small numbers of seabirds had still occasionally nested on these islands in the southeast of Mauritius, but were killed by fishermen. Putting seabirds back on Ile aux Aigrettes, which was now being carefully protected, was a clear priority. White-tailed and Red-tailed Tropicbirds *Phaethon rubricauda*, and Wedge-tailed Shearwater chicks were harvested from Round Island, an island north of Mauritius, reared on Ile aux Aigrettes, and allowed to fledge naturally from artificial nest sites. No one had tried moving these species between islands before, although I knew it was likely to work, since when these birds fledge they fly out to sea and can look after themselves. They also usually return to the same island from which they fledge. Some of the birds we released have returned, and have been seen flying over or around the island, but have yet to settle and breed.

I also wanted to release some terns, since these common colonial nesting birds were likely to have been found on, or close to, Ile aux Aigrettes. Seabird biologists were skeptical and told me it would not be possible, since young terns are looked after by their parents after they leave the nest. I was not convinced, since we can release other species of birds, such as kestrels, that also have post-fledging care. I hatched tern eggs and reared the young at home in my kitchen. I experimented with rearing and releasing techniques, and, when I was happy with these, we harvested young Sooty Terns *Onychoprion fuscatus* and Common Noddies *Anous stolidus* from Serpent Island north of Mauritius. These nestlings were reared on Ile aux Aigrettes and fed pieces of octopus and small fish. At feeding time we whistled to them, and when older, but before they could fly, the terns and noddies would come running up to their carer for food. They grew well and started to fly at the expected age, and late every afternoon we whistled and in they flew to get their meal. Their development was comparable to that of wild birds: they started fishing in the lagoon around the island and soon started missing feeding days, when they had found enough food themselves. The terns, one by one, became independent and stopped returning for their free handouts—it was possible to rear and release terns. This seabird work is still in its early stages, and we are still developing our skills and approaches. In the future we hope to bring back other missing seabirds.

The vision we developed for Ile aux Aigrettes was of a site where we can have free-living populations of some of our rarest species, and also a functioning ecosystem benefiting the maximum number of native species. The major block to this is that we know little about the systems we are trying to rebuild: many species have become extinct, and the impacts these had on others are largely unknown. This is something we have long pondered, trying to understand how the original systems worked.

In the early days, when dreaming about what we could achieve on Mauritius, I had thought that perhaps we could find replacements for some of the extinct species by using closely related forms that had similar ecologies to the lost ones. Perhaps we could find a suitable pigeon and parrot to replace the Blue Pigeon and the Raven Parrot *Lophopsittacus mauritianus*? When I suggested this to colleagues, I encountered a barrage of opposition. How could I think of using introduced species to repair systems, when it was introduced species that caused many of the problems? These negative feelings ran deep. I did not let these views cloud my judgement. I could understand why it would be difficult to justify releasing alien pigeons or parrots, since if it went wrong it would be difficult to reverse the damage, but other species could be more tractable.

The early settlers wrote about vast herds of giant tortoises on Mauritius and the other Mascarene Islands. Of the five original species, Mauritius had two: a dome-shaped grazing tortoise *Cylindraspis inepta* and a saddle-backed browsing tortoise *Cylindraspis triserrata*. All are now extinct, killed by the early settlers. The more I pondered what function these tortoises may have played in the ecosystem, the more I became convinced that they must have had a huge role in shaping the native vegetation communities. I spoke to tortoise experts and visited other islands with tortoises, such as the Galápagos, to try to understand how the tortoises would have interacted with the plants. The tortoises on Mauritius would have been grazers, browsers, and tramplers, keeping some areas open. They would also have been dispersers of seeds. I examined the native plants and a large number seemed to have adaptations to cope with tortoises. Many small endemic herbaceous plants and native grasses were now very rare, and I suspected they would have been part of an open vegetation community maintained, closely cropped, by the grazing of tortoises.

I wanted to see how the tortoises and plants would interact. Some of my academic colleagues were far more open-minded than the conservationists I had spoken to—they agreed that we may be able to use an existing tortoise to replace an extinct form and reactivate some long-lost ecological interactions. It was an exciting idea, and I secured the necessary support from Christine Mueller, Zurich University, Switzerland, and Stephen Harris, Bristol University, United Kingdom. We developed a PhD position and one of our volunteer fieldworkers, Christine Griffiths, who worked with our tortoises, became the student. The Aldabra giant tortoise *Aldabrachelys gigantea* was the nearest proxy we could realistically hope to get, and fortunately we had some. Our group was a mixture of ex-pets and some that had come from a sugar estate, where they had lived in a large enclosure. I had collected them in the hope that one day I could use them for our studies.

The tortoises were released on Ile aux Aigrettes, and we followed them. Where did they go? What did they eat? Slowly we built up a picture of their lives. They tended to feed on introduced grasses and fallen leaves and fruit, and helped maintain tortoise lawns, which they frequently visited. During the heat of the day, and at night, they hid under dense vegetation. They also started to breed, and we soon found young tortoises. Then something remarkable started to happen. Young ebony trees started to grow in parts of the island where there had been none. The ebonies, a coastal tree with a population on Ile aux Aigrettes, were not regenerating properly. An occasional young tree would grow under the adults, but these were usually poor specimens. Now we had young vigorous trees growing well away from the parent plants. The tortoises had eaten the fallen ebony fruits and spread the seeds in their droppings. The seeds that pass through the gut of a tortoise are spread by them, and these seedlings are also a lot stronger.

Rebuilding lost and damaged ecosystems has become our goal. It started modestly, by replacing some missing species, and has grown into trying to reconstruct functional systems. Ile aux Aigrettes was an early effort, although there have been other initiatives. One of the most spectacular has been the replanting of native forests on Rodrigues. Rodrigues is the smallest and, ecologically, the most damaged of the three main Mascarene Islands. When Wendy Strahm and I visited in the early 1980s, the 108 km^2 island was largely denuded as a result of deforestation, overgrazing, drought, and cyclones. The people were friendly and open, seemed happy, and were always smiling, even though they had few resources; they lived mostly by subsistence farming and fishing. Most of the wildlife was extinct and those few species that had survived were perilously rare. We were to discover that much damage had been done in recent times. In the 1960s, when Rodrigues was still part of the British Empire, an agricultural adviser had suggested that most of the then-remaining forests be chopped down to make way for agriculture. The result was that he had sanctioned the destruction of many of the island's watersheds and, in the following years, there had been bad droughts.

During our first visits, we wanted to get an idea about how the native wildlife was faring. Wendy did a survey of the native plants, and I went looking for the three remaining endemic animal species, the Rodrigues fruit bat and two passerine birds, the Rodrigues Warbler *Acrocephalus rodericana* and Rodrigues Fody *Foudia flavicans*. No native forest was left, just secondary woodland on some hills, and deep in valleys, with the odd native plant scattered among a sea of introduced weedy species. The location where the bats roosted was well known, in the biggest valley, Cascade Pigeon, which led down into the capital, Port Mathurin. The warblers and fodies were also concentrated in and around this area.

Cascade Pigeon was the water catchment area for the capital, and the government had reforested its slopes and tried to protect its vegetation—although on our early visits into the valley we encountered cattle, goats, pigs, woodcutters, and families collecting firewood. The understory was open and the forest patchy and unloved. The bats roosted in a cluster of tall trees left on a poorly accessible slope. The fodies and warblers were in the densest patches of brush and around some of the few mature trees that were growing next to the forestry station.

The bat had suffered badly from the deforestation, and many had likely died in the droughts and been killed in cyclones that had hit the island in 1972 and 1973. When Gerald Durrell visited the island in 1977 to collect bats for a captive breeding program, he thought fewer than 60 were left, and some believe the population may have been as low as 20 or so animals in the early 1970s. By the early 1980s the population had grown: we counted bats as they left the roost at night and found numbers in the low hundreds.

The Rodrigues Fodies are very inquisitive and easy to find. The male has a bright yellow breast and a black mask surrounded by orange. The females are a dull green-brown. They are bold and confiding, and when you enter their territory they will often fly down and perch on nearby bushes to investigate you, especially if you make squeaking noises. I crisscrossed their habitat, marking any birds I found on a map. In all, I found birds in 41 territories and estimated that, allowing for birds that I missed, there could have been as many as 150 individuals. This was a substantial increase over previous estimates since, in 1967, a Mauritian birdwatcher had counted them and could find only 12 birds.

The warblers are often quiet skulking birds that like dense vegetation and occasionally make a beautiful throaty warbling call. They have longish bills, a long tail, short, rounded wings, and their plumage is various shades of olive-green. As I walked slowly along trails through suitable habitat, occasionally stopping and making squeaking calls, they too would come to investigate. Most were in one small area, in the upper reaches of Cascade Pigeon, around a natural spring called La Source. In all I found 21 birds, and I thought there could be as many as 30–45. In the early 1960s, they were so rare that a Mauritian birdwatcher could not find any. In 1964 a museum ornithologist visited the island and thoroughly searched for the warbler. He found one, which he shot and is now in a museum, and heard another. During the 1960s the species was listed as critically endangered, and its future looked grim; a weeklong search for the species by two Mauritian naturalists in 1969 failed to find any. Luckily, though, it had avoided extinction.

The situation with the native plants was equally dire: most were down to tiny populations. One, the café marron (wild coffee) *Ramosmania rodriguesii*, was down to the last forlorn individual, in a hedge next to a house by a main road. We desperately wanted to do something to help Rodrigues, but it all seemed overwhelming and hopeless. Wendy had an idea: we could find small amounts of money from our sponsors, hire a volunteer, and work with the Forestry Department to grow some of the rarer plants in their nursery. That would be a first step and would generate some local and international interest in the desperate state of Rodrigues fauna and flora.

Over the next few years we had a series of young international volunteers helping us develop the nursery and grow rare plants. To support them, we—and especially Wendy—made many visits to Rodrigues. It was an island we both loved. The pace of life was much slower than Mauritius and it was our bolt-hole whenever we needed a change of scene. The international aid community was interested in helping Rodrigues; they wanted to reestablish their watersheds and fence them to keep out domestic livestock. This was our opportunity. By working with the Rodrigues Forestry Department and the overseas aid workers, we were able to suggest what areas were a priority and how they could be best managed to secure them as watershed and help the native animals and plants.

In parallel to this work, we established a small native-plant nursery and started to grow some of the rarest plants from seeds and cuttings. We wanted to use these plants for rebuilding the watersheds, although this was unrealistic, since there were not enough plants available. Nevertheless, we had sufficient to start replanting in the most important nature reserve, called Grande Montagne. Here we removed the introduced weedy scrub and replaced it with native plants. These were small, modest steps, since initially we were replanting only tiny areas. We got lots of help from the Forestry Department, and one young forester was to take this work to new levels. His name is Richard Payendee.

Rodrigues is part of Mauritius, although Rodriguans have a strong sense of self-identity—they love their island. Richard is a man with an easy smile and a natural charm. He is a leader. He embraced the idea that the plants and animals belonged to Rodrigues, and it should be Rodriguans that looked after them. Soon Richard had mobilized his friends, and youth groups; we had young Rodriguan volunteers clearing exotic scrub, growing plants in the nursery, and planting the seedlings in Grande Montagne and in a drier lowland area, a valley called Anse Quitor. The youth of Rodrigues were rebuilding their native forests, and this work has now continued for the past three decades. Many rare plants have been grown in large numbers—up to 40,000 plants a year—

the watersheds have been restored, and the amount of forest cover has increased. Most of the forest cover is made up of exotic plants, although substantial tracts of native forest are reaching maturity. This work has been driven by Richard Payendee, who became the manager of the Mauritian Wildlife Foundation's Rodrigues branch, then subsequently a politician, and is now a senior minister with a portfolio of the environment, fisheries, and tourism.

The fruit bat, warblers, and fodies have all responded to the reforestation of Rodrigues. In the 1980s and 1990s the populations grew steadily, and as the forests began to mature, their numbers increased exponentially. These species are found in high densities in the areas of native forest in the nature reserves, but they are also using the areas of secondary exotic vegetation. The bats have established several roost sites in the forested valleys, and the fodies and warblers have spread widely. In 2019, the populations were about 20,000 Rodrigues fruit bats, 17,000 Rodrigues Fodies, and 20,000 Rodrigues Warblers—some of the most spectacular species recoveries ever for 3 species that, in the 1970s, were battling extinction.

Our work was primarily in species conservation, which in turn has driven the much bigger agenda of whole-habitat reconstruction. There is no quick fix—species conservation can take decades, and restoring whole systems very much longer. Nowhere has this been more apparent to us than on Round Island. Mauritian naturalists had long recognized Round Island as a very special place. It was one of the largest tropical islands that had been spared introduced rats, which can cause extensive damage. Rats have been accidentally introduced to islands worldwide, wreaking chaos and driving many species to extinction. On both Mauritius and Rodrigues, they are the likely causes of many extinctions, especially of reptiles and birds.

Round Island, a dome-shaped island 22.5 km north of Mauritius, about 2.15 km^2, is home to a community of native reptiles, seabird colonies, the last area of palm savannah in the Mascarenes, and some endemic invertebrates. It is uninhabited but had been badly degraded by introduced rabbits and goats, which had eaten much of the vegetation and caused widespread soil erosion. In the 1970s and early 1980s, Round Island was a sad sight: the last remnants of the palm savannah hung onto the steep slopes and were dying. The reptile populations were depleted, and the seabirds were being regularly poached by raiding bands of fishermen.

Gerald Durrell had visited Round Island and, awestruck by the wonderful animals and plants that still lived there, pledged to help the island. The priority was to remove the rabbits and goats. One of the big problems facing islands worldwide has been the impact of introduced mammals. The pioneers in restoring islands by removing unwanted mammals are the New Zealanders, and one of the experts was our old friend Don Merton. In 1979 the last of the goats was shot by a Mauritian hunter, but the rabbits were going to be more problematic. Don visited in 1984 and, together with Wendy Strahm, we went across to the island to see how we could get rid of them.

Wendy and I had visited the island several times before; this was to be our longest stay, allowing us to get to know it better. We camped in an erosion gulley that provided some shade in the heat of the day. Don, who had spent nearly half of his working life camping on remote islands, was the most perfect companion—he had developed camp living into an art. Don was highly organized and had brought all the stores we would, or could, need, carefully packed and labeled in cardboard boxes; each day was planned with military precision. The conditions on the island were harsh, hot, dry, and rugged, in contrast to the relative genial luxury of our field camp. This comfortable and dynamic camp was to become a haunt for some of the reptiles. Telfair's skinks *Leiolopisma telfairii,* lizards a foot long, raided our kitchen area every day to look for scraps and were bold enough to feed, or snatch food, from the hand. A retinue of up to a dozen was always searching among our pots and pans for leftovers. Small Bojer's skinks *Gongylomorphus bojerii,* the color of burnished copper, also came scavenging, moving among our stores with the fluidity of quicksilver; one evening a Round Island boa *Casarea dussumieri* glided gracefully through our living area.

Each day we searched the island carefully. Where were the rabbits living, and how many were there? We estimated there were about 3,000, living mainly in the last vegetated areas, hiding under fallen palm fronds and in burrows in the few areas that had any soil. The rabbits and goats had eaten most of the vegetation that had been holding the soil in place and, with the heavy summer rains, the soil was being washed down deep erosion gullies, bleeding into the sea. Don was a consummate field man and amazing naturalist. When not studying the rabbits, we explored the island together. I banded seabirds and took field notes on them and the reptiles. Wendy compiled information on the plants. The vegetation was in poor shape; there was little regeneration. Some rare native plants survived on ledges the rabbits could not reach. Of the palms and screwpines scattered across the island, most were adult and old, and some were fruiting, although any seedlings were being nibbled to death by the hungry rabbits. The last remnants of the palm savannah were dying. Surprisingly, the native tussock grasses had survived in large clumps, under which we found reptiles and nesting seabirds.

Four known species of seabirds were nesting on the island: the Wedge-tailed Shearwater, two species of tropicbird, and the Round Island petrel. As we systematically searched the island, we found the remains of hundreds upon hundreds of seabirds that had been killed by poachers; they had removed the heads and wings and taken the bodies. The island had once had thousands of tropicbirds, which had been reduced to scattered pairs breeding in nooks and crannies and under tussock grass. The shearwaters and petrel populations had also been greatly reduced. The remaining sea-birds added a special ambience to the island. During the day the tropicbirds, with their long streamer tails, performed aerial courtship ballets over the island, calling with their rasping *kara-karakara . . . kikiki-kik . . . clik . . . clik . . . clik,* and every evening the petrels flew over our campsite, sky-racing and calling *keh, keh, keh, klou, klou, klou,* a machine gun kecking followed by deep wa-tery utterances. These Round Island petrels were of great interest, and their species much debated by ornithologists. Many thought the petrels were Trindade Petrels *Pterodroma arminjoniana,* al-though Don felt that many were inseparable from the Kermadec Petrels *P. neglecta* that he had seen on the Kermadec Islands, north of New Zealand in the South Pacific Ocean.

Living and camping on Round Island gave us a new, and more intimate, understanding of this magical place. After supper we went on night walks, and in the relative cool of the night, an island of a completely different character revealed itself. Shearwaters, the first of the year to return to the island after their winter wanderings, sat calling at the entrance of their burrows with a low haunting *ohwooo, ohwoo-oo-woooo-urr.* The few areas of vegetation were alive with the rustling of invertebrates: large glossy black cock-roaches and small pale almost translucent ones, chirping crickets, and, in the palms, pale green or brown stick insects. As we walked through the last remnants of the palm savannah, we walked though clouds of micro-moths. Scurrying along the ground, hunting, were large wolf spiders and small centipedes, and sitting quietly among the vegetation were small greenish scorpions. Feeding on the in-sects were Telfair's skinks and night geckos, while hunting in the palms were the large, 25 cm long Guenther's geckos *Phelsuma guen-theri,* with their soft velvety skins and large bright eyes. The apex predator in this system was the Round Island boa, of which there were perhaps as few as 75 left. We searched hard and found some among the palms, where they were hunting lizards.

Round Island had become famous for its reptiles: three species of skinks, three geckos, and the snake. This was the most complete reptile community left in the region, but it was disappearing, and it had lost species. The last wild tortoises anywhere in the Mascarene Islands were recorded on the island in 1844; as recently as 1975, the last burrowing boa *Bolyeria multocarinata* was seen, now believed extinct. At least three or four other lizard species may have lived here before the introduction of rabbits and goats. As we hiked around the island, experiencing its moods and enjoying its surprises, we became increasingly aware that we were witnessing a dying island.

In the evenings, after supper, when we were not going out for a night walk, we sat outside under the moon and stars, chatting. The ambience was deeply soothing, with the mournful song of distant shearwaters. The calls added an unworldly atmosphere to the island. Many locals think the shearwaters are the spirits of the departed. To me, their cry is soothing—I associate it with quiet, reflective evenings when we would enjoy the breeze coming in off the sea and the gentle background rustle of palm fronds.

Don was a great storyteller and entertained us with tales of his adventures working with wildlife on remote islands. At the time, Don was one of the foremost conservation biologists, a pioneer of clearing islands of invasive mammals and then using the islands as refuges for New Zealand's most endangered animals. Don had saved the Saddleback *Philesturnus carunculatus*, a species of wattlebird, and the Chatham Island Black Robin *Petroica traversi*. He had recovered the black robin population from five individuals, including just a single female, using a range of techniques similar to those we had been using to boost the population of our birds. Don was an inspiration and a doer, for many years the main person driving the restoration of the Kakapo, the large, flightless nocturnal parrot. There was so much to learn from him.

During our evening discussions, we developed a vision for the island once the rabbits had all been removed. The vegetation could be restored and the island allowed to recover. Eradicating the rabbits would not be easy, and Don reckoned that the most effective and humane approach would be to use a poison named by us Bunny Slumber, an anticoagulant that would kill them painlessly. Any rabbits that did not take the poison could be shot by an experienced hunter. This would be a dramatic approach, but necessary if we were to save this amazing island and prevent its reptiles, plants, invertebrates, and seabirds from dying. As a conservationist, I have always had a deep respect for life, and killing one species to benefit others does not sit easy. Seeing the complex, vibrant, and beautiful ecosystem of Round Island being reduced to a bare rock brought home how devastating introduced species can be. The rabbits were causing the unraveling of a complex system, and the only way to heal the harm was to get rid of them.

A plan to eradicate the rabbits was developed by Don. Permissions and funding was secured, although these took a while, as bureaucratic procedures often do. In 1986 we were ready to start this exciting restoration. Don returned with two colleagues, one of whom was a marksman—a rabbit sniper—and two and a half tons of Bunny Slumber. The blitzkrieg lasted ten weeks and, by the end, all the rabbits were gone. When the team was brought off the island, they were worn out and suffering from island fever—an extreme form of cabin fever brought on as a result of two and a half months on a hot, dry, barren, uninhabited island. They had had enough of each other's company. Conservation successes do not come easily, and there is often a personal cost.

Flushed by the victory of eradicating the rabbits, we sat back and waited, watching for the island to recover. Wendy and I made regular visits to the island to see how it was progressing. Soon we started to see the regeneration of palms and screwpines, and also the growth of numerous pan-tropical weeds, many of which had never previously been recorded on the island. Some of these weeds could be harmful and suppress the recovery of the native plants. Wendy contacted experts on invasive plants, and they urged that some of the worst species should be eradicated before they took hold.

To battle the weed invasion, we made several expeditions to the island with conservation colleagues from the government. These expeditions were usually for a few days and we camped in one of the gullies. To avoid the heat of the day, we rose before dawn so we could be at the weeding site by first light. In the middle of the day we took a siesta, before the second weeding session in the late afternoon. It was backbreaking work and Wendy was a task-master, keeping us working at a steady pace, so she had good data on effort, and a recording of the number of weeds removed per person-hour. We removed thousands of weed seedlings, and, yet, on subsequent trips we found even more. Our efforts were not working and we may even have been making the situation worse, spreading weed seeds on our boots and creating disturbed soil for other weeds to colonize. This was not how we had imagined the island would react to the removal of rabbits. It had been expected that we would see the regeneration of missing native plants that had remained dormant in the seed bank in the soil. None of the missing plant species appeared—there was not a lot of soil, and any seeds that may have existed had long ago been washed out to sea. Wendy and our colleagues took native plant seeds, collected from the main island, and did some trial sowing. Few germinated. Re-storing the vegetation was not happening as we had expected and, even worse, the island was being invaded by exotic weeds.

The information on the plants was carefully considered; while some native plants were regenerating, others were declining. The native tussock grass that had survived the rabbits and goats was now becoming rarer. What was happening? The tussock grasses formed clusters, with gaps and hollows between the plants that were an important microhabitat for seabirds, reptiles, and invertebrates.

These tussock grasses had strong, fibrous, silica-filled leaves that made them unpalatable to the rabbits and goats and were an adaptation that had evolved to allow the grasses to live alongside grazing animals such as tortoises and geese. A grazer was required that would selectively eat the weedy grasses and avoid the native tussock grass. What grazer would be appropriate? The rabbits and goats had been grazers, but were too severe in their feeding habits.

It was obvious. The way forward was to use an exotic tortoise to replace the extinct one. Tortoises had survived on Round Island until 1844, and it was now time to put them back again. My thinking was too radical for my colleagues. In Jersey, my bosses distanced themselves from the idea and government colleagues were not impressed. I examined the evidence: in addition to the tussock grass, there were several species of prostrate, herbaceous, sun-loving plants found on Round Island that were now very rare, which I suspected had adaptations for tolerating grazing and trampling by tortoises. I imagined that, historically, Round Island would have been covered by a palm savannah with open areas, maintained by tortoises, where these plants would have been found. These open areas, and their attendant vegetation, were missing. The more I looked at the challenges facing Round Island, the more I was convinced we needed tortoises to help rebuild the plant community.

Convincing people about the value of tortoises, and then obtaining the necessary permissions to put them on Round Island, was going to take time. In the meanwhile, we had to ensure we had the information to be able to manage the island properly. A priority was to look at all the other islands around Mauritius and find out what animals and plants they had. We would be able to identify the most important for conservation, and which islands had species we could use to replenish Round Island and vice versa.

Our work on Round Island and other islands around Mauritius and Rodrigues went into high gear. Every island was visited, and we made inventories of the plants and animals. I worked on the reptiles and birds. New Zealand colleagues, Brian Bell and his team, looked for invasive mammals, and my friend Eshan Dulloo, from the National Parks and Conservation Service, studied the plants. More than forty islands were visited; some were close to the shore and were being used for tourism, while others had been badly damaged by people and invasive species and had little of interest on them. A small number had relict populations of native lizards, seabirds, and plants, and we found some unexpected surprises in new populations of lizards and plants.

At the end of the survey, we were able to identify the priority islands that were of conservation value. The islands off the southeast of Mauritius, part of a group that included Ile aux Aigrettes, were important, as were some close to Round Island in the north. These islands could be managed as two different units. To be able to restore the islands in these groups, we would first need to get rid of the invasive mammals that were present. Brian Bell and his team, most of whom were his children, returned to Mauritius and cleared islands of mice, rats, and hares. The Mauritius Wildlife Foundation and the National Parks and Conservation Service got rid of shrews from one small island and rabbits from another. We could now start doing some conservation work. Ile aux Aigrettes could be the base for managing the southeastern islands. The islands in the north, including Round Island, were more of a problem to work on, since we did not have any place to stay and had to camp.

A field station on Round Island was a priority so people could remain on the island for extended periods. Then we would be able to conduct the important studies needed to better understand and conserve the island and its wildlife. There was some feeling against building on such a precious reserve, but we argued that a field station was essential if we were going to restore the island. Eventually, we all agreed that any building should have minimal environmental impact and be modest and practical, so in 2001 a small wooden hut was constructed. Solar panels were erected to provide power for lighting and electrical equipment, and we built a system to collect rainwater and store it in tanks. A compost loo and a small plant nursery were erected; we were now equipped to get our teeth into the problems on Round Island. Staff was hired to work on a rotation system, staying on the island for a month at a time. A schedule of work was drawn up; restoration of native plants, removal of any new problem weeds, studies on the reptiles, banding of seabirds, and some research on the petrels—and we needed to find out more about invertebrates, soil formation, and how to minimize erosion.

As soon as we had a field station and a permanent presence on Round Island, the poaching of seabirds stopped and their populations started to recover. Islands with seabird colonies are more productive and support higher densities of reptiles and invertebrates, because the birds pump nutrients onto the island from their droppings, regurgitated food, unhatched eggs, eggshells, dead birds, and molted feathers. These add to the soil, and the nutrients improve soil fertility. Understanding what birds we had on the island was important. We soon found that the island held some interesting seabirds that had been previously overlooked. A small colony of Bulwer's Petrels *Bulweria bulwerii* was found nesting in rocky cavities, and several Black-winged Petrels *Pterodroma nigripennis* were using the island but not breeding.

I was keen to try to work out what species the Round Island petrels were. I, and others, had collected information on their biology, banded them, and measured numerous birds on the island and in museums. This information was scattered in my field notebooks and on data sheets and needed to be compiled and analyzed. My right-hand man at the Mauritian Wildlife Foundation, Vikash Tatayah, wanted to do his PhD. I suggested he work on the petrels, looking at the details we had collected. Vikash studied the birds on the island, recorded their breeding biology, worked on museum specimens, analyzed the field data, and reviewed the historic accounts. This type of knowledge is important when setting up conservation projects: broad ecological studies, reviews of what we know about natural history, populations, and breeding biology are the foundations on which subsequent work can be based. The work by Vikash and others was suggesting there were more than one species of petrel on Round Island, and that there were hybrids between them. This story is still being written: there are at least three species, including Trindade Petrels from the Atlantic; Kermadec Petrels, as suggested by Don; and Herald Petrels *P. heraldica* from the Pacific. Some birds show the characters of all these species, which are three-way hybrids. The biology of these petrels was extraordinary, with hidden surprises—and it was going to get more exciting.

The petrels spent several months away from the island, and we had little idea where they went. One of our banded birds had been found, storm-driven, inland in India, and another, a recently fledged bird, grounded in the north of Mauritius. These records added to our curiosity. To learn where they went, we designed a tracking study, led by my colleagues Ken Norris and Malcolm Nicoll from the Institute of Zoology, London. They caught more than 150 petrels and placed a small geolocator on a leg; by capturing the bird a year or more later, we could download information from the tag that told us where the bird had been. Remarkably, they were flying virtually all over the Indian Ocean, traveling many thousands of miles every year. Some birds flew to the islands north of Australia, and one went close to Lord Howe Island. Another went into the Atlantic and flew close to Trindade Island, wandering north of the equator before flying back home around the Cape of Good Hope to Round Island.

Round Island was revealing its secrets, showing how important the island was. We realized that with sympathetic management, we could enhance its value as a biodiversity hotspot. Restoring the vegetation was a priority, and we drew up a list of plants that would likely have been growing on the island before the vegetation was denuded by the rabbits and goats. We based this list on the work of Ehsan Dulloo and Wendy Strahm, both of whom knew the flora well. Seeds and seedlings were collected on Mauritius, which we took across and grew in our nursery. After a year we had grown 1,500 plants, ready to plant out on Round Island.

Our first year had gone well—we had an enthusiastic Mauritian staff being helped by international volunteers. There was a buzz in the air and a feeling that we were moving forward. The island team planted out all the seedlings and watered them well. They were elated we were rebuilding Round Island. A year later we surveyed the plants—all but one had died, and that was a plant next to the field station that had been nurtured carefully. The team was depressed—restoring the island was going to be harder than anyone had thought. The plants had died because they had been unable to cope with the harsh, hot, dry conditions and had been dug up by burrowing shearwaters. Some felt it was "natural selection": if they could not make it without our help, then so be it. Most felt we needed to support the seedlings until they were well established. Our birds have required a lot of help to improve their survival, and so it seemed the same would apply to the plants.

To survive, our seedlings needed more frequent watering and protection from the shearwaters, which were competing for the few patches of soil where they could dig their nesting burrows. Our rainwater collection system was expanded: we built a dam on one of the island's bare, rock-slab slopes, and the collected water was fed by a series of pipes into storage tanks. From there, with hoses and taps, we could deliver water to all the planting areas. The shearwater problem was harder to solve, since we wanted to encourage them while still being able to grow plants in the same areas where they nested. After some experiments we came up with cages, tubes of wire mesh lined with shade net. These we sunk deep into the soil to prevent the seabirds digging them up, and in each we planted a seedling. These cages also provided a micro-climate, protecting the delicate young plants from harsh conditions. With our new planting strategy, putting the seedlings in their cages and watering them frequently, survival improved—a year later about two-thirds were still alive. After being out on the island in all its seasons, these plants were hardy and well established and did not require extra care. Slowly, we were restoring the hardwoods on Round Island, and in response the reptile populations were increasing.

There was still much to learn about the reptiles, and I invited a friend, Nick Arnold from the Natural History Museum, London, to help us. Nick had had a long-term interest in the reptiles of the region and made two expeditions to visit us with a colleague, Jeremy Austin. Together we visited several of the islands and caught reptiles and dug for bones to try to identify what was once present. With all the information we had, and various specimens that had been collected, Nick and Jeremy worked on the evolutionary genetics of the reptiles. They constructed evolutionary trees, and there were revelations. One of the skinks, the orange-tailed skink *Gongylomorphus* sp. nov. collected from one of the northern islands, Flat Island, was new to science, and the night gecko on Round Island was different from other species. Nick and I described the gecko, and named it after Gerald and Lee Durrell, in recognition of the efforts they had put into highlighting the plight of Round Island and championing its recovery. This lizard became Durrell's night gecko *Nactus durrellorum*. Our work also discovered four undescribed extinct geckos from Rodrigues, and some other undescribed lizard populations from the small islands around Mauritius.

All these exciting finds inspired a series of studies on the skinks, day geckos, and night geckos. On Round Island we conducted a study on the whole reptile community, looking at their ecology; this research was done by a talented young Mauritian, Nicolas

Zuel. After he had finished his doctorate, Nicolas worked for the Mauritian Wildlife Foundation and became manager of Round Island. All this inquiry gave a clearer picture of where the reptile populations were found, and their needs, and from historic research we also had an idea of what other species once existed and where. I wanted to rebuild some of the lost reptile communities, as best we could, by moving reptiles onto the islands we were restoring. This would need someone with a range of skills in animal and human management to drive and nurture this work.

One of the students who had worked on the reptiles was Nik Cole, an extraordinarily talented herpetologist who did his doctorate on the night geckos. Here was the person we needed to implement our plans for restoring the reptile populations of Round Island and the other islands around Mauritius. In addition to his obvious scientific and animal management skills, he had a mild, genial temperament, was blessed with practical and diplomatic skills, and was well liked. He became the person to drive the reptile and island restoration work. Nik and his team moved lizards onto several of the small islands in the southeast, establishing new populations, including putting Telfair's skinks and Guenther's geckos on Ile aux Aigrettes.

The most important translocation was when we moved some of the newly discovered orange-tailed skinks from Flat Island to another of the northern islands, Gunner's Quoin. This translocation was rushed, since the highly invasive musk shrew *Suncus murinus* had been accidentally introduced to Flat Island. This was a fortuitous move on Nik's part, since the orange-tailed skink on Flat Island was wiped out by the shrews. Without this move, the orange-tailed skink would now be extinct. In addition, Telfair's skinks were moved from Round Island to Gunner's Quoin, and when they were well established, we also introduced their predator, the Round Island boa. In the years to come we will put additional lizards and tortoises on the island. The seabird populations are very depressed, the result of years of poaching. With a greater presence on the island, this killing has decreased and the seabird populations, tropicbirds and shearwaters, are increasing.

Our island restoration work was developing momentum, and it was time to reconsider putting tortoises back on Round Island—we had a field station and a permanent presence. Our friend and supporter Nick Arnold, the greatest authority on Indian Ocean tortoises, had encouraged us to forge ahead with the idea. The hardwoods were being restored, and the palms and screwpines were coming back. The native tussock grass and some of the small endemic herbaceous plants were, however, still declining. I reframed the problem, and at every opportunity explained to all the doubters that without the restoration of a grazer on Round Island, we would lose several plant species—they would become extinct and a whole plant community would be lost. A species was needed to crop the grass and herbaceous plants, to restore an ecological function. Perhaps tortoises would be the answer? Slowly, my colleagues began to accept the need for a grazer and agreed we should conduct similar studies to those we had done on tortoises on Ile aux Aigrettes, but this time on Round Island, with some in pens and others free-ranging.

Christine Griffiths, who had done the studies on Ile aux Aigrettes, designed and conducted the research. Ten Aldabra tortoises and ten radiated tortoises *Astrochelys radiata* were taken to Round Island for a comparative study. The tortoises behaved as we had predicted, feeding on the weeds, creating open areas—"tortoise lawns"—that they maintained by grazing; they kept the grass short by feeding on the fresh growing shoots. They also found water that was seeping out of some rocks, and in the wet season created a mud wallow. The Aldabra tortoises fed on the fallen fruits of the screwpines, spreading the seeds in their droppings. The Aldabra tortoises were better adapted for life on the island than were the radiated tortoises, a species that typically lives in flat scrubland and found the slopes of the island tough going. The tortoise study was positive, and Christine could quantify the benefits—we could assuage the doubts people may have had. The tortoises were filling important ecological roles.

The results were enough to convince the government's National Parks and Conservation Service that tortoises were a good idea; they gave their full support to the project. Subsequently, we have concentrated on developing the Aldabra tortoise population and have released additional young tortoises. Survival has been very high: in 2020 we had more than 600 tortoises on the island, including some recently hatched young, progeny from the first introduction. The tortoises are living in the smoother, flatter areas and avoid the steep and rocky areas, and their differential use of the island is creating a habitat mosaic. Within the grazed areas, the tussock grasses are beginning to regenerate. The tortoises are restoring some of the original ecological interplay.

The tortoise is a keystone species that helps shape its world, as do all species, although some are more important actors than others in their ecological theatre. We have only just begun rebuilding Round Island, restoring what is there, bringing back missing species, and, for some of the extinct forms, finding understudies. Restoring ecosystems is a multigenerational job, and we are developing a hundred-year vision, bringing back animals and their ecological functions. Mauritius had a browsing saddle-backed tortoise and the Española giant tortoise *Chelonoidis hoodensis* from the Galápagos, the only surviving saddle-backed tortoise anywhere, is the only possible substitute. Flightless rails were once widespread, found on virtually all tropical islands, and the Aldabra rail *Dryolimnas aldabranus* is a good proxy to play the part of scavenger and lizard predator. Now that the seabird colonies are recovering, and new species are colonizing the island, we need to consider returning seabirds that are unlikely to recolonize themselves. The obvious example is Abbott's booby *Papasula abbotti*, which historically occurred on Mauritius and was likely lost from the Western Indian Ocean in the 1830s. It is now found only on Christmas Island, north of Australia, where it is endangered.

Looking forward a hundred years is a realistic proposition, a mere two and half times my working life in Mauritius, and perhaps the minimum time required to get the Round Island system in a good functional shape. We are not necessarily trying to re-create the past, since that is, in many cases, unrealistic because of extinctions and irreversible changes brought on by human influence and climate change. The aspiration is to use knowledge of the former systems to build workable wildlife communities that will benefit the maximum of biodiversity.

In badly damaged systems, like those in Mauritius, some enduring assistance will be required. This has been brought home forcibly to us with the Mauritius Kestrel. The recovery of this lovely falcon is one of our most well-known successes, yet in recent years it has been declining. We recovered the population, took our eye off the ball, and withdrew our care, rather than stepping back gradually and monitoring closely. Kestrels in the Bambous Mountains, which nest in boxes, have a stable population, while those in the Black River Gorges, which nest in cliffs, are less productive—and this population is decreasing. We suspect that if we could get the Black River Gorge population to nest in safe, roomy boxes, their productivity will improve. The management of this population is being stepped up again. As this example shows, there are few quick fixes—recovering endangered animals and plants takes time and is an iterative process, learning from mistakes and building on success.

Our work started with relatively modest goals, and we have progressed from managing captive populations to applying many of the same approaches to look after the species in the wild. Even though these free-living birds are being cared for, they are under natural selection and fulfilling their ecological roles. Support may be reduced as we find out more about what is limiting the population and are able to correct it.

Our work in Mauritius, Rodrigues, and on the surrounding islands is still developing, having grown organically from species to systems. This is the natural path many conservation projects follow, if given the room to grow and time to mature. We have been lucky not to have been burdened by constipated committees, with their attendant politics and risk-averse philosophies that shackle so many recovery efforts. When I look at our projects, our successes have been due to having had three of the most talented conservation biologists as mentors. Gerald Durrell, Tom Cade, and Don Merton were very different personalities, yet all were blessed with the ability to see the way forward with clarity, through the maze of politics, uncertainty, and white noise. They could evaluate and use evidence and be directed by well-honed intuition. They taught the value of deep knowledge, to be able to think like the species we work with and experience the world through its senses.

There are great uncertainties about the future, although, far from the doom and gloom of the naysayers, solutions can be found for the world's challenges, and the future can sparkle. The techniques we have learned working on island species are applicable to all, and they put us in good stead when having to confront the challenges that are being wrought by climate and other human-induced change. Slowly we are learning how to recover even the most endangered animals and plants, which means that, if we can save the rarest, we can save them all. Efforts to restore species are, if sustained, a powerful driver for larger conservation challenges, often unlocking the problems and showing how to progress.

Our modest examples are providing a window into what may be possible in the future, since islands in microcosm tell the story and problems of the world. They have taught us about extinction and evolution, about invasive species and their eradication. Islands are

Professor Carl Jones is credited with bringing the Mauritius Kestrel—once the world's rarest bird—back from the brink of extinction. Their populations are now more than 400. Courtesy: Paul Turcotte

providing answers to reversing global harm—we are learning about recovering endangered species and how to use these to build new systems pulsing with life.

Further Reading

Adams, D., and M. Cawardine. 1990. Last Chance to See. Ballantine Books.

Cheke, A. S., and J. Hume. 2008. Lost Land of the Dodo. Yale University Press.

Durrell, G. 1978. Golden Bats and Pink Pigeons. Simon and Schuster.

Quammen, D. 1996. The Song of the Dodo: Island Biogeography in an Age of Extinction. Scribner.

CHAPTER 9

FORESTS AND PRIMATES WORLDWIDE

A Lifetime of Challenges, Opportunities, and Triumphs

DR. RUSSELL A. MITTERMEIER
2018 Recipient of the Indianapolis Prize

Indri
Indri indri

My interest in and commitment to wildlife and wild places can best be attributed to a combination of factors, principally my mother and the legend of Tarzan. I'm a native New Yorker. I was born in the Bronx, moved to Brooklyn at age 7, and then to Long Island at age 9, where I lived until leaving for college at age 17. My mother was a housewife, an immigrant from Germany who came over during the Great Depression in 1929, and who had somehow acquired a great interest in wildlife. She took me to the American Museum of Natural History and the Bronx Zoo almost weekly. During these visits, I usually gravitated toward the reptile and primate houses, my two favorites. I was especially fond of the large snakes and the turtles, especially ones like the reticulated python and the king cobra, and was fascinated with the goliath frog, the largest frog on Earth. I also distinctly remember a white uakari monkey from the Amazon, which looked to me like a mini version of the abominable snowman, a media sensation at that time. I was so taken with this red-faced monkey, with its long shaggy white fur and short tail, that I committed myself to someday go out and see it in the wild. During these early visits, I started to make a mental list of those cool and charismatic species that I needed to see face-to-face, in the wild, a list that I still maintain and that I have, little by little over the years, ticked off on visits to remote parts of our planet.

The legend of Tarzan influenced my life in a major way. I was exposed to the Tarzan films and the Tarzan books from childhood and was totally fascinated by Tarzan's endless adventures and friendship with so many different kinds of animals, especially the primates. To me, Tarzan was an early conservationist, although I didn't call him that or even fully realize it back then. Some of my favorite scenes from those early movies were of Johnny Weiss-muller or Lex Barker riding on the backs of elephants, dodging charges from rhinos, or swinging through the trees on lianas, and also when Tarzan fought against unscrupulous people coming to destroy his jungle or capture its animals. I also connected with the Tarzan character because, although he was a superhero with amazing strength and knowledge, his abilities were within the realm of possibility of a normal human. I never felt any affinity with characters like Superman, Spiderman, or others of the Marvel Comics universe. I thought their superpowers were unrealistic, unscientific, and frankly somewhat silly. Tarzan, on the other hand, was a mortal man, just a very special one.

I was so taken with Tarzan that when my mother enrolled me in Catholic school at age 6, the School of the Immaculate Conception in the Bronx, I informed the nun in charge that I wanted to be called Tarzan and not Russ. She informed me that they would have to call me by my real name, and I immediately replied that I would not go to her "lousy school" if they didn't call me Tarzan. My mother pulled me outside, told me to shut up, and, remarkably, they still accepted me into the school. Later that same year, in the first grade, we were all asked what we wanted to be when we grew up. I quickly replied, "Jungle explorer," secretly thinking to myself that what I really meant was "Tarzan," which today would probably translate as "biodiversity conservationist focused on tropical rain forests."

My love for Tarzan also extends to the history of his films, books, and other products, and I have become over the years an avid collector of Tarzan memorabilia, especially pins, buttons, toys, games, comics, and books. My collection now includes well over a thousand pieces and continues to grow.

I also had an early love of reptiles and amphibians, especially turtles and snakes. I grew up in North Babylon, in Suffolk County, Long Island, about 40 miles from New York City, when there were still some natural areas left before the large-scale conversion to suburbia. I caught turtles, snakes, frogs, and salamanders in the forests and swamps, and kept many as pets. I also participated in the New York Herpetological Society and was one of the founders of the tiny Long Island Herpetological Society, in the journal of which I published my first scientific papers at the age of 17.

My early experiences on Long Island also helped forge a lifelong conservation ethic. Over my first few years there, I watched as the nice little forest patches in my neighborhood were cut down and converted to still more suburban housing, destroying the habitats and driving away the species I loved. I was several times so infuriated by this that I broke the windows of some of the new houses going up to show my displeasure—an early foray into juvenile delinquency that fortunately did not escalate.

I acquired every book available on reptiles and amphibians at the time and learned how to identify every North American species and as many tropical species for which information was available. This early love of books soon expanded to other topics, such as nineteenth-century explorations of the tropics, indigenous peoples, and tribal art. This fascination continues to the present day, and my house is filled with thousands of books on these very same topics, sometimes creating space and curatorial nightmares for me and my family. Among the items that I collect are blowguns (I believe I have the largest collection in the world), bows and arrows, spears, clubs, paddles, masks, dance costumes, spoons, combs, peanut grinding boards, wooden plates, and many others.

When I wasn't reading books about reptiles and amphibians and the exploits of the early explorers, I read over and over again the 75 or so books by Edgar Rice Burroughs, which include not only Tarzan but many other adventure stories as well. I particularly liked the seven-book series on Pellucidar, the prehistoric world inside the earth that Tarzan actually visited in one of the Tarzan series (*Tarzan at the Earth's Core*, my all-time favorite). I also placed great emphasis on physical fitness, started lifting weights at age 13 (which I continue to do to the present day), played all the usual ball sports popular at that time, and ran track and field at the varsity level in high school (starting with the shot put and high jump and winding up in the long jump and triple jump). After all, like Tarzan, I had to be strong to live in the jungle.

Fortunately, I also focused on my studies in school, graduated salutatorian of my high school class at North Babylon Senior High, and also had a perfect attendance record of five years duration. I didn't like school, but I understood its importance and the need to excel if I wanted to move forward in my life. I had also been fascinated by John F. Kennedy and wanted, like Kennedy, to go to Harvard. That didn't work out the first time around, but I never lost my focus on that goal. Fortunately, I did get into Dartmouth College in Hanover, New Hampshire, another great school. Dartmouth provided me with a full scholarship, and my time there turned out to be very fortuitous in many ways.

I had wanted to study biology in college. However, during my first trimester at Dartmouth in the autumn of 1967, I found out that almost all the biology majors were pre-med and that the major included rigorous requirements in chemistry and physics as well—two subjects that I had really disliked in high school. During that first trimester, I got my first-ever C—in chemistry, as it turned out, and getting such a low grade was devastating to me. I also had a hard time in the winter trimester, and even thought about dropping out. Fortunately, I pulled it all back together in the spring trimester and got straight As once again.

During the summer after freshman year, I worked for about a month filing insurance claims for Allstate, an incredibly boring job. But it gave me the funds to take a surfing trip to Puerto Rico for a few weeks with several buddies. I had taken up surfing a year earlier, fell in love with it, and even had my own surfboard (a 10-foot-long, 30-pound tank that still today occupies a place of honor in my home). I had never been to the tropics before and had no idea how strong the tropical sun could be, so I got an awful case of second-degree sunburn, with blisters all over my chest and back. On top of that, I had never encountered coral reefs before, there being none on Long Island, and wound up with a number of nasty coral cuts on my body. By all counts, I should never have wanted to return to the tropics, but the opposite was true. I truly fell in love with the tropics, in part because I also saw my first tropical rain forest on that trip, in what is now Puerto Rico's El Yunque National Forest.

I did not like the long cold winters at Dartmouth, so I started to look for ways to spend time elsewhere, beginning in my sophomore year. Most fortuitously, Dartmouth had an amazing foreign-language/foreign-study program, among the first of its kind back in the late 1960s, headed by a visionary professor by the name of John Rassias. I took full advantage of it. This was not only to escape the cold but also to immerse myself in new cultures and to learn new languages. I had been fortunate to grow up bilingual, picking up German and English at the same time (my father was also a German immigrant), and I had always enjoyed speaking more than just English—and of course Tarzan was multilingual as well. So, aside from polishing up my German in high school, I also took French, and then, in my sophomore year at Dartmouth, spent two of three trimesters doing foreign study at the University of Mainz in Germany and foreign-language training in Bourges, France. I wound up fully fluent in both by the middle of 1969. Right after those courses ended, I followed another of my early dreams— to see the world. I bought a Eurail Pass, spent the three months of summer traveling around 18 European countries, and even made a short foray into Asia, crossing the Bosporus to visit Istanbul.

I used this trip around Europe to sample European culture in the broadest possible way, taking in opera and ballet and visiting dozens of world-renowned cultural sites, including art museums like the Louvre in Paris, the Prado in Madrid, and the Rijksmuseum in Amsterdam; religious sites such as Westminster in London, Notre Dame and the Sacré-Coeur in Paris, the Vatican in Rome, and the Blue Mosque and Santa Sofia in Istanbul; and amazing monuments like Stonehenge, the Acropolis, and the Coliseum. But everywhere I went, I was most strongly drawn to the zoos and natural history museums, and in those institutions, I invariably found myself looking for the primates.

Immediately prior to my trip to Europe, which began in January 1969, I took a class in anthropology, which was being taught by an inspiring young professor by the name of Jim Fernandez. He really brought the subject to life, and I began reading books like Robert Ardrey's *The White Nile* and *The Blue Nile*. This further strengthened my interest in Africa that had originated with Tarzan, and also opened the door to physical anthropology (aka biological anthropology), which historically had been the study of human bones and human evolution, but which had recently started looking at living nonhuman primates as models for human evolution. After speaking to Professor Fernandez, I decided that I should switch majors from biology to anthropology, because it opened the door for me to look at both culture and biology. Even better, I could avoid taking the dreaded chemistry and physics classes, and never needed to take calculus again (I was not intended to be a mathematician).

For my foreign-study program in Germany, I attended classes at the University of Mainz. While there, I was also able to advance my interest in reptiles and amphibians. I made contact with the German herpetological community through one of my professors, Professor Erhard Thomas, and his friend, Professor Walter Sachsse. Sachsse was also a turtle specialist, with an amazing collection of living turtles that occupied every room in his house. He became a close friend, taught me a lot, and introduced me to two of the most famous European herpetologists, notably Dr. Robert Mertens, probably the greatest of all time and the author of more than 800 publications, and Dr. Konrad Klemmer, who had succeeded Mertens as director of Frankfurt's world-renowned Senckenberg Museum. My early interactions with these heroes of herpetology furthered strengthened my interest in this field, and also set a goal for me in terms of publishing. If Mertens could publish 800 papers, why couldn't I—and that has become another of my lifetime objectives (I am getting close).

An interesting aside about Mertens was that he died a few years later, in 1975, from the bite of one of only two venomous species of colubrid snakes (the largest family of snakes, which includes many of our common American species), a savanna twig snake (*Thelotornis capensis*). Sadly, no antivenin existed for this snake at that time, and it took Dr. Mertens 18 days to die. Like a good herpetologist, he wrote down the symptoms as he was dying from the bite (published posthumously), stating that it was "for a herpetologist a singularly appropriate end."

Equally fascinating is the fact that one of the greatest American herpetologists, Dr. Karl Schmidt, suffered the same fate in 1957, dying from the bite of the African boomslang (*Dispholidus typus*), the only other rear-fanged colubrid snake dangerous to humans. Like Mertens, he too wrote down what was happening to him as he was dying, and the results were published after his death. Unlike Mertens, Schmidt died in just 24 hours, refusing medical attention at the end because it would affect his documentation of the effects of the venom. Herpetologists are pretty hard-core!

The combination of my visits to the many zoos of Europe, my growing love for primates, and the decision to switch to anthropology really determined my future path as a primatologist. This direction was also facilitated by Professor Elmer Harp, the chairman of Dartmouth's Anthropology Department, who was a physical anthropologist by training and who had also taken an interest in the emerging field of primatology. He and Professor Fernandez were really instrumental in determining my career path, and I don't know if I ever had the opportunity to adequately thank them.

After that momentous trip to Europe, I began my junior year at Dartmouth. Given how much I enjoyed my European programs, I decided to take a course in Spanish and to participate in yet another of Dartmouth's amazing field programs, this one to Costa Rica.

My foreign-language program in Costa Rica began in April of 1970, and it took place during tumultuous times. The Vietnam War was in full swing, Nixon bombed Cambodia, and a lot of our time in Spanish class was spent talking about the impacts of this war. Most of my fellow classmates protested the war by marching in front of the American embassy in San Jose and wound up getting thrown in jail for a night. I was never one for public protests and watched from a short distance, later visiting them in jail. But I did later get teargassed during a riot against Alcoa in San Jose.

Once again, I was not there to protest, rather just along for the show. Costa Rica back then was not the model country that it has become today,

In any case, I did learn Spanish very well during my three months in Costa Rica, and also had the opportunity for my first in-depth visit to a tropical rain forest during a field trip organized by our course. This trip took us to the northeastern corner of the country, where we visited the Rio Sarapiqui and Tortuguero, the sea turtle nesting beach made famous by Archie Carr, the greatest pioneer of research on these animals. We spent several days there, and my interest in tropical rain forests grew ever stronger.

Following the Costa Rica program, as I had done in Europe, I took the summer to explore Central America, traveling to Nicaragua, Guatemala, Honduras, El Salvador, and Belize (then still known as British Honduras—it didn't become Belize until independence in 1975). This enabled me to visit several other rain forests, and I also carried out a study of turtle exploitation in the markets of Central America. The result was my first-ever publication in a glossy journal, "Turtles in Central American Markets" in the *International Turtle and Tortoise Society Journal*. It was also during this trip that I saw my first nonhuman primate in the wild, a spider monkey (*Ateles geoffroyi vellerosus*), swinging through the trees in the forest surrounding the magnificent Mayan ruins of Tikal.

Several interesting life-changing events happened in the winter trimester prior to the Costa Rica foreign-language program. Given my long-term interest in Africa, stimulated first and foremost by Tarzan but also by the amazing stories of nineteenth-century explorers like Stanley, Livingstone, Burton, Speke, and Grant, I really wanted to do fieldwork on the so-called Dark Continent. The obvious person to ask for a position was Louis Leakey, the famous paleontologist who had not only discovered critically important human remains at Olduvai Gorge in Tanzania but had also gotten Jane Goodall and Dian Fossey on track to do their pioneering studies of chimpanzees and gorillas. I wrote to Dr. Leakey, asking him if I could come and work in Kenya at his Tigoni Primate Center, the first of its kind in Africa. Unfortunately, he turned me down, in spite of three letters and my offer to cover all of my own costs, a disappointment at the time but something that turned out to be fortuitous in my career.

Before going to Costa Rica, I applied for a senior fellowship at Dartmouth. This was an interesting program that allowed a small number of students who had performed well in their first three years to dedicate their senior year to independent research on a topic of their choice. I applied to work in East Africa, still thinking that Leakey might give me a spot. The Senior Fellowship Committee liked my application, but they were nervous about having me travel to Africa on my own. I remember one question from a member of the committee, who asked me if I would camp out in the middle of the savanna with leopards and lions all around. I told them no problem, because I already had a lot of field experience (which was definitely not true at the time). Field biology was still a new discipline back then; the committee members had little or no familiarity with it, and they were right to question me. Nonetheless, in spite of their skepticism, they didn't reject my application outright. Rather, they put a final decision on hold until further information became available.

When I headed down to Central America to start the spring trimester in Costa Rica, I made a stop in Panama, invited by a Panamanian classmate from Dartmouth. He introduced me to Dr. Neil Smith at the Smithsonian Tropical Research Institute, which managed (and still manages) the Barro Colorado Island Research Center, the longest-running biological research station in the Neotropics. Neil, already an accomplished biologist, was very kind and invited me to come and work at Barro Colorado. I didn't think much of it at the time, as I was still focused on Africa, but remembered it later when my plans for Africa fell through.

After the rejection from Leakey and my trip through Central America, I thought that I should perhaps shift my focus to Latin America. After all, it was still poorly studied at that time, and, aside from a few pioneering studies of primates, in need of much further attention. I therefore decided to take up Dr. Smith's offer and asked permission to work for the fall trimester of my senior year on Barro Colorado Island. To my delight, my application was accepted. I decided to focus on the mantled howler monkey (*Alouatta palliata*), which had actually been the subject of the first-ever modern primate field study by Clarence Ray Carpenter in the 1930s, and off I went. While there, I wrote to the Senior Fellowship Committee, and said, hey guys, I decided to go to the Panama jungle instead of East Africa, I'm here already, so why don't you just give me the senior fellowship and help me move forward with my career? Happily they said yes, probably thinking that Panama was a little safer than Africa and figuring that this crazy guy was going to do whatever he wanted anyway, so we might as well give him a green light.

This field study was instrumental in launching me profession-ally and resulted in several publications on primates and one on turtles, since I also did the first-ever study of a little forest turtle called *Rhinoclemmys annulata*. This rather small brownish animal is not spectacular, but it was the only terrestrial turtle on the is-land, and working on it enabled me to study my two favorite groups of animals at the same time. Fortunately, I gathered enough data on both the howler monkeys and this little turtle to publish a couple of peer-reviewed papers on them.

Since I had already gotten my work under way on Neotropical primates, I decided to fulfill my written thesis requirement for the senior fellowship by doing an in-depth analysis of everything that was known at that time of the monkeys of South and Central America. This study, carried out during the winter and spring tri-mesters of my senior year, resulted in a 300-page compendium on these monkeys, which laid the groundwork for much of the rest of my career. It was also sufficiently appreciated by my two advisers in the Anthropology Department, Jim Fernandez and Elmer Harp, that they also made sure I graduated Summa Cum Laude and Phi Beta Kappa.

During my senior year, when not writing my thesis, I often participated in guest seminars offered by my Department of Anthropology. Once—I think it was in the spring trimester—we had a presentation by a Harvard professor by the name of Irven DeVore. I had already heard a little about DeVore and his pioneering research on baboons, but when I heard him speak I was blown away. Irv had enormous charisma and confidence, and what could best be described as a golden tongue. And on top of that, he was from Harvard! Throughout my time at Dartmouth, one of my strongest motivations was to get into graduate school at Harvard to fulfill my childhood dream. They had rejected me the first time around, but that was not going to happen again. So here, with Professor DeVore, we had the perfect storm—Harvard professor, charismatic personality, and a primate field biologist. OK, he worked on savanna baboons, which weren't my favorite primates, but everything else was perfect. I talked to him right after his lecture, got his contact information, wrote him a letter, got a response, and, when it was time, applied to be his graduate student in the Department of Anthropology. He accepted me, and another major childhood dream was fulfilled.

During the last few months of that senior year at Dartmouth, my great friend and classmate Anders Rhodin and I made one last attempt to get a position in Africa. We wrote to Dian Fossey to see if we could work with her on mountain gorillas in Rwanda. Since I was already on track to work in the Neotropics, I was less committed than was Anders, but who could have turned down a chance to work with Dian? The first response, as with Leakey, was a rejection letter. I gave up. Anders tried again but didn't hear back.

Only later did he learn that a letter arrived from Africa while he and I were traveling in South America. His parents forwarded it to an address in Brazil, and he never received it. Who knows what it might have contained, or how it might have changed both of our careers?

I will always be grateful to Dartmouth for opening the door to so many opportunities, and especially for facilitating my interest in languages. This interest came naturally to me because of my bilingual upbringing and because of my fascination with other cultures and worldviews. However, during my college years, I also made the decision that, if I was going to be a truly global researcher and explorer, languages would be an extremely important tool for me. I also realized that by learning the main colonial languages—French, Spanish, and Portuguese, in addition to English—I would have a large part of the tropical world open to me. I continue to love languages to the present day, and keep trying to learn new ones, but unfortunately one's language acquisition ability declines dramatically with age, so I think I am probably stuck with the six that I speak well (Sranan-tongo from Suriname being the sixth), with a smattering of Dutch, Malagasy, and Bahasa Indonesia, and remnants of the Swahili that I briefly learned on my first trip to Africa in 1972.

Upon graduation from Dartmouth in June 1971, Anders Rhodin and I embarked on an expedition to South America to learn more of the field research possibilities there. We began the trip in Panama, with a follow-up visit to Barro Colorado Island, where I had done my first field study the year before, and then proceeded to Colombia. It was in Colombia that I got my first glimpse of the mighty Rio Amazonas at Leticia, after a flight in a cargo plane. My stomach had been bothering me, and I took a drug called Enterovioform, which made me quite ill. So my first day on the shores of the Amazon was spent violently vomiting. That soon passed, and we spent a couple of days exploring the Leticia area. We then took a flight from Leticia to Manaus, in the heart of the Brazilian Amazon. This first foray into Brazil was truly a trial by fire. Our small propeller plane ran through several storms, the back door slid open, and everyone was vomiting, including me. After this first high-stress introduction to Amazonia and to Brazil, as with my first trip to the tropics in 1967, I should have lost all desire to return. However, once again the opposite was true. I fell in love with the Amazonian region, and Brazil as a whole has been my favorite country for nearly 50 years.

While in the Manaus area, Anders and I did a short trip on the Rio Cuieiras, the first little tributary north of Manaus on the Rio Negro, then flew to Belem at the mouth of the Amazon, where we visited the world-renowned Museu Goeldi, which houses some of the most important zoological collections for Amazonia. From there we took a bus on dirt roads to Brasilia, the strange modernistic capital of Brazil that had been built in the middle of nowhere in the Cerrado region of central Brazil a little more than a decade earlier. The bus trip was grueling and took about 50 hours, so we arrived in Brasilia thoroughly exhausted. After visiting sites in Brasilia, we continued, again by bus, to Rio de Janeiro. There I had the great good fortune to meet Professor Adelmar F. Coimbra-Filho, then the only real primatologist in Brazil. Primatology was still in its infancy globally, and in Brazil it really hadn't started yet, except for this visionary gentleman who was doing work on the golden lion tamarin (*Leontopithecus rosalia*), an endemic species found only in the state of Rio de Janeiro and severely threatened by habitat destruction and live capture for the pet and zoo trade. Though I was little more than a teenager, Coimbra treated me like family, and we began a 45-year relationship of close collaboration that ended only when he passed away in 2016 at the age of 92.

From there, Anders and I traveled to Sao Paulo, where Anders decided it was time to go home and see his girlfriend and pursue his medical career. I opted to continue on and complete the remaining circuit of seven more South American countries. Thanks to Coimbra-Filho, I was able to make contact in Sao Paulo with Paulo Nogueira Neto, a wealthy businessman who was to become one of the great pioneers of the Brazilian conservation movement. Once again, as with Coimbra-Filho, the wonderful Brazilian hospitality kicked in, and Paulo took a personal interest in my work. He dedicated a week to drive me all the way across the state of Sao Paulo to the Morro do Diabo State Reserve, where just the previous year Coimbra-Filho had rediscovered the black lion tamarin (*Leontopithecus chrysopygus*), a species that had not been seen in well over 50 years. During this drive, I observed firsthand the large-scale destruction of the Atlantic Forest region of Brazil that was taking place at that time. Where there had once been luxuriant forest, comparable to that of Amazonia, there was now an endless landscape of charred stumps and degraded grassland.

These two experiences in the Atlantic Forest convinced me that I needed to dedicate myself to conserving the primates of this region. They also helped me start focusing on high-priority regions for biodiversity that were severely threatened by human development—areas that would later come to be known as "biodiversity hotspots" and that would be a defining focus of my career. It would still be eight years before I started a full-blown survey of Atlantic Forest primates and protected areas, but the seeds had been sown.

After Sao Paulo, I continued on by train, bus, and plane to Paraguay, Uruguay, Argentina, Chile, Bolivia, Peru, and Ecuador, which left me missing only Venezuela and the Guianas on the South American continent. But these last four, and particularly Suriname, would come to occupy a very important role in my life just a few years later.

While in Peru, I made another very important contact with Professor Hernando de Macedo-Ruiz, director of the Museo de Historia Natural Javier Prado in Lima. Yet again, as with Coimbra-

Filho and Paulo Nogueira-Neto, Hernando took me under his wing, and we developed a strong relationship that would last for decades. During my senior fellowship review of all known information on the monkeys of the Neotropics, I had stumbled across a species that particularly intrigued me: the Peruvian yellow-tailed woolly monkey (*Lagothrix flavicauda*), restricted to a tiny area of the northern Peruvian Andes. It had first been described by the amazing German explorer-naturalist Alexander von Humboldt in 1812, who never actually saw a live animal but based his scientific description on skins being used as saddle covers by Peruvian muleteers. The animal was not heard from again until 1925 and 1926, when two expeditions by the British Museum of Natural History and the American Museum of Natural History collected a total of five specimens. Then, for the next 45 years, there was no news whatsoever of this species, and it was thought to possibly be extinct.

Professor Macedo-Ruiz and I discussed the importance of this species for Peru, since it appeared to be the largest mammal endemic to the country. We resolved to carry out an expedition to look for it in the near future. This did not take place until 1974. However, when we finally carried it out, we managed to rediscover the species and bring back the first-ever live specimen to Lima, where it attracted a great deal of national and international attention—a lost species brought back to life.

I began graduate school at Harvard in September 1971, and was extremely fortunate to land in the middle of one of the most exciting periods in the history of biology, the emergence of sociobiology. This development was led by brilliant scientists like Edward O. Wilson, the greatest evolutionary biologist of the twentieth century; and the equally brilliant but less known Robert Trivers; and with people like my adviser Irven DeVore also playing a key role. Sociobiology postulates that our behavior has a very strong biological and evolutionary basis, and that we need to take this into account in all aspects of human endeavor. I started out just an observer of all the wonderful and sometimes heated discussions on this topic but became so enamored of it that it has over the years become a core element of my life.

After one year of graduate school at Harvard, I did a summer of field work in Panama and Tanzania in 1972. This took me yet again to Barro Colorado Island in Panama, where this time I looked at the locomotor behavior of spider monkeys (*Ateles geoffroyi*), and then to Tanzania, where I studied the locomotion of black-and-white colobus monkeys (*Colobus caudatus*) in Arusha National Park. I had originally intended to do this work in Uganda. However, at the same time that I arrived in Nairobi, the infamous dictator Idi Amin began to expel Asians from Uganda. I consulted with the US Embassy, and they advised me that it might be better to avoid Uganda at that time. I took their advice and fortunately was able to smoothly switch to the delightful Arusha National Park in Tanzania instead.

This visit to Tanzania and neighboring Kenya was my first trip to the African continent, and like everyone who has ever gone there, I was amazed and fascinated by the great megafauna of the world-renowned national parks of northern Tanzania and southern Kenya. I visited the Serengeti, Manyara, Amboseli, the Ngorongoro Crater, and several others, fell in love with them, and have returned many times since. I also did some crazy things like taking a bus to the Serengeti, getting out, and walking on foot into the Leakey camp at Olduvai. I was on a very low budget, so how else was I going to get there? While walking alone in the Serengeti, I was picked up by Hans Kruuk, the famous Dutch pioneer researcher on hyenas. He gently informed me that it was not a good idea to be walking alone in the Serengeti (the interview committee for Dartmouth's senior fellowship had been right!). He deposited me at Mary Leakey's camp (Mary being the wife of the above-mentioned Louis Leakey, and herself a famous paleontologist), where I wanted to visit a couple of my fellow Harvard graduate students who had invited me. Mary, however, was not pleased with my unannounced arrival. She kicked me out, and I ended up spending the night in a nearby local village before getting transported back to the main road to continue my journey. Between the rejection by Louis and the expulsion by Mary, I did not have a good track record with the Leakeys!

Following my second year of graduate school at Harvard, passing my qualifying exams, and getting my master's, I began my doctoral dissertation research program. This involved a number of different trips, the most notable of which was a four-month expedition to the Brazilian Amazon in 1973. During this trip, I partially retraced the routes of the great British explorer-naturalists of the nineteenth century, Henry Walter Bates and Alfred Russel Wallace. The main purpose of this trip was to find the uakari monkeys in the wild and to explore the possibility of doing my doctoral research on them. As noted above, my interest in these bizarre monkeys had first been stimulated by that lone white uakari in the Bronx Zoo when I was a child. The uakaris at that time were considered "mystery species," since there was very little information available on them. On this expedition, I had the great good fortune to become the first outsider to see all three species of uakaris— red, white, and black (*Cacajao* spp.)—as well as the white-nosed bearded saki (*Chiropotes albinasus*), another very poorly known animal. Although both Bates and Wallace had reported on these species in their landmark books and had observed live animals being kept as pets in local villages, neither ever saw them in the wild.

One of the most memorable events from this incredible voyage of exploration was a boating accident that we had on the Rio Negro after a short side expedition. In addition to my work on the monkeys, I had also been collecting specimen reptiles and amphibians for the Museu de Zoologia in Sao Paulo and the Museum of Comparative Zoology at Harvard, again with a special emphasis on turtles. The idea for the side trip originated when we stopped at our base in the port of Manaus, the largest city in the Brazilian Amazon (back then only about 300,000 people, but now well over 3 million). Just by chance, I ran into my very good friend Federico Medem from Colombia, who was in the middle of a South America–wide survey of crocodilians, sponsored by what was then known as the New York Zoological Society, aka the Bronx Zoo (now the Wildlife Conservation Society). Fred was quite an interesting character. He was Latvian royalty, escaped from Latvia during World War II, studied in Germany, and wound up in Villavicencio, Colombia, where he created a center of excellence in the study of South American turtles and crocodilians. I met him during that first momentous trip through South America in 1971 and visited him again in 1972. We became close friends and remained so until his death in 1980.

When we met in Manaus, Fred and I discussed a little-known species of turtle, the red-headed Amazon sideneck turtle (*Podocnemis erythrocephala*). This species had started to appear in pet shops in the United States in the 1960s, apparently coming in along with tropical fish collections. All that was known about it at the time was that it occurred in the Rio Negro drainage. Fred and I decided on the spot to carry out an expedition into one of the small tributary rivers of the Rio Negro, and chose the Rio Cuieiras, just north of Manaus, which I had already visited once in 1971 with Anders Rhodin. We set off in the large motorized canoe attached to our expedition boats and took off upriver. We were successful almost immediately and found that this species nested in what are called *campinas*, patches of sandy habitat with very distinctive vegetation in the middle of the enormous terra firme ecosystem of the Rio Negro. Fred and I collected eggs and several adult turtles and got what data we could on egg size and nest characteristics. We then headed back to our expedition boats moored in the Manaus harbor.

The Rio Negro is an enormous river. As its name implies, it is a black water river that meets the mighty Amazon itself just downstream of Manaus, in the world famous "meeting of the waters," where the black waters of the Rio Negro mix with the white waters of the Amazon. As the river approaches Manaus, it can be as much as 10 km wide, and it was at one of these very wide points that we ran into trouble. The day was bright and sunny, but we suddenly got blasted by strong winds just as we turned a bend in the river. Several waves hit our canoe in rapid succession. As usually happens in such incidents (and, though this was my first, I have by now experienced several of these canoe accidents), your boat starts to fill with water. You use your bailing gourds to remove water as quickly as possible, but to no effect. As the second and third waves hit, the canoe fills with water, all your equipment starts to float away, and finally the boat turns over. Fortunately, we were fairly close to shore, so Fred and our boatman swam to the edge of the river. I will never forget the image of 250-pound Fred perched on a small tree sticking out of the water, saying "Thank God we are alive." I didn't feel so thankful, and immediately began diving in search of my camera equipment and other gear. I was 23, a strong swimmer, and not at all worried about drowning. But I thought of the impact of losing all my gear and the cost of replacing it on my tiny graduate student budget, not to mention all our field notes and the specimens we had collected. Sadly, all I was able to retrieve was one 300 mm Nikon lens that floated in its leather case and a green toothbrush cup that my mother had given me in 1967 when I left for college. (This cup, by the way, has become my good luck charm now for more than 50 years, and it travels with me everywhere). What is more, I lost all my clothes, and was almost naked, with nothing left but a ripped Speedo bathing suit.

We made it to shore, and even managed to salvage the canoe and its motor, and after a few hours were able to flag down a passing boat, which pulled us back to Manaus harbor. None the worse for the wear, but with a hugely bruised ego and budget, I proceeded to buy new camera equipment and other supplies in Manaus, and we continued our expedition upriver on the mainstream of the Amazon.

Surprisingly, I still have fond memories of this short ill-fated mini-expedition. It was my only opportunity to do fieldwork with Federico Medem, who was such an iconic figure in the history of Neotropical herpetology, and it did result in an important publication redescribing the red-headed Amazon sideneck turtle

I had intended to do my doctoral dissertation research on the uakari monkeys of Amazonia. However, after successfully finding populations of the red, white, and black uakaris, as well as the white-nosed bearded saki monkey, I realized that the logistics of working in the remote flooded forests of Amazonia presented serious difficulties. I estimated that it could take as long as five years to produce the kind of data needed for a quality thesis, and that was just too long. (It would be a decade before another researcher, Brazil's Jose Marcio Ayres, took on the challenge and studied the white uakari for the first time.) I needed to find another place to work on related species.

Fortunately, on my way down to Brazil to start the 1973 Amazon expedition, I had made a short stop once again on Barro Colorado Island. There I met a Dutch botanist named Paul Maas, who had just been to Suriname. Suriname was one of the South American countries that I had skipped on my 1971 South American research tour, and I knew little about it, except that it was still a European colony called Dutch Guiana. Paul told me he had seen good population of bearded saki monkeys (*Chiropotes sagulatus*) in the Raleighvallen-Voltzberg Nature Reserve in central Suriname, which really piqued my interest. This species is closely related to the uakaris and in the same genus as the white-nosed saki, and apparently the logistics of getting to the site were much easier than reaching the central Brazilian Amazon.

As a result, after spending a year and a half in South America, including the 1973 expedition, the 1974 expedition to rediscover the Peruvian yellow-tailed woolly monkey with Hernando de Macedo-Ruiz, and miscellaneous other projects in Colombia and Panama, I returned to Harvard at the end of 1974 and explained to my adviser Irven DeVore that I was going to start all over again with a new country. He was a bit taken aback, but wonderfully understanding and supportive, and told me to just get on with it. I will always be grateful that he was so tolerant of my idiosyncrasies and really just let me do my own thing.

In March 1975, I made my first trip to Dutch Guiana (it would not become Suriname until November of that same year), and was received by Dr. Joop Schulz, director of the STINASU, the Foundation for Nature Conservation in Suriname. When Joop met me, he was a bit shocked, saying that he thought he was going to receive an old distinguished German professor, not a 25-year-old kid. However, to his credit, he was enormously supportive and opened every possible door for me to carry out my work. He arranged for me to visit the Raleighvallen-Voltzberg Nature Reserve, where I easily located a population of bearded saki monkey, as well as populations of the 7 other species of Suriname monkeys. This was ideal, and I resolved to study not just a single monkey species, but to do a synecological study of all eight species to see how they divided up the resources of the forest.

That project kept me busy from 1975 to 1977, based in the Voltzberg area of the reserve. I was also very fortunate in that a young Dutch primatologist by the name of Marc van Roosmalen was also interested in working in Suriname. He contacted me shortly after my 1975 trip, and in 1976 we met for the first time in Suriname. Marc had never been to Suriname before and had never seen a wild primate, but he was amazingly well prepared. Not only had he kept spider monkeys as pets in the Netherlands, he had also written the first-ever detailed catalogue of all the fruits of Suriname, using the collections of several Dutch universities and herbaria. The result was that I had a walking encyclopedia of Suriname botany working with me throughout my thesis research, someone who could identify plant species from the seeds in primate feces found on the forest floor and who had an astounding knowledge of plant-animal interactions. Marc focused on the black spider monkey (*Ateles paniscus*), while I studied the interrelationships of all eight Suriname species and also traveled to villages of the Amerindian and African-origin Maroon peoples to see how they utilized primates and other species in their daily lives.

My findings from that major 1973 Amazon expedition were shared with several key conservation leaders of the International Union for Conservation of Nature (IUCN) Species Survival Commission (SSC): notably Sir Peter Scott, who was then the chair of SSC; Dr. F. Wayne King of the Bronx Zoo; Dr. Thomas Lovejoy of the World Wildlife Fund–US, himself a specialist in Amazonia; and Dr. Barbara Harrisson, the first chair of the Primate Specialist Group, which had its origins in the early 1960s and was first led by Dr. Harrisson. Barbara had spent a good part of her life in Sarawak, on the island of Borneo, and became interested in orangutans, establishing the first-ever rescue center for these animals in the 1960s. I first met her in 1970 when she was a visiting professor at Cornell University, and we developed a close relationship. Later, when I decided to carry out my doctoral research on the monkeys of Suriname, I continued to share my experiences with these people, and to make recommendations to them as to how the Primate Specialist Group could become more effective, the three chairs following Barbara in the late 1960s and early 1970s having not been particularly active.

To my surprise and delight, the leadership of SSC asked me to take over the chair position of the Primate Specialist Group in early 1977, before I had even finished my thesis. I was really surprised when I received their letter inviting me. I was in Suriname at the time and couldn't believe that they would hand this great responsibility over to a 27-year-old kid. But I was absolutely delighted and committed to engaging in this task with every fiber of my body. I have now chaired this group for 43 years—the longest-running chair in the network of the Species Survival Commission—and have built a large and effective primate conservation community over that time.

I completed my thesis, an 800-page compendium that was approved by my advisers on November 7, 1977, a day before my 28th birthday. I immediately began work on the first-ever Global Strategy for Primate Conservation, which was completed in about three months in early 1978. This 300-page document, prepared with the help of a couple of dozen early primatologists, identified priority projects for primates around the world, providing the first comprehensive overview of what was needed to ensure the survival of every single living species of primate. This early strategy laid the groundwork and set a precedent for dozens of other primate action plans that would follow.

As a result of the Global Strategy, I was hired by Tom Lovejoy at the World Wildlife Fund–US (WWF-US) to continue my work as chair of the Primate Specialist Group and also to carry out a major survey of the primates of the Atlantic Forest region of Brazil that I had first visited in 1971. Tom and I first met in 1975, when I was a graduate student at Harvard. He had first learned of my existence in 1973, shortly after taking over as vice president at WWF-US. One of the first things he found on his desk when he arrived at his new job was a carbon copy of a long, handwritten report on my abovementioned Amazon expedition. Xerox machines not being readily available at that time, I had made about 20 carbon copies of this handwritten report and sent them to every specialist I could think of, including Tom's immediate predecessor at WWF-US. Tom read the letter and was pleased to find a kindred spirit interested in Amazonia (there weren't many of us at that time). We made contact by mail, and eventually met at Harvard. Tom wanted me to work on Amazonian primates, but I told him I thought the Atlantic Forest, then already down to only about 10% of its original extent, was a more urgent priority. He agreed, and that grant followed shortly thereafter.

Although these two projects fully funded my work, WWF-US was still very small at that time and didn't want to take on any new employees. As a result, Tom asked Dr. F. Wayne King at the Bronx Zoo, one of the people responsible for appointing me as the chair of the Primate Specialist Group, whether he could take me on as a staff member. Wayne agreed to become my sponsor, and I became attached to the Bronx Zoo, although I set up my office at the State University of New York at Stony Brook, on Long Island, where my closest friend from Harvard Graduate School of Arts and Sciences, Dr. John Fleagle, had just become a professor. That also saved on office costs, since Stony Brook gave me free office space and made me an adjunct assistant professor. During that year and a half working for the Bronx Zoo, I carried out a number of expeditions, especially my first-ever trip to Southeast Asia, where I visited Thailand, Peninsular Malaysia, Sabah, Sarawak, Brunei, Kalimantan, Sumatra, and Java to learn more of the status of primates there. This was also a key trip in the development of my career and included a face-to-face encounter with a wild tiger in Khao Yai National Park in Thailand on my first-ever day in a Southeast Asian forest. But that is another story.

In the latter part of 1979, Wayne King left the Bronx Zoo to take the position of director at the Florida State Museum at the University of Florida, Gainesville. Wayne had given me free rein in my position, and I was very sad to see him go. He was replaced by none other than George Schaller, another of our Indianapolis Prize winners, as head of what was then called the Center for Field Studies at the Bronx Zoo. I was excited by this, since George was already famous for his studies of the mountain gorilla, the Indian tiger, the Serengeti lion, and the Pantanal jaguar, and was about to embark on the first-ever study of the giant panda. (Just as an aside, I had actually written to Sir Peter Scott earlier that year, offering my services to carry out that first study of the giant panda; fortunately, they made a good choice and awarded that honor to George instead.) However, on my first day with George at the zoo, he gave me a large pile of proposals to read and analyze and said that this would be my job over the next few years. I informed him that I already had a grant from Tom Lovejoy at WWF-US to carry out a large-scale survey of primates and protected areas in the Atlantic Forest region of eastern Brazil and would soon be embarking on that. George's response was "What for?" My immediate reaction was that this wasn't going to work. Back in those days, and even now, I am first and foremost a field man. I have avoided office bureaucracy as much as possible throughout my career (although some has been necessary in the positions that I have occupied), and I certainly wasn't going to start being an office bureaucrat at age 29, just as I was about to start my first major long-term field study.

I immediately called Tom Lovejoy and asked if he could take me on at WWF-US. After all, they were paying my salary, so why not have me as a staff member. He consulted with Russell Train, who had recently taken over as president of WWF-US. Russ was a key figure in conservation at that time, having already served under Richard Nixon as chair of the Council on Environmental Quality from 1970 to 1973 and second administrator of the Environmental Protection Agency, from 1973 to 1977. Fortunately, Russ was a man of quick decisions, and without hesitation he said, why don't we just hire Mittermeier and make him the head of a new primate program. Problem resolved, and I will remain eternally grateful to both Russ and Tom for opening that door for me. Not only that, this new WWF-US Primate Program included the first-ever Primate Action Fund. It started at only $35,000 for the first year, a tiny amount by today's standards, but a very important resource back then, in that it immediately enabled me to start implementing projects identified in our Global Strategy for Primate Conservation.

I then had to call Bill Conway, longtime director of the Bronx Zoo and without a doubt the greatest visionary in the history of the zoo world, and tell him of my decision. Bill was really the first zoo director to fully recognize that zoos were more than just entertainment centers. They had a key role in saving species in captivity and in the wild, and he was instrumental in creating the largest zoo-based field conservation program in the world, which now, together with four zoos and an aquarium, is the Wildlife Conservation Society. I called Bill from England, where I was attending a meeting. He was very disappointed, since he had welcomed me at the zoo just a year earlier, but I think he understood. I also had to inform George, which was equally difficult, since I have always considered him the greatest large mammal field biologist that ever lived, and someone whose accomplishments will never be surpassed. But I think that he also understood, and certainly we remain friends to the present day. What is more, one of the greatest honors for me in receiving the Indianapolis Prize was that I am now part of an elite group that includes George.

My position at WWF-US lasted for a decade, from 1979 to 1989, and enabled me to develop a very strong basis for our global primate conservation efforts. It also included a strong focus on Brazil's Atlantic Forest region, on Madagascar, which I first visited in 1984, and on Suriname, building on the work that I had done during my thesis. Since Brazil and Madagascar are the first and second countries in the world in terms of primate diversity, these efforts dovetailed very well with my interests in primates.

Over the years, we have accomplished a great deal for primates, establishing an active global network of more than 700 members that is now divided into eight regional sections, with two special sections for great apes and gibbons and one thematic section on human-primate conflicts. We are the IUCN Red List authority for primates, which means that we are responsible for assessing the conservation status of these animals on an ongoing basis and determining which are critically endangered or vulnerable, and which are of less immediate concern. Using this information and building on that early model of the Global Strategy for Primate Conservation, we have produced dozens of action plans for regions and for particular species over the past four decades. We also publish a major journal, *Primate Conservation,* and four regional journal/newsletters, and have produced a wide variety of primate educational materials over the years, all of which have formed the basis of dozens of conservation campaigns and fundraising efforts.

Our international fundraising efforts have also been quite successful. As an example, the Margot Marsh Biodiversity Foundation, established in 1996, is entirely dedicated to primate conservation. To date, it has generated more than $14 million for primate conservation projects worldwide. In 2016 we received full funding for our Action Plan for Lemur Conservation from an anonymous donor, the first time that an IUCN Action Plan has been funded in its entirely (~$8 million, in partnership with IUCN's Save our Species Program). Our Primate Action Fund—the one first created in 1980 when I was at the World Wildlife Fund and continued to the present day with funding from the Margot Marsh Biodiversity Foundation—has by now supported well over 2,000 small primate projects around the world. Many of these have provided early support for what are today some of the greatest leaders in primate conservation. One of the best examples is Pat Wright, another of our Indianapolis Prize winners, to whom we gave a small grant to look for the greater bamboo lemur (*Prolemur simus*) in 1985. Not only did Pat rediscover the long-missing greater bamboo lemur, she also discovered a new species, the golden bamboo lemur (*Hapalemur aureus*), which led to her lifelong commitment to the Ranomafana region of southeastern Madagascar.

A lot of my success in primate conservation has been made possible by an amazing team of people that I have had working with me for a very long time—some of them for 40 years or more. These include Bill Konstant, who I first met in 1980 at the State University of New York at Stony Brook and who has been instrumental in the success of many primate endeavors, as well as having created zoo conservation programs at the Philadelphia Zoo and the Houston Zoo that continue as models to the present day. Bill currently serves as an adviser to two of the most important species conservation funds, the Margot Marsh Biodiversity Foundation and the Mohamed bin Zayed Species Conservation Fund. Dr. Anthony Rylands, who I first met through correspondence in 1976, is currently one of our deputy chairs in the Primate Specialist Group and also director of the Global Wildlife Conservation Primate Program. He is the world's leading authority on Neotropical primates and the go-to person for everyone in the primate conservation community for information on primate taxonomy and Red List conservation status. Like me, Anthony, a British national, has close ties to Brazil, having spent 23 years there studying primates.

Stephen Nash, another Brit, the greatest primate illustrator of all time, has illustrated all of our books and field guides and has produced the logos and a wide variety of educational material for dozens of primate programs and organizations. I first met Stephen in 1981 and brought him to the United States to begin work on primate field guides that continues to the present day. Jill Lucena, who first began working with me in 2000 while at Conservation

International, has been an essential part of our team, keeping us organized and distributing our wide variety of publications around the world. And last, but certainly not least, is Ella Outlaw, who first started working with me as a temporary secretary in 1988 and has been with me ever since. Ella does everything from organizing my complicated travel schedule to managing grants to maintaining our primate conservation network to keeping the rest of our team fully connected. Without her, all that we have created would simply cease to function.

Over the past 15 years, I have also been promoting the concept of primate-watching and primate life-listing, following the bird-watching model. Birdwatching has become a global industry worth billions of dollars, with nearly 50 million people in the United States alone identifying as birders. My son John is a top-notch birder, and I became incredibly impressed with how interconnected the global birding community actually is. I decided that we should try to create something along the same lines for primates, to stimulate greater interest in these amazing animals and to encourage people to visit remote corners of the tropical world to see them in the wild. Aside from developing a broader constituency for primate and tropical forest conservation, this kind of ecotourism also contributes resources and creates livelihoods for local people in priority areas for primates. We have been producing many materials to support such activities, including the field guides and pocket guides mentioned below. I have also tried to develop models for community-based primate-watching in several places, most notably in Madagascar, where we have a lemur-watching app nearly ready to launch.

Not only have I promoted the concept of primate-watching and primate life-listing, I have also practiced it. I love listing (it's really just another form of collecting), and I have been keeping lists of things I have seen and done since childhood. After nearly 50 years of observing primates in the wild, I am almost certain that I have seen more primate species and subspecies than anyone else (approaching 400 at this time). What is more, as of April 2019, with observations of the kipunji (*Rungwecebus kipunji*) in southern Tanzania, I became the first person ever to see all 80 genera of primates in the wild. I should also note that all of the first sightings of these 80 genera came without the assistance of radio-tracking, camera-trapping, or other technological aids, just good old-fashioned slogging through the forests with local guides and fellow primatologists. Special for me was the fact that both my son John, the inspiration for primate-watching, and my longtime friend Hiromi Tada were with me on this special occasion.

Although many primates are considered threatened at this point, we have not with certainty lost a single primate taxon in well over a century, the only larger group of mammals that has not lost at least one species or subspecies during that period. An enormous amount of work remains to be done to ensure a zero-extinction objective for primates, but we believe that our efforts have been successful in establishing primates as a priority group for conservation worldwide

The other group of animals that has always interested me is the turtles, particularly the tortoises and freshwater turtles. My interest in turtles goes back to my earliest childhood, to my days on Long Island, when I collected and kept common species like painted turtles, box turtles, snapping turtles, and musk turtles in my backyard. When I got to Harvard graduate school, although I was officially in the Department of Anthropology, I immediately made contact with Professor Ernest E. Williams, then the curator of herpetology at Harvard's world-renowned Museum of Comparative Zoology. Although Ernest's interests had shifted to the *Anolis* lizards of the Caribbean, he was one of the greatest turtle researchers of his time and still quite interested in these animals. We immediately hit it off, and he was kind enough to offer me better office space than was available in the Department of Anthropology. I took him up on his offer, based myself in the museum from 1971 to 1978, and worked on many different turtle projects while there, including the description of three new turtle species, all with Anders Rhodin, one of which we named after Ernest.

Back in 1979, I led the process to create a separate IUCN/SSC specialist group for the tortoises and freshwater turtles, which make up the vast majority of the chelonians. Up until that time, there had only been three IUCN Species Survival Commission Specialist Groups dealing with reptiles and amphibians: one for crocodilians, one for marine turtles, and one for all other reptiles and amphibians. Given the increasing information coming in on the plight of tortoises and freshwater turtles around the world, I came to the conclusion that we really needed to have a separate focus on them as well. As a result of discussions with leading turtle and tortoise specialists, and with the leadership of the SSC, the decision was made to create two new groups, one for tortoises and another for freshwater turtles. These two got off to strong starts, and then were merged a few years later. Over the past 40 years, I have worked with five chairs of this group and have been on its executive committee for that entire period.

In the early part of 2001, I was involved in the creation of the Turtle Survival Alliance, which actually grew out of a turtle rescue effort carried out under what was then a Conservation International (CI) Turtle Program, and in the creation of a CI-based Turtle Conservation Fund, which now resides at Global Wildlife Conservation. I have also been a long-term adviser of the Turtle Conservancy, another major turtle conservation organization, and now serve on its board. Almost all of my work on turtles has been carried out with my close friend and fellow Dartmouth College graduate, Dr. Anders Rhodin. Anders has been one of the great leaders of the turtle conservation movement: he has served as the chair of our Tortoise and Freshwater Turtle Specialist Group from 2005 to 2012, founded the journal *Chelonian Conservation and Biology*, and produced some of the community's most influential and fundamental turtle publications. What is even more amazing about Anders is that he did all of this work on turtles while also being a full-time highly respected orthopedic surgeon.

In 2018, just a month before receiving the Indianapolis Prize, I was honored to receive the Behler Prize for Excellence in Chelonian Conservation from a consortium that includes the Turtle Survival Alliance and the Turtle Conservancy and is named after my good friend the late John Behler, the longtime curator of herpetology at the Bronx Zoo, and chair of the SSC Tortoise and Freshwater Turtle Group from 1990 to 2000 and co-chair, with Anders Rhodin, from 2000 to 2005. The Turtle Conservancy's Behler Conservation Center in Ojai, California, is also named after him.

The marine turtles were under a separate specialist group from the very beginning. That group was also under my program at Conservation International for nearly a decade, and is currently chaired by another close friend, Rod Mast, formerly of CI and now the president of the Oceanic Society, the country's oldest marine conservation organization. Although my role in turtle conservation has been more behind the scenes than my work with primates, I am also quite pleased with what I have been able to accomplish for this equally amazing and highly threatened group of animals.

Through my work with these Species Survival Commission specialist groups, I have developed a long-term relationship with the IUCN that dates back to 1974. In 1982, I was invited to be on the steering committee of the entire Species Survival Commission, the leadership group within this 9,000-member commission, and I continue in that role as well. My overall work with the Species Survival Commission was recognized in 2008 with the Peter Scott Award, the highest honor bestowed by the commission on its members. In 2004, I decided to run for higher office within IUCN, and was elected to the IUCN Council, the governing body of the entire union, and served two four-year terms on the council, the second as one of IUCN's vice presidents (2008–2012). Upon stepping down as a councillor in 2012, I was made a lifetime honorary member.

In line with my fascination with the diversity of life in all its manifestations, and going back to my early background in taxonomy, I have always been interested in the discovery of species new to science and in rediscovering those that have been "lost." This has been a focus of my own work and of projects that I have helped to support through various funding mechanisms. This interest really began with some of those earliest abovementioned expeditions in Amazonia and the Andes in 1973 and 1974, when I was the first outsider to see the three species of uakaris in the Brazilian Amazon in 1973 and when I rediscovered the Peruvian yellow-tailed woolly monkey in the northern Peruvian Andes in 1974. Thus far, I have been involved in the description of 22 species new to science (three turtles, seven lemurs, four tarsiers, and eight monkeys), with several others in the works, and eight have been named after me by colleagues (two lemurs, a saki monkey, three frogs, a lizard, and an ant—the ant being named after me by none other than the abovementioned Edward O. Wilson of Harvard).

I was also heavily involved in the establishment of Conservation International's Rapid Assessment Program (RAP) in 1990, which continues to the present day. This highly innovative program was aimed at creating a mechanism to quickly assess the conservation status of remote and poorly known parts of the tropical world, recognizing that we know very little about the biodiversity of most of these regions and that we can't wait decades for long-term research to be conducted. We needed a quick and dirty approach to gathering data, and we decided this could best be done by using the greatest living field biologists. RAP was initially focused on tropical rain forests but later expanded to marine and freshwater systems as well. The brainchild of the late Nobel Prize–winning physicist Murray Gell-Mann (also an avid birder), the late Ted Parker (probably the greatest birder of all time), and CI cofounder Spencer Beebe, this program was started with support from the MacArthur Foundation. RAP has now carried out more than 125 expeditions to remote corners of the tropical world. These expeditions have laid the groundwork for the establishment of many new protected areas, from Madidi National Park in Bolivia to the Raja Ampat Marine Reserves in Papua, Indonesia, and have resulted in the discovery of more than 1,500 species new to science.

The organization for which I currently work, Global Wildlife Conservation, now also has a program on lost species, a global effort to rediscover animals and plants that have not been seen in decades and sometimes in more than a century. This exciting program has thus far been successful in rediscovering six species, with more in the works, and has attracted a great deal of media attention.

I am also particularly grateful to the leadership of Global Wildlife Conservation, notably founder and CEO Dr. Wes Sechrest, president Dr. Don Church, and board chair Brian Sheth, for their belief in me and for bringing me on a chief conservation officer in December 2017, to follow my species conservation dreams in this latest stage of my career.

One of my most important contributions to conservation has been a strong focus on priority-setting in biodiversity conservation. I developed the concept of "megadiversity countries" back in 1986 and presented it at the first conference on biodiversity in that same year. (This conference, organized by Edward O. Wilson and held at the Smithsonian Institution, really marked the point at which the term "biodiversity" entered the conservation vocabulary, although it had been coined a few years earlier.) The megadiversity country concept simply recognizes that, of the roughly 200 nations on Earth, a mere 18 are responsible for two-thirds of all global biodiversity—terrestrial, freshwater, and marine. Brazil and Indonesia top the list, with Colombia in third, and with some developed countries such as the United States and France also being among the highest global priorities. This concept, though not central to global conservation priority-setting, has been used quite often, especially by some of the countries on the list, and it even led to the formation of a Group of Like-Minded Megadiverse Countries within the Convention on Biological Diversity (CBD).

However, by far the most important priority-setting concept over the past quarter-century has been the biodiversity hotspots. This one was created by British ecologist Norman Myers in 1988, in a paper in which he recognized 10 hotspots. Based on feedback from several specialists, myself included, he published another paper in 1990, increasing the total to 18. As soon as I saw this concept in 1988, I fell in love with it, and fully adopted it. I tried to make it a central focus for WWF-US, without success, and that was the major factor precipitating my move from WWF-US to Conservation International in 1989. In contrast to WWF-US, Conservation International, and its cofounder Peter Seligmann, recognized the great value of the hotspots concept, and for the next 20 years it became the strategy for CI, driving the geographic placement of our programs and serving as the basis of our fundraising activities.

Over the course of the next 20 years, CI fully embraced the hotspots concept; we updated it several times, and we used it as a basis for two very successful billion-dollar fundraising campaigns, the Campaign to Save the Hotspots and A Future for Life. In addition to these campaigns, the hotspots also became the rationale for the very successful Critical Ecosystem Partnership Fund, a multi-institutional fund based at CI and focused on providing support to civil society organizations working in about two-thirds of the hotspots. This partnership involves the World Bank, the Global Environment Facility, the government of France, the government of Japan, the European Union, and CI, with the MacArthur Foundation providing major support in the early stages, and with several other foundations now having joined as partners. To date, it has funded 2,339 civil society organizations in 24 hotspots, for a total to date of $237 million in investments.

In three books and a number of peer-reviewed publications, we increased the number of hotspots to 25 and then 34. Subsequent additions have increased the current total to 36, the two most recent additions being the forests of Eastern Australia and the southeastern coastal plain of the United States. Among the best known and most emblematic of the hotspots are the above-mentioned Atlantic Forest region of Brazil, the amazing island of Madagascar (arguably the highest priority biodiversity hotspot of all), Mesoamerica, the Caribbean, the tropical Andes, the Cape Floristic Province of South Africa, Southwest Australia, the Mediterranean, the Philippines, Sundaland (western Indonesia and Malaysia), Wallacea (eastern Indonesia), and many others.

The biodiversity hotspots focus on heavily affected areas of high diversity and endemism that are now down to only about 10% of their original extent. As a complement to the hotspots, I came up with the concept of high-biodiversity wilderness areas, also in 1988. This complementary concept also concentrates on areas of high diversity and endemism, but looks at the opposite end of the spectrum, focusing on a handful that are still largely intact, often with 80%–90% or more of their original area. The most important of these are the vast forests of Amazonia, the Congo forests of Central Africa, and the island of New Guinea. Taken hand in hand with the hotspots, these areas would conserve at least 75% of the planet's terrestrial biodiversity in only about 8% of its land area, and the two concepts should be viewed together as a part of a single strategy.

This wilderness focus has been highlighted in another book, in a series of peer-reviewed publications, and was the basis for the creation of another major fundraising mechanism at CI, the Global Conservation Fund (GCF). This fund was created in 2001 with a gift of $100 million from the Gordon and Betty Moore Foundation and was focused on creating new protected areas in wilderness areas, both terrestrial and marine, and in hotspots. It has supported the creation or expansion of 135 new parks and reserves totaling 81 million hectares (an area about twice the size of the state of California). Noteworthy among these are the 11.5-million-hectare Kayapo Indigenous Territory in the southern part of Brazilian Amazonia and the enormous 40 million hectare Phoenix Islands Marine Protected Area in the Pacific Island nation of Kiribati, the deepest and largest World Heritage site on Earth.

Starting with my early interest in the jungles of Tarzan and my later interest in primates (90% of which occur in tropical forests), I have spent a large part of my career visiting, studying, and helping to protect tropical forests around the world. My strongest emphasis has been in the Neotropics, where I began working in 1970, with a special focus on the Atlantic Forest of Brazil and the Guiana Shield region of Amazonia. Since 1984, I have also developed a very strong focus on the unique island continent of Madagascar. But I have not been limited to these areas, and have carried out research, seen firsthand, and supported projects in almost every tropical forest country. I continue to work to find mechanisms to establish new parks, reserves, and indigenous territories, and to create funding mechanisms (e.g., trust funds) to ensure their long-term viability.

In Brazil, my early work in the Atlantic Forest Biodiversity Hotspot, which began in 1971, became particularly intense in the 1980s and 1990s and was instrumental in placing this distinct forest region on the global priority map along with the much larger Amazonian forest. Prior to that, it had been largely overlooked, but began to be recognized internationally when I had it included in an international WWF Campaign on Tropical Forests in 1981. My work in the Guiana Shield, and particularly Suriname, has established this northeastern portion of Amazonia as the most intact rain forest region remaining on Earth, and has resulted in the

establishment of very significant new protected areas and indigenous lands. Among these are the 1.6 million-hectare Central Suriname Nature Reserve, created in 1998, recognized as a World
Heritage site in 2000, and now with a $16 million trust fund; the
600,000-hectare Wai Wai Community-Owned Conservation Area
in southern Guyana, established in 2006; the 611,000-hectare
Kanuku Mountains Protected Area in central Guyana, created in
2011; and the 7.2-million-hectare Southern Suriname Conservation Corridor, a huge indigenous reserve for the Trio and Wayana
Indians in the far south of Suriname that was declared by the indigenous people in 2015. Our work in Guyana over a quarter-
century was responsible for the passage in 2011 of the first protected areas legislation for that country; for the Guyana Protected
Areas Trust Fund, now at $8 million; and for the preparation of a
Low Carbon Development Strategy, which led directly to a gift of
$250 million from the Norwegian government.

In Madagascar, I was responsible for the WWF-US Madagascar
Program from 1984 to 1989, established the Conservation International Madagascar Program in 1990, and have been using lemurs as flagship species and symbols for the unique biodiversity
of that amazing island ever since my first visit there in 1984. In
2003, I was very much involved in convincing then-president Marc
Ravalomanana to commit to tripling protected-area coverage, a
process that has continued to the present day through three suc-
cessive governments; and in raising the funds to support this process, a Madagascar Biodiversity Trust Fund that now has more
than $50 million in it. I also helped to get UNESCO to recognize
the protected areas of Madagascar's eastern rain forests as a series of World Heritage sites. Last but not least, I have led many donor trips to Madagascar, created a wide variety of media opportunities, and supported a wide range of in-country and international
NGOs to work on lemurs, tortoises, and other Malagasy species
through a variety of grant mechanisms, from the Critical Ecosys-

tem Partnership Fund and the Global Conservation Fund to the most recent, the abovementioned $8 million fund to implement our Lemur Conservation Action Plan.

In late 2008, I was about to write a paper titled "Madagascar: An Incipient Success Story," because of the success of the tripling of the commitment by President Ravalomanana. Then, all of a sudden, there was a coup in which the mayor of the capital city of Antananarivo, a 34-year-old former disc jockey named Andry Rajoelina, toppled the Ravalomanana government and declared himself president. He remained in power until 2013, but his government did not receive recognition from any country, and most foreign assistance was suspended. There also ensued a period of lawlessness, with an increase in the illegal wildlife trade and large-scale illegal logging of valuable rosewood from several protected areas in the northeast. A huge setback.

A new president, Hery Rajaonarimampianina, was elected in 2013. He brought back foreign investment but was otherwise largely ineffectual. Elections were held again at the end of 2018, with both Rajoelina and Ravalomanana emerging from a pack of several dozen candidates to contest a runoff election. We thought that Ravalomanana would win, but he did not. Rajoelina won with a decisive majority. At first, I was inclined to despair, but then reality set in. We would have to deal with Rajoelina as president for the next five years, and quite possibly much longer, so why not try to make the best of it? With this in mind, I arranged to meet with the new president in January 2019, just four days before his inauguration. To my surprise, this meeting turned out to be quite positive, and we have maintained contact since that time; I am guardedly optimistic that President Rajoelina will see biodiversity as a major underpinning of his country's future development strategy.

Conservation in Madagascar continues to be a major challenge, and success is still a long way off. But at least we have put in place some resources, and international interest in the country and its very special biodiversity is at an all-time high. However, from a global perspective, what this situation clearly demonstrates is that there are *no final victories in conservation*. Even when we think we have achieved great things, the slightest change in politics can set us back years or even decades. Another example is the recent election of President Jair Bolsonaro in Brazil, whose policies could negate five decades of progress in that critically important megadiversity country. We must always remain vigilant, and recognize that wherever we choose to work, we are in it for the long haul.

Over the course of my career, I have also paid a great deal of attention to indigenous peoples, in recognition of the fact that they are perhaps our most important partners in efforts to protect more of the natural world. I have visited dozens of tribal communities around the world and have had particularly close relationships with quite a few, from the Trio Indians of southern Suriname and the Saramaccaner, Matawai, and Aucaner Maroons of central Suriname to the Kayapó of the Brazilian Amazon. I have engaged them in a variety of conservation endeavors, have worked to improve livelihoods, and have placed special emphasis on protecting, expanding, and creating indigenous territories, the latest of which is the abovementioned 7.2-million-hectare Southern Suriname Conservation Corridor with the Trio and Wayana people of that country. In addition, I have published on the strong connections between biodiversity and human cultural diversity, demonstrating how the highest priority areas for each overlap globally at a remarkably high level.

At a broader scale, beyond my focus on species and protected areas, I have also been very much involved in promoting nature-based solutions to climate change for more than a decade, with a particular emphasis on tropical forests. We estimate that protection and restoration of tropical forests represents at least 30% of the solution to climate change and possibly 50% or more, and that this is clearly the most cost-effective and immediate remedy. Although less than 2% of the investment in climate change currently goes to nature-based solutions, there is increasing interest in this approach, especially after the Paris Agreement in December 2015. Together with several colleagues, we worked early on to promote the concept of "avoided deforestation," now better known as REDD (Reduction in Emissions from Deforestation and Degradation) and were instrumental in putting the "+" in REDD+, highlighting the importance of biodiversity. In particular, we have pushed the very significant role of the high forest cover, low deforestation rate (HFLD) countries such as Suriname, Guyana, and Gabon, which have been largely overlooked in those global discussions that have highlighted the importance of REDD+. This dovetails very nicely with my long-term focus on the biodiversity hotspots and the high-biodiversity wilderness areas, since wilderness areas like Amazonia, the Congo forests, and the island of New Guinea are where much of the tropical forest carbon currently exists and needs to be protected, and the hotspots are where the vast majority of the restoration needs to take place, building out from those core areas that still remain.

As I look back over the course of my career, I see a number of accomplishments of which I am particularly proud. In particular, I think that my work on several major groups of species, notably primates and turtles, have been transformational, and I believe that this impact should be sustainable over the long term. Beyond these particular species groups, I believe that I have also had an important impact on biodiversity in general, through my role in creating and popularizing priority-setting concepts like the biodiversity hotspots, high-biodiversity wilderness areas, and megadiversity countries, through my work on protecting tropical forests in key regions, and through the establishment of funding mechanisms to support others in their critically important efforts. What is more, I have always made a major effort to get the word out and reach a wide variety of audiences through publications of various kinds. Indeed, my list of publications, now well over 750 (and rap-idly approaching Robert Mertens's 800+), includes peer-reviewed scientific papers, articles in popular magazines, and more than 40 books. What is more, I am doing my best to make a generational shift and start using the power of social media as well. A list of my books and several of my key publications is provided below in the Literature Cited section.

Last but certainly not least, over the years, I have managed to have some semblance of a personal life as well, in spite of my in-tense travel schedule that usually has me flying at least 100 times and visiting at least 20 countries every single year for the past 5 de-cades. I have been married twice to very fine women, first to Isa-bel Constable from Cambridge, Massachusetts, who I first met on a Harvard Museum tour to Suriname in 1979. We were together until 1987 and had one son. Isabel is a committed conservationist who travels the world, loves nature in all its manifestations, and is a gifted writer. I met my second wife Cristina when she was working for Conservation International in Mexico. She picked me up at the airport in Mexico City, and it was love at first sight. We were together from 1991 to 2011 and had two children. She has become a world-class photographer, has a conservation organ-ization called Sea Legacy based in British Columbia, and is a master communicator, with 1.3 million followers on Instagram. Indeed, these days, upon meeting me for the first time, people are apt to ask, "Are you related to Cristina Mittermeier?" Cristina and I continue to work closely together, producing one book per year in the long-running Cemex series on nature conservation.

As for my children, I am particularly proud that I have been able to instill in them a strong, lifelong commitment to conservation and to have all three pursue careers in conservation. My son John, Isabel's son, is now 35 and just completed his doctorate at Oxford. He has become a world-class ornithologist and has traveled to more than 120 countries to follow his passion. My second son,

Michael, Cristina's son, is now 28 and finishing his undergraduate studies at the University of South Florida. He started life as a herpetologist but has now become an accomplished specialist in tropical plants, notably aroids, bromeliads, orchids, and ferns. He has been to more than 80 countries pursuing his interests. My daughter Juliana, my second child with Cristina, is now 24, and is currently studying anthropology at the University of Victoria in Canada. She has been to some 40 countries, and, at age 12, became the youngest member of the family to travel to all 7 continents.

I was often an absentee father, but fortunately my children put up with my crazy schedule and adapted to it very well. What is more, I never told my children what to study, I just exposed them to as much of the world as possible through multiple international trips and visits to zoos, museums, botanical gardens, and aquaria from their earliest days. I also provided hands-on experience for them with many pets, mostly reptiles and amphibians, which enabled them to be in direct contact with animals every day. They then figured out what they wanted to do on their own.

What I always told my children, and what I recommend to any young person who asks, is that you have to pursue your dreams. And your dreams have to be yours and not someone else's, not those of your parents, not those of your friends or teachers—just yours and yours alone. What is more, don't let obstacles and setbacks get in your way, don't even recognize them as obstacles but only as learning opportunities. Always remain positive and optimistic, be respectful of others, and count on a little luck from time to time, because luck can be a key ingredient. I have always followed this philosophy and view of life, and I think that my children are doing so as well.

To be sure, our planet is facing enormous environmental challenges, and will continue to do so for the remainder of this century and perhaps beyond. However, in spite of the many threats that our living Earth and its multitude of species face, we cannot

Dr. Russ Mittermeier with a Madagascar big-headed sideneck turtle (*Erymnochelys madagascariensis*) in the Morondava area, southern Madagascar, 1985.

descend into gloom and doom. We must learn from our many successes and from our failures, and develop strategies that both improve the quality of life for people around the world and simultaneously benefit, protect, and preserve the other species, ecosystems, and ecological processes on which our own quality of life ultimately depends. After all is said and done, we are still the only planet in the entire universe where we know with certainty that life exists; we are part of that intricate, interconnected, and truly unique web of life; and we should do everything possible to make sure that this fragile web remains functional, fully intact, and as amazing and as diverse as it was when our own species emerged onto the scene. There never has been and likely never will be another planet like ours. Let's work together to make sure that it does not lose any of the endless manifestations of life that make it so unique.

Further Reading

Coimbra-Filho, A. F., and R. A. Mittermeier, eds. 1981 and 1988. Ecology and Behavior of Neotropical Primates. Vols. 1 and 2. Brazilian Academy of Sciences.

Gorenflo, L. J., et al. 2012. Co-occurrence of Linguistic and Biological Diversity in Biodiversity Hotspots and High Biodiversity Wilderness Areas. PNAS 109 (21): 8032–8037.

Mittermeier, R. A., P. R. Gil, and C. G. Mittermeier. 1997. Megadiversity: Earth's Biologically Wealthiest Nations. CEMEX and Agrupación Sierra Madre.

Mittermeier, R. A., N. Myers, P. G. Robles, and C. G. Mittermeier, eds. 1999. Hotspots: Earth's Biologically Richest and Most Endangered Terrestrial Ecosystems. CEMEX and Agrupación Sierra Madre.

Mittermeier, R. A., et al. 2005. Pantanal: South America's Wetland Jewel. David Bateman.

Mittermeier, R. A., et al. 2007. Las tortugas y los cocodrilianos de los paises andinos del tropico. Bogota, Colombia.

Mittermeier, R. A., et al. 2009. Warfare in Biodiversity Hotspots. Conservation Biology 23 (3): 578–587.

Mittermeier, R. A., et al. 2010. Lemurs of Madagascar. 3rd ed. Conservation International.

Mittermeier, R. A., D. E. Wilson, and A. B. Rylands, eds. 2013. Handbook of the Mammals of the World. Vol. 3. Primates. Lynx Edicions.

Myers, N., et al. 2000. Biodiversity Hotspots for Conservation Priorities. Nature 403:853–858.

THE STEEP AND RUGGED PATHWAY

MICHAEL I. CROWTHER

CEO, Indianapolis Zoological Society (2002–2019)

Chimpanzee
Pan troglodytes

So here's the most arrogant statement you're ever likely to hear from anyone:

I think I know what our species' biggest problem is.

In my opinion, it's our tendency to respond strongly to those things that are right in front of our noses while ignoring challenges and opportunities that are a little way down the road.

Now, I understand why we do this. When we taste something nasty, we spit it out. When it's delicious, we take another bite. When a saber-toothed tiger emerges from around the corner, we immediately return to the trees, but when we spot a bear on the other side of the river, we keep gathering berries.

Unfortunately, this tendency to strongly favor *present utility* over *future utility* has become embedded in our cultures and politics. And, as we have developed greater technological resources, we have also acquired the ability to act so quickly and powerfully that our short-term actions could result in permanent change; in other words, our ability to act has surpassed our ability to think. One of the results of the speed and power of human action is the extinction of other species. The example everyone knows is that of the Dodo.

In his chapter Lessons from the Dodo, 2016 Indianapolis Prize winner Professor Carl Jones reminds us that Dodos disappeared from our planet in 1662. Dodos were, of course, endemic to Mauritius, a 2,000 km² island in the Indian Ocean that was uninhabited by humans until colonized in 1598. Carl's lectures include an image of a 1601 woodcut that illustrates humans applying our technology of the time to harvest Mauritius' abundant resources: fish, timber, and even tortoises, which could be rendered for their oil. On the right side of the woodcut, the first-ever representation of a Dodo shows it—with a symbolism not apparent until later—walking out of the frame.

Mauritius' isolation meant that Dodos had evolved without significant predation, and humans were able to exploit their resulting lack of defenses. Additionally, we were equipped to quickly harvest their forest environment; the combination resulted in the Dodo's complete elimination within 70 years of their first being sighted by people.

A perhaps even more ominous commentary is that their extinction was not recognized for another two hundred years or so. In other words, we didn't understand the risk of our actions for two centuries after it was too late to do anything about it.

I hope that if we had known that our actions in Mauritius would exterminate the species we would have acted differently, but I'm not sure. Dr. Paul R. Ehrlich, the brilliant Stanford biologist who awakened us to the dangers of unchecked human population growth, has written that humans need to "culturally evolve" in response to our ever-growing ability to impact our environment. Without that cultural evolution, the shortsighted actions even of individuals and small groups can quickly result in permanent environmental devastation.

In order to drive cultural change, the thought-leaders and institutions that touch society must move beyond the shiny or scary distractions immediately before us and invest in ethics, policies, and programs that focus on ensuring we have an enriching, wondrous, and joyful future that is capable of sustaining us for generations to come. Whether we want the job or not, we *are* the custodians of the home we inhabit. That responsibility includes adopting a different philosophy toward the harvesting of our planet's resources, with sustainability and biodiversity—its vital factor—trumping appetite.

In Ehrlich's 2002 paper "Human Natures, Nature Conservation, and Environmental Ethics," he wrote that "The key [to environmental sustainability] is finding ways to alter the course of cultural evolution." Awarding the Indianapolis Prize, which celebrates those who succeed in improving the sustainability of species, is an attempt to do that. Our plan was to elevate those who are saving our world's future to the level of popular-culture heroes. If the human world celebrated those who protect the natural world, might not our values shift, too?

In early 2002, I interviewed for the position of president and CEO of the Indianapolis Zoological Society. I'd held the same position at the New Jersey State Aquarium, where brilliant and thoughtful leaders like Brian Duvall, Frank Steslow, and Julie Johnson opened my eyes to the paradigm of first *engaging*, then *enlightening*, and finally *empowering* people in order to change behaviors and improve the sustainability of the natural world.

The search committee that interviewed me was an assemblage of many of the smartest, most seasoned, and most committed leaders of Central Indiana. And Indianapolis was a community that had amazed America with its transition from "Indian*o-place*" to one of the most vibrant, successful, and forward-looking cities in the nation.

The committee pushed, probed, and challenged. I told them, of course, that I knew how to build attendance at the Indianapolis Zoo, but I also said that my primary interest was being part of a new kind of wildlife conservation organization. I was interested helping create a bridge—between the people, demands, and resources of developed nations and the needs and opportunities of the natural world—that would be a tool in Paul Ehrlich's cultural evolution.

They liked the idea. Indianapolis is full of people who are more interested in reality than image, and they like being useful. Then someone asked, "How could we make enough of a difference to actually move the needle? We're a young organization. We don't have massive resources to throw at the challenge."

With no prior thought or existing concept, I blurted out, "Well, we could create the world's most important award program for wildlife conservationists. We could give them a big cash award and develop an exciting and glamorous event and tell their stories in a way that helps change people's paths!"

They hired me anyway.

There are just a few core ideas behind the Indianapolis Prize. First, we know that the human impact on the natural world can't continue its present trajectory: as I write this, the IUCN Red List of Threatened Species includes more than 27,000 species that are threatened with extinction, including 25% of all mammals . . . our own taxonomic class. Second, people tend to identify more closely with other people than with abstract concepts, and we love when heroes and champions elevate us all. Finally, we know that story-telling plays an important role in driving change, and that conservation champions have exciting and compelling adventures and victories to share.

We believe that if we can recognize and reward these conservation champions, providing them with the financial support and public adulation that has been frequently missing from the field, then more people will become *engaged* in their stories, *enlightened* about their challenges and solutions, and *empowered* to join them on their quests in some way. Humans love quests, even if their only participation is as observers. But when we truly believe in a cause, we may find joy and fulfillment even in the face of hardship.

When I was in school in England in the early 1960s, we'd begin every day with a religious service. One of the hymns we sang regularly began,

> Father, hear the prayer we offer:
> Not for ease that prayer shall be,
> But for strength that we may ever
> Live our lives courageously.
>
> Not for ever in green pastures
> Do we ask our way to be;
> But the steep and rugged pathway
> May we tread rejoicingly.

I think that most of the thousand boys in that old school believed that message—that there is more joy in strength than in indolence—and personal experiences during the past fifty years of my life have confirmed it. Even today, most people I know well have found far more real bliss on "steep and rugged pathways" than in their recliners in front of their televisions. Steep and rugged pathways reward effort with actual accomplishment and incredible views, and they remind us that we are far more than "consumers."

I hate the word "consumer," which sounds like a creature whose essence is to eat and defecate! Is that our lot, to slavishly follow that cycle until our degrading bodies can no longer maintain it, leading inexorably to our deaths? Wouldn't our lives be better spent on "rejoicingly treading" those steep and rugged pathways, soaring beyond the limits of our physical shells, experiencing spectacular sights, and becoming explorers, artists, inventors, poets, and champions?

In his book *The Greatest Generation*, Tom Brokaw wrote that those whose lives began around the Great Depression, fought in or supported the Allied efforts in World War II, and drove America's postwar technology and wealth boom did so primarily "because it was the right thing to do," not because they sought personal gain. They trod the steep and rugged pathways that had not been worn smooth by countless others, but that were the only way to a better outcome for all concerned. And they found a far greater understanding of being alive than those who sought simply ease.

There are many *Homo sapiens sapiens* finding their way on our world's less-traveled roads. And some of them—those who save other species along the way—become Indianapolis Prize finalists and winners. Those finalists and winners are not simply people who have tried hard in a noble struggle to defend wildlife. They are true champions who have invested the preparation, thought, resources, and effort to save species, and whose accomplishments have been vetted, verified, and valued by committees of experts.

One of the surprises we've learned about the champion conservationists we've come to know through the Indianapolis Prize is that most of them didn't start out with the critical and objective eyes of scientists. Instead, they tended to begin with a deep interest in animals and the natural world, and they simply wanted to spend as much time as they could getting as close and as immersed as possible.

Of course, that interest turned into caring, and caring turned into responsibility, which resulted in action. First, they began to acquire the tools they needed, particularly knowledge and education. Then they learned how to use the tools well, through years of grunt work, sometimes under the eye of brilliant mentors, but other times in circumstances of stifling frustration. Then they put their tools to work in innovative ways, and with care and skill and persistence they created solutions that benefit us all. The idea of sharing the message that protecting our planet's biodiversity is essential to our own survival, however, was not a concept that all conservationists—including me—immediately embraced.

Most conservationists were forged by the philosophy that every being has an inherent right to exist; that, for example, elephants deserve a place in our world simply because they are what they are. At the 2008 Indianapolis Prize Gala, however, winner Dr. George Schaller challenged "ethical conservationists" with a firm wake-up call.

George Schaller is regarded by many as the most influential field biologist since Charles Darwin: he went to Central Africa to study mountain gorillas before Dian Fossey; he told Jane Goodall, "If you see tool using and hunting, it will have made the whole study worthwhile"; he conducted the definitive study of African lions, establishing a model that is still followed; he was the first Westerner to work with giant pandas in China; he led the protection of vast swaths of South America and Asia.

As he accepted the Indianapolis Prize, however, George told us that, in today's world, if we want a species to continue to find a place, we will need to ascribe "extrinsic value" to it. Essentially, Dr. Schaller said that this crowded, hectic, ambitious, and hungry world will demand that animals answer the question, "What have you done for me lately? How do you contribute to this planet?"

But we have to make some effort, too, especially when it comes to understanding how our planet works.

Our own very survival as a species requires that we understand that we depend on the spectacular *diversity* of animals, plants, and people. This diversity forms a living tapestry that supports and enriches our lives and our spirits in countless interconnected ways. And while the individual threads can be fragile, the fabric they form has astonishing beauty and resiliency. Think of how easy it is to break a single thread, but how, when many threads are woven together, they can create fabrics that gently bring skydivers to Earth, form the shells of boats, and even stop bullets. And what beauty they can bring to our lives, as countless hues reflect and refract light in different ways, often surprising us with glimpses of wondrous natures so different from our own!

The good news is that the Indianapolis Prize conservation champions have found innovative approaches to creating a better future that includes the preservation of life's glorious tapestry. They're not only enthralled by the ethics and aesthetics of conservation but also compelled by the *ecosystem services* the natural world provides. The complex machinery of planet Earth depends on the interplay of ecosystems that provide the supporting, provisioning, regulating, and cultural resources that makes life possible. From water purification and carbon sequestration to raw material extraction and food provision, and even on to climate regulation and artistic inspiration, our health, happiness, and even national security depends on keeping Earth's machinery running. And as ecology pioneer Aldo Leopold wrote, "To keep every cog and wheel is the first precaution of intelligent tinkering."

We know that if too many of our living tapestry's threads fray and break, our planet will lose its integrity. Our world will literally fall apart, often in ways we may not anticipate.

This is not always self-evident. We may be able to accept that bees are important, for example, but how about bats? Or hawks? Or elephants?

What is worth saving?

Do we really *need* African lions? Lemurs? Bald Eagles? When Aldo Leopold wrote about the importance of keeping "every cog and wheel," his logic was that when any part of a complex machine is missing, its loss may cause the overall mechanism to fail. And we just don't know which bits—if any—we can do without. But there are prices to pay if we are to keep them, and those prices involve our willingness to move beyond our focus on the things immediately in front of us.

Indianapolis Prize Honorary Chair E. O. "Ed" Wilson is a legend, and that's not an indulgence in hyperbole. He's been called the "father of biodiversity," and his academic affiliations include Harvard and Duke University. He's a two-time Pulitzer Prize winner, and is simply one of the most influential biologists of all time. Ed's famous for his work with ants, and one of my most prized possessions is a copy of his groundbreaking work *The Theory of Island Biogeography* (which he cowrote with Robert H. MacArthur), inscribed to me with his hand-drawn sketch of an ant. Ed supported Aldo Leopold's notion of "keep[ing] every cog and wheel" with his paper "The Little Things That Run the World (The Importance and Conservation of Invertebrates)."

But Dr. Wilson has now gone further. His book *Half-Earth: Our Planet's Fight for Life,* written in 2016, builds on Tony Hiss's ideas to propose that half of our planet's land should be established as a preserve without humans to maintain Earth's biodiversity. Ed isn't being silly here; our world works because of its interacting cogs and wheels, and they need appropriate environments in order to keep doing their jobs.

It is irrational of us to say, in effect, "We're going to keep taking more and more of Earth's resources for ourselves, and we expect you other species to keep providing life-sustaining ecosystem services for our geometrically increasing population with less and less for yourself." Imagine saying, "I'm not going to add any oil to my car engine because I'd rather spend that money on a burger." How would that work out? A mature and responsible person would say, "Sheesh, I really want that burger, but if I don't spend the $5 I have in my wallet to bring the oil level on the dipstick back up to FULL, then I probably won't make it back from the drive-through."

We've seen the disappearance of species cause entire ecosystems to crash. But the Indianapolis Prize helps consistently successful wildlife conservationists keep those cogs and wheels in place and turning by rewarding them financially, elevating their status in the professional community, and sharing their stories and missions with the people, organizations, and governments of the world. And now the Indianapolis Prize has itself become an essential part of the machinery of conservation.

The Prize is a lever that helps proven champions do more, do it better, and do it for longer. It is a bridge connecting the people and resources of the developed world with the needs and opportunities of wild things and wild places. If we don't have a bridge from which to see the wonders of the natural world, those who are protecting it can't take our hands and lead us across to share their spectacle and importance. And if we never have those experiences, we may be content to let those wonders die.

The Indianapolis Prize works hard to share the journeys of its champions with the rest of us. We don't just provide information about our nominees, finalists, and winners, but tell their stories through essays, articles, and spectacular short films. Indianapolis Prize films have become an iconic highlight of the world's leading award for animal conservation, and the response they generate at the biennial Prize Gala is powerful and uplifting.

Joining a brilliant, dedicated, and accomplished conservationist on his or her quest helps us understand not only the importance of the goal but the emotional and intellectual richness of the roads they travel. I'm convinced that we need a combination of journeys and destinations to experience the greatest joys and wonders in life. If we only wander, we are likely to limit the value we provide to others and constantly fall short of the greatest possibilities and achievements. Yet if we are exclusively fixated on iconic goals, we may become—like Captain Ahab in *Moby Dick*—fanatical, desperate, delusional, and unfulfilled. For me, it's the combination that can be so fulfilling.

When we identify a place we want to go to, and pay equal attention to the adventure of getting there, we can delight in every step of the way, even when that pathway is challenging. I remember driving to Spain with my family in the early 1960s when I was about 10 years old. My father packed my mother, grandmother, aunt, brother, two sisters, and me into our Ford Consul sedan, along with two weeks' worth of clothing and supplies, and set out from our home in Bedfordshire in the middle of England. I certainly remember our time in the little fishing town of Palamos on the Costa Brava, but I also recall the adventure of loading our car onto the ferry that carried us across the English Channel to France; the incredible traffic jam in Marseilles, during which an exuberant French taxi driver happily encouraged us to join everyone else in blowing their car horns just because it turned an impediment into a party; and the point at which our car overheated while crossing the Pyrenees, and a farmer who spoke English with a Cockney accent refilled our radiator from a jug on his bicycle.

The best expeditions don't simply start out with everything they could possibly need. That's usually unwieldy and wasteful. Instead, they are planned carefully and realistically, and then feedback loops allow for adjustments along the way. And they include people who contribute both expertise and teamwork to the traveling party.

Colonel John Hunt (later Brigadier Sir John Hunt) is a name most people don't know and therefore don't associate with what is often listed as one of humankind's greatest achievements: the summiting of Mount Everest by Sir Edmund Hillary and Sherpa Tenzing Norgay. Hillary and Tenzing are so closely associated with each other and the awesome achievement that for years it was not known which of them had been the first to set foot on the summit. But Colonel Hunt was the one that made it possible.

John Hunt was born in India, the son of a British army officer. He began mountaineering at age 10, but then attended the British Royal Military College at Sandhurst, where he excelled. After receiving his commission he was posted to India, where he became a military intelligence officer and climbed in the Himalayas.

During World War II, Hunt returned to Europe and was recognized as a visionary, ambitious, and accomplished leader. He established far-reaching goals, developed thoughtful and thorough plans, and implemented them brilliantly and successfully. After the war, he was assigned to the Supreme Headquarters Allied Expeditionary Force, and when Britain mounted its 1953 expedition to summit the world's tallest peak, he was—to the surprise of many—named the leader of the massive effort.

John Hunt was an inspired choice. He understood mountaineering. He understood logistics. He understood human nature. And he understood the importance of balancing both journey and destination. Brigadier Sir John Hunt never summited Mount Everest, but he made it possible for others to do so.

I'm no John Hunt. When I told our board and our staff that I wanted the Indianapolis Zoological Society to create the most important wildlife conservation award in the world, I outlined our destination. I was sure that it could be an important tool in advancing our strategy of connecting the people and resources of economically developed nations with the needs and opportunities of the natural world, but that was pretty much the extent of my plan. I could see that if we elevated successful, heroic conservationists to the level of screen, sports, and music stars, we could bring more attention to their causes, their work, their victories, and their needs. Actually planning, mounting, and sustaining an expedition, however, is not my strength.

But we had Karen Burns. And she became our John Hunt.

Karen is executive vice president of the Indianapolis Zoological Society and executive director of the Indianapolis Prize. If we say that we want to get to the top of Everest, she develops the plan, defines the resources, establishes the team, and makes sure everyone comes back alive. The Indianapolis Prize has become the world's leading award for animal conservation because we do *all* of that, not just because we had a great idea.

Karen dreamt up many of the concepts and strategies that have grown the prize from a seed to something that's flowering and begetting its own seeds, but her biggest contribution to the Indianapolis Prize is that she has institutionalized it. It's no longer just a program; it's an academy, a business, a center of excellence. It has become part of the fabric of global wildlife conservation, becoming a bridge that allows everyday people to travel from their world into the wild places where the wild things are, to see and learn what extraordinary people are doing to ensure that our planet retains its richness and ecological functions. Of critical importance is that this bridge allows two-way traffic, so scientists and field researchers can cross into the daily lives of bankers, teachers, nurses, factory workers, politicians, and everyone else who makes up our societies. In crossing that bridge, conservationists can tell enthralling, powerful stories of uplifting victories and urgent needs, and they can change our stars.

Then there's Amy Kerrick. Amy's title is executive assistant, and it didn't take me long to realize that didn't mean she's an assistant to an executive, but rather that she's an executive whose specialty is assisting others. She's very much like a lever and fulcrum, allowing small thoughts and actions in one place to result in large movements far away. But, as with Karen, Amy's real strength is that she cares so much about our mission—empowering people and communities, both locally and globally, to advance animal conservation—that the filters and amplification she applies add their own texture to the outcome.

Perhaps Amy's most indispensable value to the Indianapolis Prize has been that she makes sure that the balls I am constantly tossing into the air never hit the ground (except occasionally, when they should . . .). Her experience and attention to detail allow others to be as scattered and creative as they need to be, while she acts as a very effective ground-control officer.

If my family had never made it to Palamos in 1962, I think that I'd recall endless hours in a hot, crowded car. But because we *did* get there, the diversions and adventures of the journey became fond memories. The Indianapolis Prize is a trove of fond memories, which we owe to the team that has shaped them and constantly propelled us toward the next destination.

Many other people have helped make the Indianapolis Prize useful and effective, but Myrta Pulliam is in a category of her own.

Myrta is a past board chair of the Indianapolis Zoological Society and was part of the search committee that conducted my job interview back in 2002. She is a journalist and a founder of Investigative Reporters and Editors, a nonprofit organization committed to improving all aspects of investigative journalism. She was part of a team that won a Pulitzer Prize for investigative reporting. Her family owned and operated the *Indianapolis Star* newspaper for decades, and she is part of the fabric of Indianapolis. She's been my boss, my collaborator, and my colleague, and she will always be my friend.

Myrta may have more real friends than anyone I know, and that's in spite of her short temper, abrasiveness, and absolute confidence in the correctness of her opinions. I believe that's because people know that she is scrupulously honest, impossibly hardworking, thoughtfully generous, and a genuinely good person. She's obviously very intelligent and experienced, so she usually *is* right . . .

I suspect that most people present during my job interview regarded our discussion of a conservation prize as nothing more than a thought experiment at the time, a way for us to explore how we address challenges. Myrta was different. I started work at the

Indianapolis Zoo on Monday, July 8, 2002, and on Thursday, July 18, I met with her—at her request—to discuss how we could activate the concept. Five days later I met with Indiana governor Frank O'Bannon. The fifth bullet point on the meeting outline I prepared for him said, "We are also creating an annual cash award to the year's most notable conservation program. We will hold a major award program every year, attracting stars and others to an Academy Award–type program."

Myrta made her first major contribution to the process by suggesting that we interview what she called "smart people" to brainstorm the concept, and then went about scheduling meetings with a dozen people who became our "kitchen cabinet." Purdue University president Martin Jischke recommended that we award the Prize every two years rather than annually. Central Indiana Community Foundation CEO Brian Payne strongly endorsed calling it the *Indianapolis* Prize. Anthem EVP and CFO Mike Smith encouraged us to be outrageous, to reach for the stars and not settle for anything less than becoming the most important conservation award in the world. Eli Lilly and Company Foundation president Tom King not only emphasized the importance of program continuity but also came up with the seed money for the first several years of the program. There was not a single wasted meeting, and Myrta's personal credibility and reputation ensured that her dozen "smart people" paid attention and shared their best thinking.

Seventeen years and seven Indianapolis Prize Galas later, I cannot imagine any scenario in which the Indianapolis Prize would have actually become the "world's leading award for animal conservation" without Myrta Pulliam leading the way. She has made a difference in the world we will bequeath to future generations.

Beyond the basic concepts that drove the vision of the Indianapolis Prize, there are a few fundamental elements that have proved to be central to its success:

- We decided that the award should be limited to a living individual, rather than a team or an organization. This has been critical in the development of our storyline that a single human being can make a difference, and that the thoughts, words, and actions of each of us shift our collective direction in some way. The stories of George Archibald, Iain Douglas-Hamilton, George Schaller, Steve Amstrup, Patricia Wright, Carl Jones, and Russ Mittermeier are the stories of people who have done extraordinary things, and their brilliance, sacrifice, effort, heroism, and accomplishments are illustrated by the compelling stories we can share about them.

- We launched the Indianapolis Prize with an unrestricted personal award of $100,000. The amount was based on two key points: first, we wanted an amount of money that emphasized the importance of the winners' accomplishments—we shouldn't tell the world that saving a species from extinction is worth $500; second, Karen Burns pointed out that placing $100,000 under the unfettered control of a conservationist who has proven that he or she knows how to succeed has the potential to be a far better investment than turning it over to a bureaucracy with formulas and overhead and the possibility of conflicting priorities. In 2013, we decided to increase the award to $250,000, beginning with the 2014 prize.

- We created a selection process involving a nominating committee and jury of highly accomplished conservation experts from around the world, and added representatives from our board, our community, and our staff. Each nine-person body engages in spirited and thoughtful discussion over a period of several weeks, and they have absolute freedom from lobbying or any kind of pressure. Their decisions have been unassailable.

- We envisioned a spectacular, celebratory gala for the award, and it has exceeded our imaginations. The first description—written well before the first Prize Gala in 2006—stated "The Gala will not be a quiet, academic, scientist-focused event, but instead be a great, enthusiastic, spectacular celebration of victories, reaching out to and embracing attendees, inspiring and exhorting them to start caring in a way they've never cared before, and placing heroes who live in tents and live in danger of both wild beasts and angry men with guns on the same pedestal that we usually reserve for sports and entertainment stars." The core of the Indianapolis Prize Gala is a series of six short videos, shot on location, featuring each finalist. Filmmaker Matt Mays has played a huge role in bringing the worlds inhabited by wild creatures and the conservationists who protect them into the consciousness of Prize Gala guests.

· The Indianapolis Prize, as the world's leading award for animal conservation, specifically recognizes remarkable individuals who have achieved *measurable* accomplishments in advancing the sustainability of a species or group of species. They have saved whooping cranes from extinction, established multinational habitats for wide-ranging antelope, and developed groundbreaking techniques for monitoring elephant movements, managing their ranges, and combating poaching activities. And yet, during the first few award cycles, we heard the winners and finalists consistently speak of the critical importance of conservation voices who are *not* scientists or field workers in remote parts of the globe.

At the 2006 Indianapolis Prize Gala, celebrated actress Jane Alexander told the audience, "We need more than professional conservationists. We need everyone else, too. We can't save things that we don't care about, so our task is to help teach people to care more about wild things and wild places. It's critical for the natural world, but we're learning more every day about how important it is to all of us."

Jane has been a friend and honorary chair of the Indianapolis Prize since the beginning and has decades of commitment as a voice and champion for the wild things and wild places of our world. We decided to create a new award for a different kind of conservation champion, and to name it in her honor. Those who receive the Jane Alexander Global Wildlife Ambassador Award are those who support the natural world by leading others to action. The Jane Alexander Global Wildlife Ambassador Award is presented to an individual who has been a credible, consistent, and effective public voice for the sustainability of wildlife. As Jane said, "My hope is that sharing the stories and the passion of wildlife conservation will change people's lives. Then we will all truly be winners."

We named Jane herself as the inaugural Jane Alexander Global Wildlife Ambassador. The second ambassador was actress Sigourney Weaver, who portrayed gorilla researcher and conservationist Dian Fossey in the film *Gorillas in the Mist* in 1988. Sigourney is the real deal. She's been honorary chair of the Dian Fossey Gorilla Fund International since then, and is one of the most eloquent and passionate conservation voices we have. She's a wonderfully effective conservationist because she combines being very smart, very skilled, very passionate, and very well known. She commits herself to thoroughly understanding issues, and then is hugely effective at influencing others to take action and create change.

Harrison Ford was named Jane Alexander Global Wildlife Ambassador in 2018. Harrison's commitment to wildlife conservation is evident and includes extensive work both in the field and in the boardroom. Whether patrolling the Hudson River by helicopter to get a bird's-eye view of polluters or trekking through Indonesia to understand the challenges of deforestation, he makes sure he understands things himself, then he shares that understanding with others.

Harrison has been an honorary chair of the Indianapolis Prize since 2010 and has been board member of Conservation International for more than 25 years, serving on the executive committee and helping shape the organization's design and growth. He influenced the establishment of its Center for Applied Biodiversity Science and its Center for Environmental Leadership in Business.

We haven't committed to naming a Jane Alexander Global Wildlife Ambassador every two years. Rather, we've decided that we'll select an ambassador when someone achieves the level of commitment and accomplishment exemplified by Jane. Sigourney Weaver and Harrison Ford meet those criteria, and it will be interesting to see who else emerges.

- The most important factor behind the Indianapolis Prize's success has been the corps of smart, connected, experienced people who have given us their time, talent, treasure, and influence:

  Jane Alexander, Christel DeHaan, Harrison Ford, Gil Grosvenor, Carl Hiaasen, Roger Sant, Sigourney Weaver, E. O. Wilson, Dan Appel, Anne Nobles, Myrta Pulliam, Mary Clare Broadbent, Mitch Daniels, Jim Danko, Lori Efroymson-Aguilera, Suzie Fehsenfeld, Tony George, Rob Manuel, Mickey Maurer, Mark McCoy, Michael McRobbie, Sam Odle, Jeff Smulyan, Pete Ward, Bart Peterson, Greg Ballard, Joe Hogsett, Tom King, John Lechleiter, Tim Solso, Tom Linebarger, Ed Sherin, Alfre Woodard, Sam Waterston, Josh Duhamel, Marvin Hamlisch, Angela Brown, Saba Douglas-Hamilton, Sylvia McNair, Frank Pope, Anne Thompson, Ben Fogle, Max Graham, Mike Wells, Annie Wells, Katie Betley, Kate Appel, Bill McCarthy, Anne Murtlow, Beth Cate, Al Smith, Denny Bassett, Sally Brown Bassett, Karen Fuson, Mark Miles, Cathy Langham, Susan Williams, John Ketzenberger, Elizabeth Ahlgrim, Weezie Combs, Cheri Dick, Nancy Elder, Nancy Hunt, Lisa McKinney, Aril Sasso, Lauren Sparkman, Emily Dindoffer, Karen Burns, Amy Kerrick, Rob Shumaker, Teri Baker, Melanie Laurendine, Michele Schilten, Liz Mok, Judy Palermo, Kristin Kraemer, Maribeth Smith, Ellen Saul, Matt Mays, Laura Mays, Mike Marker, Emily Brelage, Pat Rhoda, Johnny Moore, Adam Rife, Lisette Woloszyk, and dozens of other volunteers, contractors, consultants, sponsors, and donors.

I don't think that our "steep and rugged pathway" will ever become overcrowded. The key is that it has a built-in filter, a requirement that one's presence on the path must be forward-looking and for the greater good.

Nevertheless, it will continue to be rewarding. It will provide us with the opportunity to *go beyond* in every way, while also carrying our species and our planet with us. And that's a lot better than just being a "consumer" in my book. That's something that future generations will thank us for.

I think about those future generations a lot. I wonder what they'll see and hear when they wake in the morning; what they'll eat and drink; and whether they'll look forward to the days and weeks to come. I wonder if they will feel in control of their lives or if they will be merely *consumers* . . . just doing what it takes to stay alive.

There are many factors that contribute to our actions, including the much-debated nature versus nurture, and the values we develop along our lives' journeys. One of the most well-known maxims in conservation is Senegalese environmentalist Baba Dioum's dictum, "In the end we will conserve only what we love, we will love only what we understand, and we will understand only what we are taught." I've supplemented that lesson with the words of those late-twentieth-century philosophers Crosby, Stills, Nash, and Young. Graham Nash wrote:

> You, who are on the road
> Must have a code
> That you can live by.
> And so
> Become yourself
> Because the past
> Is just a good-bye.
> Teach your children well
> Your father's hell
> Did slowly go by.
> And feed them on your dreams
> The one they pick
> The one you'll know by

What is the "code" we are living by and teaching our children? What are the dreams they observe us following?

I've been blessed with a wife whose "code" is not only clear but lived out through her actions every day. As a mother, Eileen provided our daughters with a broad and sturdy backing cloth on which they could weave their own tapestries of life, with clear dimensions. Morality, integrity, effort, ambition, responsibility to others, and joy were embedded in the foundation she gave them. Neither Megan nor Erin felt constrained by it, but rather were empowered to create their own designs. Megan became a veterinarian, and Erin a conservation development specialist.

The Indianapolis Prize also seeks to give everyone a backing cloth on which they can create their own paths. By revealing the glory and majesty of life on Earth, illuminating challenges, revealing solutions, and acclaiming its champions, we hope to give

Mike Crowther assists with GPS collaring efforts in Africa alongside Dr. Iain Douglas-Hamilton's Save the Elephants team.

everyone the vision to "teach our children well" as they both enjoy and contribute to Earth's magnificent living tapestry.

The pathway before us may be steep and rugged, but we'll have great companions along the way—and it leads to a far better destination than any of the alternatives.

Further Reading

Dinerstein, E. 2007. Tigerland and Other Unintended Destinations. Island Press.

Sodhi, N. S., and P. R. Ehrlich. 2010. Conservation Biology for All. Oxford University Press.

Stolzenburg, W. 2008. Ecosystems Unraveling: Conservation. University of Washington.

Sutherland, W. J., et al. 2018. A Horizon Scan of Emerging Issues for Global Conservation in 2019. Trends in Ecology and Evolution 34 (1): 83–94.

Wilson, E. O. 1975. Sociobiology: The New Synthesis. Harvard University Press.

INDEX